Accounting
and the
Global Economy
After
Sarbanes-Oxley

Accounting
and the
Global Economy
After
Sarbanes-Oxley

Don E. Garner, David L. McKee,
and Yosra AbuAmara McKee

M.E.Sharpe
Armonk, New York
London, England

Library of Congress Cataloging-in-Publication Data

Garner, Don E.
Accounting and the global economy After Sarbanes-Oxley / Don E. Garner, David L. McKee,
Yosra AbuAmara McKee.
  p. cm.
 Includes bibliographical references and index.
 ISBN 978-0-7656-1376-9 (cloth : alk. paper)
1. Corporations—Accounting—Standards. 2. Corporations—Auditing—Standards.
3. United States Sarbanes-Oxley Act of 2002. 4. International economic relations.
I. McKee, David L. II. McKee, Yosra AbuAmara, 1948– III. Title.

HF5686.C7G297 2007
657.02'1873—dc22   2007005349

Printed in the United States of America

The paper used in this publication meets the minimum requirements of
American National Standard for Information Sciences
Permanence of Paper for Printed Library Materials,
ANSI Z 39.48-1984.

BM (c)   10   9   8   7   6   5   4   3   2

Contents

Part II. Some Specific Issues Facing
Accounting and Auditing Practice

Part III. The Firms in the New Global Environment

Introduction

The major international accounting firms and other purveyors of business services have developed significant roles in the global economy. In the post–Enron-Andersen debacle environment, the playing field for the accounting firms has been drastically altered. At the same time, ongoing changes in the needs of the global economy are forcing significant adjustments in the roles of all business service providers and in the manner in which business services are provided. Nowhere is this more evident than in matters relating to international accounting and auditing standards.

Prior to Enron-Andersen, a consensus had developed with respect to the need for standardized accounting and auditing standards on a cross-border or global basis. Efforts and, indeed, progress were being made in the development and acceptance of global standards. In the post–Enron-Andersen environment, the global economy, corporations, and other business interests appear to have a heightened need for global uniformity and practice. Yet, the events surrounding the accounting and auditing failures may have caused some nations, notably the United States, to be less receptive to acceptance of such global standards.

In the United States, accounting standards have periodically come under close and specific scrutiny by the U.S. Congress, in some cases resulting in the Congress setting specific accounting standards. In 1934, U.S. securities law made the Securities and Exchange Commission (SEC) responsible for governing accounting and auditing. From inception, the SEC allowed the U.S. accounting profession to be essentially self-regulated. The SEC also delegated the authority to set U.S. accounting standards to the profession and related private-sector boards.

Over the years, the SEC has maintained active oversight. The U.S. Congress has also maintained its oversight both by specific members of Congress and as a legislative body. The Congress has directly intervened where it deemed necessary by passage of specific legislation. These interventions have frequently been in highly politicized cases and in cases where congressional constituencies were involved.

In 2002, a long series of accounting and auditing failures culminated with the collapse of Enron Corporation, closely followed by the bankruptcy of WorldCom. The U.S. Congress reacted by revamping U.S. securities laws in a number of significant aspects, including ending the self-governance of accountants who audit public corporations. The Sarbanes-Oxley Act became Public Law 107-204 in July 2002, creating a governmental board, the Public Company Accounting Oversight Board, as an arm of the SEC with total authority for U.S. auditing practices and standards for public corporations.

In an atmosphere where the accounting profession, if not the entire private sector, has been seen to be deficient, the U.S. Congress, and in all probability the U.S. electorate, cannot be expected to be receptive to housing authority for U.S. accounting and auditing standards in a global organization, particularly one that has no world-spanning enforcement ability.

Standardization of global accounting standards did appear to be moving ahead in the years prior to the Sarbanes-Oxley legislation. A set of standards useful for cross-border stock listings was in the later stages of development by international bodies. A new International Financial Accounting Standards Board, with a supporting organizational structure similar to the U.S. Financial Accounting Standards Board, had begun operations in spring 2001. The European Community declared it would use the International Accounting Standards beginning in 2005. No such intention was expressed by the U.S. SEC. In fact, when corporations list their stock on U.S. exchanges but prepare financial statements using other than U.S. generally accepted accounting principles, the SEC requires that a reconciliation to U.S. generally accepted accounting principles be filed. The outlook for a change in this requirement and thus the outlook for the future of global standardization of accounting standards certainly was not enhanced by the failures leading up to enactment of Sarbanes-Oxley.

In the international arena, reviews and major reforms of audit practices and standards have also taken place. The changes continue apace in both the U.S. and other jurisdictions around the world. Of major importance in the review of auditing practices is the issue of independence of auditors from attestation clients. For a number of years, international accounting firms had continued to increase their management advisory service role for clients in both local jurisdictions and on an international basis. In many cases such consulting-type services were performed for clients for whom attestation services were also performed, notably the audit of financial statements. Many believe that this gave rise to the conflicts of interest that ensnared Arthur Andersen and, essentially, all of the international accounting firms.

Attestation services by their very nature require that accountants performing attestation engagements not have a financial interest in the attestation client and not act in a management capacity for the client. The former would be a conflict of interest and the later a case of auditing or attesting to one's own work or actions. With the advent of the Sarbanes-Oxley Act, accounting firms are now prohibited from performing engagements involving specified management advisory and other consulting services for audit clients that are public corporations. This has created a completely new market environment for the way in which such service engagements are obtained. Large firms formed new strategies to adjust to the new competitive situation. Firms of all sizes are, in fact, benefiting from the restrictive changes made in the public accounting services market by the Sarbanes-Oxley Act. The firms are benefiting as well from the increase in work necessary to meet the act's requirements, particularly those for corporate internal control.

Despite the problems of auditors and those they audit, the global financial market system continues to expand at a rapid pace. This expansion is placing new and increasing demands upon facilitating service providers such as public accounting firms. This continued expansion, as in the past, has required geographic changes to serve expanding global markets. Superimposed upon the situation have been the locational rearrangements in the accounting and auditing services markets caused by the collapse of Arthur Andersen and the resulting Sarbanes-Oxley Act, as well as related reforms in many other world jurisdictions. Locational adjustments caused by accounting firm reduction from Big Five to Big Four have been substantial, increasing complexity and, more importantly, market concentration.

Technological advances continue contributing to rapid improvements in communications and computer systems. These advances have made and are making profound changes in the environment of world business. Truly great advances in productivity have been made in recent times in the methods available to business and accounting. The Internet, which some observers believe is among the most important innovations of our times, has been implemented in newly efficient and effective ways, becoming an indispensable tool for accountants. Advances in computer use have transformed public accounting practices. On the horizon is wide implementation of the computer innovation Extensible Business Reporting Language (XBRL), which is making financial information more easily accessible and adaptable over wide-ranging uses. XBRL has the potential to not only vastly improve the use of financial information but to produce it more quickly. Technology will undoubtedly continue to add more complexity and scope to economic life, continuing to change the environment of business and accounting.

This volume examines these issues in the hope of providing a coherent appraisal of the significance of accounting firms and the accounting profession in the global economy of today and tomorrow. We begin with four chapters on the general frame of reference: accounting and auditing standards as operating parameters in the global market-based economy; an overview of accounting standards in the global economy; the role of auditing standards in a global context; and the effects of changing realities in the post–Enron-Andersen era.

Specific issues facing public accounting firms and the accounting profession will be covered in four following chapters: harmonization of auditing standards, independence as a growing problem for accounting firms, locational adjustments facing the global financial system, and the impact of the Internet and communications systems on accounting firms.

The volume's concluding section deals with an examination of public accounting firms in the new U.S. and global environment: firm effectiveness in the face of new and emerging standards and the practical issues involved with firm adjustments in the global economy. In this section, the results of adjustments already made by the accounting profession will be analyzed. The major international accounting firms in recent years have been offering broad menus of facilitative business services to clients in various jurisdictions across the globe. The firms' strategies and abilities to continue effectively in that role, given new realities forced upon them by recent events, are considered. Finally, significant, seemingly intractable problems, most of them long standing, facing the profession are considered along with possible practical adjustments. Thus it is hoped that this book will provide a useful analysis of how the U.S. and the global economy will be affected by adjustments that accounting firms are facing as service providers.

Part I

The General Frame
of Reference

1

Accounting and Auditing Standards as Operating Parameters in the Global Economy

In the market-based world, annual financial reports are the primary media by which those who have been entrusted with private resources must periodically report both to those who own the private resources and to the general public. Proper preparation and content of financial reports are vital to the effective functioning and success of market-based economies. True, fair, complete, comparable, and transparent financial reporting is the goal to provide necessary information to investors for the best economic decisions and results.

Accounting and auditing standards are in effect operating parameters for the process of periodic accumulation and reporting of relevant accounting information through the media of financial statements. The accounting and auditing standards, along with standards and requirements for all who are involved in financial reporting, are in effect national legal requirements for the content of and for the periodic preparation, verification, and dissemination of financial accounting reports. These standards and requirements are both set and are enforceable by law within nations. Although global standards are increasingly needed, such world-spanning codifications remain a work in progress.

Investors sometimes mistakenly view periodic financial reports as verified statements of company operations and financial condition that are fact. Yet, given the nature of the information desired, such periodic statements are subject to the advantages and disadvantages, strengths and weaknesses inherent in the processes and standards by which they are periodically prepared. Subsequent chapters will examine these attributes in some detail.

In his book *Financial Shenanigans,* Howard Schilit rightly points out that reported profits can vary considerably and still be in accordance with generally accepted accounting principles (GAAP). Managers must make numerous estimates when keeping accounting records and preparing financial statements, and they must select from a variety of acceptable methods when accounting for many items in a financial statement. Schilit suggests that honest managements try to find accounting choices that will report fairly on the company's performance. Unfortunately, unscrupulous managers can distort financial reports for their own ends by choices made in selection and application of accounting alternatives (Schilit, 2002, 30).

Certification of the exact numbers in financial statements is unfortunately out of the question. Financial statements are in most respects truly approximations designed to provide relevant information periodically. Auditors attempt to highlight this inconvenient truth by issuing opinions on financial statements rather than certifications of statements and their contents. Even this approach has proven to be a tall order considering the myriad transactions to be accounted for and properly included periodically in financial reports. Thus, the promulgation of accounting and auditing standards are meant to provide the operating framework within which fair periodic financial reporting should take place.

Over the years, the vast majority of financial reports have fallen within established national parameters. Most have been issued in accordance with the GAAP of the jurisdiction in question, and an unqualified audit opinion is properly reported after the auditor has performed appropriate examination of the financial statements in accordance with the Generally Accepted Auditing Standards (GAAS) of the jurisdiction in question. Despite the glaring exceptions, most audit work and financial reporting do appear to have been conducted within parameters set by standards. The American Institute of Certified Public Accountants (AICPA) reports that approximately 17,000 successful audits are completed each year in the United States alone (AICPA, 2002, 5).

Even so, it is certainly clear that matters can stray and, in the course of financial history, have often strayed from prescribed standards, with disastrous results for stockholders and other stakeholders. Leon Levy has suggested that such disasters occur more frequently when economic and financial times are good. "Good times breed laxity, laxity breeds unreliable numbers, and ultimately, unreliable numbers bring about bad times" (Levy, 2002, 3). Levy conjectures that this is the rhythm of Wall Street and is "as predictable as human avarice" (Ibid.).

The final years of the twentieth century and the early years of the twenty-first century surely must be viewed as years containing a series of the largest debacles in financial reporting history. In this period, Levy's paradigm seems to have rung true for a good many companies and for their auditors. In the late 1990s, stock markets were riding the good times of a long bull market. Laxity, using Levy's description, was more than ample on the part of government regulators, market makers, corporate managements, and, most surprisingly to the investing public, the major accounting firms that audited the books of large global corporations.

The auditors, it was reasonable for the investing public to believe, would provide the final bulwark for the protection of corporate assets by operating within the parameters of standards set for the jurisdictions in question. The accountant's role in society has long been one of preserving the integrity of record-keeping and reporting systems. From the scribes of the ancient Middle East to the Exchequers of England to modern-day certified public accountants, public trust has been the accountant's comparative advantage.

Mike Brewster, in his *Unaccountable: How the Accounting Profession Forfeited a Public Trust,* observes that throughout history great respect and responsibility have been given to accountants. He wrote: "It is not an overstatement to say that modern society would have never developed without the people who brokered, sanctioned, recorded, and organized economic transactions" (Brewster, 2003, 7). Without honest record keeping and reporting, society is adrift without the means to assess productive efforts and to assign the fruits of production to best future uses.

In 1996, Arthur Levitt, then chairman of the Securities and Exchange Commission (SEC), stated that the accountant's stock-in-trade is the truth and declared that the accountant's role is one of the most valuable in a capitalist economic system. Levitt believed that accountants are very knowledgeable and sophisticated professionals who should maintain a critical view as they perform their societal function (Brewster, 2003, 9).

Yet, increasingly as the twentieth century came to an end, and in far too many large engagements, auditors failed to ensure honest record keeping and reporting. In far too many companies across the globe, the laxities, perhaps created by the good times, allowed wholesale misstatements of accounting numbers to be reported to unsuspecting publics. In any number of cases, outright management fraud was perpetrated. The initial frauds were accompanied, in some cases, by fraudulent positive investment-house market recommendations in return for investment fees or other service fees paid by client companies to the investment houses in question.

Accountants and auditors straying from the truth and from the parameters of standards aided and abetted the looting of investors' assets in epic proportions. In many cases, this was accomplished through the use of stock options granted to management and employees. Stock options, which clearly are an expense to existing shareholders, were not recorded as an expense on corporate income statements. In the United States, for example, this stock option accounting treatment was in accordance with GAAP, courtesy of the U.S. Congress, which, in a sordid display of political power, forced the Financial Accounting Standards Board (FASB) to accept the alternative of disclosure of employee stock option expenses in footnote form should a company choose not to book the expense on the income statement (Granof and Zeff, 2002).

The laxity, the frauds, the unreliable accounting numbers, the incorrect investment-house recommendations once uncovered led to the decline of stock market prices estimated at over $7 trillion (Levy, 2002, 2) from the market high. By Levy's assessment, such gargantuan losses destroyed the retirement plans and financial dreams of countless Americans (Ibid.). At the time Enron filed for bankruptcy, for example, the stock market priced its shares at 72 cents each. Less than a year before, Enron stock stood at $75 per share. Shareholder and employee losses from the Enron Corporation's demise were described by the AICPA in its information section on the Enron case: "Many employees lost their life savings and tens of thousands of investors lost billions" (AICPA, 2004, 1).

Surely this period must be viewed as giving rise to one of the largest debacles in financial history. Harvey J. Goldschmid, SEC commissioner, in a speech before the Association of the Bar of the City of New York, put the period in perspective. He indicated that, "The corporate and financial scandals of the 1990s and early 2000s are the most serious that have occurred in this country since the scandals of the Great Depression" (Goldschmid, 2003, 2). During this time, a systemic failure occurred because the checks and balances that were supposed to be operating were not. Goldschmid listed the groups that often failed in their responsibilities as independent directors, independent auditors, securities analysts, investment and commercial bankers, rating agencies, and lawyers. Neither the laws and regulations of the SEC and other federal and state jurisdictions nor the legal enforcers provided proper constraints. Goldschmid indicated that scarce regulatory resources, together with legislation and case law that was overly protective, contributed to the debacle (Ibid.).

This period cannot be said to be unique in most of its aspects in the history of stock markets. Other financial disasters and other periods must surely be viewed as just as bad, or worse. The fact that congressional measures had earlier weakened U.S. market and accounting oversight and regulation is surely not new in history. Nor is it new that corrective legislation was passed only after the damage had been done. Nor are the acts of market makers who fraudulently touted stocks "even as the companies recommended hurtled toward bankruptcy" (Levy, 2002, 2) unprecedented. On the financial stage, there have been many past cases where earnings, based on one or another proposition, have been reported as strongly increasing, indicating a rosy and profitable future, right up to the point where a lack of cash caused default on obligations and collapse.

Accounting and Audit Failures Unique in Financial History

The debacles of the late twentieth and early twenty-first centuries, however, are unique in the annals of stock market history because of the wholesale failure of accounting and auditing service providers to perform their duty to a remarkable number of large international companies. Parameters set by accounting and auditing standards that should have been operating were not being honored. Literally all of the Big Five international accounting firms have been shown to have participated in audit failures. The great international accounting firm of Arthur Andersen has ceased to exist.

The very accounting firms that the public had viewed as guardians of their assets have been shown to have had other objectives in mind, which they served in place of the public trust. And, these firms operated in the international arena. Their actions were not restricted to any one country. Broadly based as they were, these accounting debacles go to the fundamental roots and heart of the market system. In that aspect, they are unique in financial history.

Some misstatements of corporate financial statements were undoubtedly caused by unintentional errors. Many, however, were the result of large-scale fraud accompanied by audit failures of equal size. Whether the auditors participated in the frauds is today an open issue. The conclusions of ongoing court proceedings remain to be seen in many cases.

Audit failures and attendant public company financial restatements had

become increasingly common in the 1990s. Clients of each of the large
public accounting firms had issued restatements of earnings with attendant
instances of audit failures or suspected audit failures. And, despite the fact that
17,000 or so successful audits were being performed each year by certified
public accountants CPAs (AICPA, 2002, 5), the large, high-profile failures
caused increasing concerns throughout the world about audit performance
in general. In a prophetic speech in 1998, Arthur Levitt, then chairman of
the SEC, stated that there was erosion in the quality of earnings and in the
quality of financial reporting. He observed that managing might be being
replaced with manipulation, and integrity might be turning into illusion.
Chairman Levitt asked: "Today, American markets enjoy the confidence of
the world. How many half-truths, and how much accounting sleight-of-hand,
will it take to tarnish that faith?" (Berenson, 2003, xx–xxi).

The extant parameters set by accounting and auditing standards for
financial reporting clearly were not working. The public had witnessed
any number of corporate failures that centered on accounting failure and
fraud. The end of U.S. auditor self-regulation came as political pressure
mounted on the U.S. Congress to fortify safeguards for the public, for
investors, and for other stakeholders in the wake of two titanic bankruptcies. The collapse of American-based Enron Corporation occurred in
the midst of the bursting of the tech bubble and seemed to solidify an
already mounting skepticism about Wall Street, corporate managements,
and financial reporting.

A few months later, WorldCom's financial restatements revealed a by
now all-too-familiar scenario of financial reporting gone astray. The public response left skepticism behind as the dishonesty of those charged with
protecting shareholders, employees, and the general public was revealed
in full public view. The situation came to a head as the public response
indicated that enough was enough. It appeared that the electorate was truly
up in arms. The U.S. Congress, influenced as it is by special interests,
not the least of which is the accounting establishment, nevertheless was
finally able to muster the congressional votes to act.

Both Enron and WorldCom corporations were clients of the audit
firm Arthur Andersen. In late 2001, Enron Corporation management
announced that the corporation's earnings had been overstated in annual
financial reports since 1994 by a total that approached $600 million.
These overstatements were caused, Enron said, by accounting errors.
The announcement set off the collapse of the house of cards that had
been constructed by Enron in large measure through manipulation of its

financial statements and by the perpetration of frauds. Any number of apparent frauds that were carried out by Enron are described by Lynn Brewer in her book *House of Cards: Confessions of an Enron Executive* (2002) and in the book *What Went Wrong at Enron* by Peter C. Fusaro and Ross M. Miller (2002).

Less than a month after its announcement, Enron filed for bankruptcy protection as its cash flows dried up. Enron's financial statements, in which ever-increasing earnings had been reported, had been deemed fairly presented by auditor Arthur Andersen, it seems, right up to the point where company cash flows dried up.

Enron, with $60 billion in booked assets, had become the largest bankruptcy in history up to that time, overshadowing the Texaco bankruptcy with $35.9 billion in assets filed in 1987 (AICPA, 2004, 1). By 2004, the Enron bankruptcy professional fee charges topped $780 million. Accountingweb reported in December 2004 that Enron creditors would receive an average of 20 cents on the dollar after sale of all assets. "Shareholders, including former Enron employees, will get nothing" (Accountingweb, 2004a, 1).

No less an authority on the subject than former California governor Gray Davis said that the importance of Enron Corporation's rise and fall cannot be overstated. He believes that "the collateral damage is almost endless" (Clark and Lavelle, 2006, 45).

Enron traders had created false shortages of energy to inflate the traders' earnings and Enron profits. Their manipulations of the California energy market were probably criminal. In a regulated market, this would not have happened.

California had partially deregulated its energy market in an administration prior to the Davis term as governor. The state, in efforts to avoid brownouts and complete failures of electrical grids, turned to borrowing to pay the manipulated power costs. Billions were borrowed, and the state's debt ballooned. Davis was recalled from office in a special election. These fraudulent activities by Enron and the resulting aftermath have delayed further deregulation in this market (Clark and Lavelle, 2006, 45).

To construct its elaborate, almost unbelievable, house of cards, Enron management had used complex transactions and complex organizational structures in conjunction with inappropriate accounting rules and methods to misstate financial results. Based primarily upon its analysis of the Powers Report (Powers, 2002), which had been prepared for the Enron board of directors after the stock market debacle, Benston and Hartgraves

(2002, 12) concluded that a number of faulty or false accounting constructs were used extensively by Enron. The constructs were used with the concurrence of Arthur Andersen auditors.

Andersen's reputation in the years leading up to the Enron collapse had been increasingly spotty because of a number of problem audits. Andersen had gained a reputation for settling lawsuits for audit engagements gone wrong. There is little question from the public records that Andersen was involved in restatements of financial statements and audit failures in a number of notorious cases in the years leading up to Enron. Many of these were settled out of court.

There seemed to be a question of whether Andersen's business strategy was to act as an audit firm or as an insurance company. The firm did take on lucrative non-audit work for audit clients. Profit margins for non-audit work were substantially larger than those received for audit engagements. Was the audit work that led to the non-audit work used as a loss leader? Was audit work inadequate, resulting in less than a duly diligent job being done? Were the audit work and reports affected by company management using its leverage based on the total remuneration paid to the audit firm? The whole truth may never come to light because records have frequently been sealed by agreement between the parties involved.

Light is shed on the probable answers to these questions by J. Edward Ketz in his book *Hidden Financial Risk: Understanding Off-Balance Sheet Accounting,* which describes how the Big Five auditing firms used audit engagements as loss leaders to generate consulting business (Ketz, 2003, 184). The danger in this, Ketz believes, is that the audit becomes a vehicle in the firm's profit maximization schemes instead of being of paramount importance in its own right. Cutting costs on the loss-leader audit would surely follow.

Ketz describes how audit firms, including Andersen, used analytical reviews in place of appropriate random audit samples to cut audit costs. Increased reliance on computer programs also cut costs but left the audit team open to undetected management fraud when changes to computer programs or other actions were used to thwart auditor intent. Ketz describes how one executive had a computer program written to flag five-month-old inventory, so that the items could be moved to another location to make the auditor believe that the inventory was no older than a six-month cutoff, which the auditor had set to classify inventory as obsolete (Ibid.).

The Walt Disney Company case is an example of Andersen's problem engagements, and one in which document shredding occurred, at least by the client company Disney. Andersen had been the outside expert from 1994 to at least 1998 for the Walt Disney Company in lawsuits on Winnie the Pooh royalties, appearing in over a dozen court hearings as Disney's accounting representative.

A report by Joe Shea indicates that during these years "thousands of pages of documents related to the case were destroyed in violation of a court order" (Shea, 2002, 1). Shea believes that Andersen's full involvement is hidden because Disney asked the court to seal many documents concerning accounting activity. Monetary damages of $90,000 were paid by Disney as a fine "for destroying 40 boxes of documents, including some which were shredded as late as 1998" (Ibid.). The case was settled out of court with payments by Disney to the plaintiff.

In the Enron case, the public record concerning Andersen's relationship and actions does certainly seem to suggest that Andersen was more concerned with profits even at the expense of its public responsibilities. Andersen billed Enron for its auditing, consulting, and tax work a total of $52 million in 2000 up from $46.8 million in 1999 (Bryce, 2002, 237). Robert Bryce, in his study of Enron, indicates that "By the late 1990s Andersen had become so reliant on Enron that it simply could not afford to lose the company as a client." Bryce believes that Enron understood that and used that fact to its advantage (Ibid.). Bryce reports that when Andersen partner Carl Bass began raising questions about the accounting at Enron, Enron officials indicated that they wanted Bass removed from any work on Enron and Andersen quickly complied (Ibid., 238).

Alumni from Andersen working for Enron were numerous. In his study, Bryce commented that Enron had become packed with ex-Andersen people. The same had been true at Waste Management, another failed Andersen client (Ibid., 237). Jeff McMahon, the Enron treasurer, and his replacement Ben Glisan were both Andersen alumni, as was the Enron chief accountant, Rick Causey (Ibid.). The relationship between Causey and the Andersen partner in charge of the Enron audit was, in the opinion of Bryce, extremely close. Bryce reported that the two played golf, ate lunch, and vacationed together (Ibid., 238).

Bryce describes a meeting of Enron managers with an Andersen auditor, reported to him by an Enron executive who had been present. The meeting was called by Enron people because they needed an opinion letter from an Andersen auditor to support a claim for $270 million in tax credits. The auditor at first refused. Enron employees indicated that they would not let the auditor out of the room until they got the opinion letter desired. This and other heavy-handed methods resulted in the Andersen auditor agreeing to the tax credit scheme (Ibid., 232). This event was reported by Bryce as though it were typical of the relationship between Enron and Andersen.

As noted previously, after studying the relationship of Enron with its auditor, Mike McNamee in a *BusinessWeek* article concluded that because of the rule-based U.S. accounting standards, Enron management used accounting treatments for financial reports that served its purposes in any matter where the Andersen auditors could not cite a specific rule prohibiting such treatment (McNamee, 2002, 1).

It seems that Andersen was active with Enron personnel, many of whom were former Andersen auditors, in the aggressive use of accounting to keep earnings figures rising. A former Enron top executive was reported by Robert Bryce in his book *Pipe Dreams* to hold the opinion that the company's aggressive accounting was the cause of its bankruptcy (Bryce, 2002, 11).

Based on their study of the Enron Board of Directors' Powers Report, Benston and Hartgraves believe that Enron used a number of methods to "manipulate its reported earnings" (Benston and Hartgraves, 2002, 125–27). The company did not consolidate special purpose entities (SPEs), which allowed substantial losses and debt to be hidden from public disclosure. Sales made to controlled SPEs were recorded as if arm's-length transactions had occurred. Fees for services to be rendered in future periods and revenue from sales of forward contracts, which were really disguised loans, were recognized as current income. Mark-to-market fair-value accounting was used to restate profits from merchant contracts where no trustworthy numbers were available. Enron stock issued to and held by SPEs was not accounted for properly. Disclosures were non-existent or were inadequate for related party transactions and conflicts of interest (Ibid.).

Benston and Hartgraves indicate that problems with U.S. GAAP, as structured and administered by the SEC, the FASB, and the AICPA (Ibid., 125), are substantially responsible for the Enron SPE accounting debacle. In their view, Enron management, its outside counsel, and its auditor all felt comfortable in following the specified accounting requirements for not consolidating SPEs (Ibid.). The SEC had the responsibility and opportunity to change these rules to reflect the known fact that corporations were using this vehicle to keep liabilities off their balance sheets, although the sponsoring corporations were substantially and in many cases entirely liable for SPE obligations (Ibid.).

Early guidance given by the Emerging Task Force, an AICPA entity, was cited by Enron and Andersen as the guidance for their treatment of SPEs. This guidance involved accounts receivable securitization and perhaps leasing, which envisioned a very low probability of the securitized accounts receivable becoming a liability of the sponsor or parent entity. This low probability condition generally prevails when SPEs raise funds through selling securities to purchase accounts receivable of the sponsor. Thus, banks, for example, were permitted to leave such securitizations off balance sheets.

To use this guidance in the Enron case does not appear appropriate. The conditions of the Enron SPEs were that they were very thinly capitalized and contained risky assets. Further, the ownership risks of the SPEs remained with Enron. Enron also used FASB guidance for lease accounting inappropriately in that Enron itself was on both ends of the deal and no sale could conceivably have taken place.

Benston and Hartgraves' view that the SEC bears responsibility for the accounting debacles is bolstered by SEC approval for the use of mark-to-market accounting for Enron Gas Services. The use of mark-to-market accounting allowed huge revenue growth to be reported without the accompanying cash flow to pay its debts (Bryce, 2002, 11). The mark-to-market accounting was originally adopted by Enron for its Gas Services division. The method was approved by the Enron Board in 1991 for such use (Ibid., 66). Once board approval had been gained, Bryce reports that Enron and Andersen lobbied the SEC to permit its use by Enron. In a letter from the SEC dated January 30, 1992, such permission was granted. This was the first SEC approval of the use of mark-to-market accounting by a nonfinancial company (Ibid., 67).

SEC approval had been received during the first quarter of its fiscal year ended December 31, 1992. Bryce reports that this implementation date was ignored and the method had been instituted in Enron financial statements a full year before. Enron, with Andersen agreement, claimed that the difference was not material. The evidence seems otherwise, because without the change to mark-to-market accounting in 1991, earnings in the fourth quarter of 1991 would have been down, which would almost certainly have resulted in downgrading of the Enron stock price (Ibid.).

The mark-to-market accounting method was so successful in inflating accounting earnings that, according to Bryce, the company began to use mark-to-market accounting in every part of its business, although board approval had been only for use in Enron Gas Services. In the mark-to-market process, many of the estimates used for out-year returns were unreasonably optimistic at best and fraudulent at worst (Ibid., 68).

The desire of Enron executives to keep accounting earnings rising was driven in large measure, it seems, by the enormous bonuses and stock options granted to them. By 2000, options to purchase Enron stock made up more than 13 percent of all outstanding Enron stock (Ibid., 11). Bryce commented that "those options were going to make everyone at the company rich, that is, if Enron could just keep impressing Wall Street with big profits" (Ibid.).

Andersen Failed to Follow Professional Standards

Any reasonable reading of the Enron events seems certain to indicate that Andersen auditors did not carry out GAAS as promulgated and had violated the existing AICPA *Code of Professional Conduct* (AICPA, 2006a). This is not to say that Arthur Andersen was alone or that the other international Big Five firms were not also in violation on numerous occasions.

AICPA bylaws make the code mandatory for all AICPA members. In addition, states and regulatory agencies have codes of conduct or ethics that apply to various services provided by CPAs. Most states have a separate ethics test that must be passed before the CPA certificate or license to practice is issued. The essentials of the state codes of conduct are included in the AICPA code. In revisions of the AICPA code since 2001, members are cautioned to consult ethical requirements and standards set by the appropriate state CPA society, state board of accountancy, the SEC, and any other governmental agency that may have different ethics regulations that apply to an engagement in question.

The AICPA code consists of two primary parts. The first part, Principles, provides a framework of positive statements of responsibilities of AICPA members to fellow practitioners, clients, and the public. It sets forth the basic tenets of ethical and professional conduct to guide CPAs in performing their duties with "an unswerving commitment to honorable behavior, even at the sacrifice of personal advantage" (Ibid., 1). The second part consists of enforceable rules, based on the first part's Principles, and are designed to govern conduct of members in performing professional services. Should members fail to self-enforce these rules, enforcement ultimately can take the form of disciplinary proceedings, the results of which are made public.

The AICPA code also encompasses Interpretations of Rules of Conduct and Ethics Rulings, which are the responsibility of the Professional Ethics division's Executive Committee. These are afforded a period of public exposure before being issued in final form. Both are enforceable through the AICPA disciplinary hearings process. The rules and interpretations are generally enforceable, while the rulings, being applications of rules and interpretations to particular factual circumstances, are enforceable only to a similar set of factual circumstances (Ibid., Other Circumstances, 1).

The code requires that when performing an engagement to report on financial statements such work should be performed in accordance with GAAS. The GAAS require that, in all matters relating to the assignment, independence in mental attitude is to be maintained by auditors, due professional care is to be exercised in planning and performing the audit and report, and the audit should be performed by persons having adequate technical training and proficiency as auditors.

According to the GAAS, in fieldwork, the audit work is to be adequately planned and assistants are to be properly supervised. This provision, of course, means that higher echelons of CPA firms must properly supervise all audits. In the standards for reporting, informative disclosures in the financial statements are to be regarded as reasonably adequate unless otherwise stated in the report.

It seems that some Andersen practitioners failed in their responsibilities for every one of these requirements. Andersen's independence from Enron has been shown to lack any substance. The AICPA code or GAAS did not prohibit consulting work for attestation clients. Rules and expectations for independence did not specifically cover a situation where the audit firm received such enormous fees for other non-audit types of services that the firm would be considered financially dependent on its client. Due professional care, it seems, was lacking up and down the Andersen organization. The machinations used within Enron were clearly not disclosed adequately by Andersen auditors. Higher echelons of the firm did not adequately supervise the audit work.

The AICPA code at the time (Whittington and Pany, 2006, 32–83) contained a number of specific rules enforceable by the AICPA. Existing Rules 101, 202, and 501 seem especially to have been violated by Andersen: "Rule 101-Independence. A member in public practice shall be independent in the performance of professional services as required by standards promulgated by bodies designated by Council"; "Rule 202-Integrity and Objectivity. In the performance of any professional service, a member shall maintain objectivity and integrity, shall be free of conflicts of interest and shall not knowingly misrepresent facts or subordinate his or her judgment to others"; "Rule 501-Acts Discreditable. A member shall not commit an act discreditable to the profession."

The Arthur Andersen partner in charge of the Enron audit, David Duncan, pled guilty to obstruction of justice in April 2002 and was convicted in June 2002. Seven guilty pleas in all had resulted from the Enron case by November 2003 (Accountingweb, 2003, 1). Andersen as a firm was convicted of obstruction of justice in the Enron case for shredding audit and other documents. Nancy Temple from Andersen's legal department and David Duncan, the managing director for the Houston office, were cited as the responsible managers (Wikipedia, 2006d, 2).

On August 31, 2002, Andersen surrendered its right to practice before the SEC. As a result of its conviction, Andersen lost nearly all of its clients. Over 100 civil suits were filed against the firm related to audits of Enron and other former client companies.

The firm in effect ceased to exist as all but about 200 employees left the firm. This was remarkable since Andersen had 28,000 or so employees in the United States and 85,000 worldwide (Ibid.). Most of these, as well as the Andersen clients, went to competing audit and consulting firms where they continued their practice of public accounting.

Upon appeal, the conviction of Arthur Andersen & Co. was unanimously overturned by the Supreme Court of the United States on May 31, 2005, because of flaws in jury instructions. The jury was allowed by the Court's instructions to convict Andersen without proof that the firm knew it had broken the law or without proof that there had been a link to any official proceeding that prohibited the destruction of documents. The Supreme Court opinion was also highly skeptical of the government's definition of "corrupt persuasion" as persuasion with an improper purpose even without knowing an act is unlawful (Ibid.).

The firm had been founded in 1913 by Arthur Andersen and Clarence DeLany as Andersen, DeLany & Co., changing its name to Arthur Andersen & Co. in 1918. The firm, up until the 1980s, had been a zealous supporter of high ethical standards and accepted, it would seem, that accountants were responsible to investors, not just client companies. The firm insisted upon following appropriate accounting standards that reflected the truth as the auditors saw the truth. In those times, prior to the 1980s, accounting firms were seen as a bulwark of honesty, trust, and decency. Reputations were enhanced by the character displayed in taking strong stances on accounting issues. Most client companies, the thinking went, wanted an auditor who would keep them clear of current or future trouble. Client companies therefore expected the auditor to object rather than allow the company to follow accounting policies that would lead to future trouble (Wyatt, 2003, 2).

At various times in its history, Arthur Andersen & Co. resigned engagements rather than follow accounting treatments with which it disagreed. The firm resigned from a large railroad company engagement in disagreement with an industry-accepted accounting principle. In another case, the firm resigned from all of its savings and loan engagements when it disagreed with an acceptable treatment of deferred income taxes in the savings and loan industry. Strong increases in audit revenue were experienced by the firm as a result of these strong stances. The firm took a strong stance on the issue of proper accounting without regard to the loss of current fees, which was rewarded by increased future business (Ibid.).

Consulting Became an Overriding Concern

Consulting services as such began in the Andersen firm as well as in other prominent accounting firms in the 1960s and grew at an accelerating pace. Consulting grew during the 1970s and 1980s at a much faster pace than did the traditional services of auditing, accounting, and tax preparation, at least in part because firms used their traditional businesses as springboards to the more lucrative consulting business.

Increasing frictions between Andersen's consultants and accountants began to appear over the fair sharing of firm profits. This turned into a bitter, long-standing dispute. Although Arthur Andersen and Andersen Consulting were made separate units of Andersen Worldwide in 1989, the dispute continued until, in 2000, it was settled by arbitration. The arbitrator granted Andersen Consulting its independence from Andersen Worldwide. Andersen Consulting changed its name to Accenture (Wikipedia, 2006d, 1).

After the split-off from Andersen Consulting in 1989, Arthur Andersen had created a second consulting group, Arthur Andersen Business Consulting, which directly competed with Andersen Consulting. In 2002, as Arthur Andersen was imploding, parts of Arthur Andersen Business Consulting were bought out by other consulting companies, including Hitachi Consulting and KPMG Consulting, which later changed its name to BearingPoint (Ibid., 2).

Arthur Wyatt, in his address before the American Accounting Association in 2003, indicated that the growth of consulting services and associated changes was gradual, occurring over thirty years or so. During this period, concerns were raised about the expanding scope of services offered by auditing firms, usually centering on impairment of auditor independence. These concerns were consistently rebuffed by firm leadership, who seemed to overlook the potential for attestation independence problems. The emphasis continued on increasing the range of lucrative consulting services offered, attendant with the downgrading of traditional audit services, which were now viewed, even by some firm insiders, as a commodity with attendant problems of low profit margin (Wyatt, 2003, 4).

By the 1990s, the SEC had become concerned about the increasing variety of consulting services as well as the large increases in consulting billings. Several accounting firms were charged by the SEC with impaired independence, but a direct link between consulting and impaired independence could not be established. The firms, with the support of the AICPA, stonewalled all efforts to limit consulting services (Ibid., 4–5).

Wyatt indicated that leadership in public accounting firms failed to recognize the conflicts of interest that were being built and, more importantly, failed to see the internal changes in their firms that increased consulting was making. There had been a change in the firms' reason for being. The firms were now growth and profit oriented. Public duties, responsibilities, and professionalism were no longer the focus and hallmark. It was no longer central to provide the assurance needed by the markets that clients' financial statements were fairly presented (Ibid., 5). Instead audit service was seen as commodity-like and used to advantage as a loss leader for lucrative consulting work for audit clients to grow revenues and profitability.

The culture of the large firms had been changing slowly as their staff hires came to include more and more individuals who were not versed in accounting professionalism and did not appreciate the importance of the unique attestation role that society had placed on these firms. They became profit-maximizing organizations that gave advancement to the best rainmakers, those who brought in increasing revenues and profits, regardless of their skills as auditors. This put pressure on the audit side to take more risk to maintain or increase revenues and to cut audit costs (Ibid., 5).

The new focus of the firms was "on an ever expanding range of services offered to a client pool fighting to achieve the short term earnings per share growth expected of them in the marketplace" (Ibid.). In this climate where auditors were attempting to maximize profit, it is not surprising that accounting, auditing, and ethical standards fell both within the audit firms and within their client companies. The gatekeepers became part of the problem, and the situation was ripe for fraud.

Between 2000 and 2002, four of the Big Five international accounting firms sold or disposed of their consulting practices. As discussed above, Andersen Consulting separated from Anderson Worldwide in August 2000. The company was renamed Accenture in January 2001 and became a publicly owned company in July 2001. Ernst & Young Consulting was sold to Capgemini in February 2000 and was renamed Cap Gemini Ernst & Young, although the new company is not affiliated with Ernst & Young. KPMG Consulting was spun off in an initial public offering in February 2001. The company was renamed BearingPoint in October 2002. Price-waterhouseCoopers Consulting was acquired by IBM in 2002. Deloitte Consulting announced plans in 2002 to separate from the accounting firm and establish a private partnership to be named Braxton. In March 2003 the group terminated its separation plans. Deloitte & Touche is the only Big Four firm not to have disposed of its consulting operations established prior to 2000.

The breaking up of auditors and consultants seems to have had more to do with the struggle, publicly most evident at Arthur Andersen, for distribution of profits, rather than any considerations involving auditor independence. All of these firms are still actively engaged in consulting. Deloitte & Touche announced that it will comply with the new Sarbanes-Oxley requirements and professional independence rules while still retaining their consulting arm (Arens, Elder, and Beasley, 2004). Consulting for non-attestation clients and nonpublic companies is permitted under both.

Andersen had been a leader in the industry, adding consulting earlier in its history than other audit firms. The change in the firm's culture may have advanced it further than its competitors, and it became the leader in a pack of profit-seeking entities. The firm Arthur Andersen was alleged to have been involved in fraudulent accounting and auditing at Sunbeam Products; Waste Management, Inc.; Asia Pulp and Paper; and the Baptist Foundation of Arizona (Wikipedia, 2006d, 2) leading up to the Enron debacle.

As the Enron bankruptcy broke on an unsuspecting public, Congress was placed under considerable political pressure to act. It was becoming clear to the general public that existing operating parameters for financial reporting were inadequate. Yet Congress wavered. It had weathered such storms in the past. Within three months of the Enron collapse, unfortunately, another gigantic Arthur Andersen client went into bankruptcy. The WorldCom bankruptcy, with $100 billion in booked assets, dwarfed the Enron affair.

Fraud was at the heart of yet another Arthur Andersen audit failure. Cynthia Cooper, former vice president of internal audit at WorldCom, took her findings of financial misstatement and fraud to the WorldCom board of directors. The company admitted, in short order, to having inflated reported profits by a total of $3.8 billion, a total which has since grown to a reported $11 billion (Accountingweb, 2004a, 2004b). Bernard Ebbers, former CEO of WorldCom, was found guilty in March 2005 of one count of securities fraud, one count of conspiracy, and seven counts of filing false statements with the SEC (Accountingweb, 2005, 1). Cynthia Cooper was hailed as one of the Persons of the Year by *Time Magazine* in 2002 and elected in 2004 to the AICPA Business and Industry Hall of Fame (Accountingweb, 2004b, 1). This seems somewhat overdone, since as WorldCom internal auditor, it was Cooper's job and duty to WorldCom shareholders to report financial reporting failures to the board. Yet, in this environment, her actions in doing her duty were, apparently, viewed as courageous.

The ensuing public furor over Enron and now WorldCom had forced the Congress to act. The resulting Sarbanes-Oxley Act put an end to self-regulation of auditors in the United States. The regulation of financial reporting and the regulation of accounting and auditing remain under the purview of the SEC. Within the SEC, Congress created the Public Company Accounting Oversight Board (PCAOB) as an SEC arm to govern U.S. accounting and auditing.

Rise and Demise of Self-Regulation
of Public Company Auditors

From its inception in 1934, the SEC, while retaining oversight, had delegated the establishment of U.S. accounting and auditing standards to the accounting profession. These public responsibilities were first entrusted to the American Institute of Accountants (AIA), later to be renamed the American Institute of Certified Public Accountants. The AICPA today has grown to a membership of over 330,000 certified public accountants.

The formulation of accounting and auditing standards took different paths over the years. Accounting standards were formulated from 1939 to 1972 by a part-time standing committee of the AICPA and its predecessor AIA. In 1972, responsibility for accounting standards migrated to the part-time AICPA Accounting Principles Board and, still later, to the private-sector-sponsored full-time Financial Accounting Standards Board. The FASB organizational structure provides for stakeholder representation from outside the AICPA, including investors and financial statement issuers. Pronouncements by the FASB and its predecessors constitute the basis for generally accepted accounting principles in the United States (AICPA, 2002, 1). The SEC and the Public Company Accounting Oversight Board have indicated that the FASB will continue to set accounting standards, with continuing oversight by the SEC and the PCAOB.

As for auditors, the authority for certification and regulation of all U.S. certified public accountants is housed in the individual states of the union through their state boards of accountancy. These state boards control accountancy practice within their various jurisdictions. The state boards recognize national standards and practices. CPAs who desire to include the audit of U.S. public companies in their services must register with and meet the standards set by the newly formed PCAOB.

The state boards also retain their authority to discipline CPAs practicing within the state in question. For example, the California Board of Accountancy in September 2004 took disciplinary action against Ernst & Young LLP as a result of independence issues when the audit firm engaged in joint ventures with PeopleSoft Inc. while engaged as the company auditor. In April 2004, the SEC had sanctioned the Big Four firm for these independence issues. The California Board placed Ernst & Young on three years' probation. The New Mexico Board also issued a notice that it was considering action against Ernst & Young for the same audit independence failures (Accountingweb, 2004c, 1).

Beginning in 1939, U.S. auditing standards were formulated by the AICPA's Committee on Auditing Procedures. In 1972, the committee's name was changed to the Auditing Standards Executive Committee (Aud-

Sec). The Auditing Standards Board (ASB) succeeded AudSec in 1978 and continues to operate today. The ASB issued Statements on Auditing Standards, which in effect constituted the detailed standards to carry out generally accepted auditing standards for all U.S. company audits until the advent of Sarbanes-Oxley mandated PCAOB. ASB pronouncements currently are followed for the audit of entities other than public corporations, which are under SEC jurisdiction (AICPA, 2007, 1).

What happened to the AICPA as a professional organization during the latter part of the twentieth century? Arthur Wyatt addressed this issue in his American Accounting Association presentation. In reviewing the long, productive, and professional history of the AICPA in its earlier years, Wyatt said, "The AICPA operated as a professional organization when John Carey was its director" (Wyatt, 2003, 1). His focus was on "heightening the awareness of the importance of ethical professional behavior." The AICPA had, however, turned into what in effect was a trade organization, which had limited effects upon members' "professionalism and ethical behavior" during the years of its profession's greatest crisis.

In the final decades of the twentieth century, professional leadership was to a large extent left to the individual Big Five firms. These firms, it seems, had moved from an emphasis on public duty squarely to an emphasis on profit maximization with little regard for public attestation responsibilities. It also seems as though their professional organization, the AICPA, had either followed suit or led the industry down that same profit-seeking path.

The bar has now been raised by the Sarbanes-Oxley Act, and by similar legislation in nations across the globe. Penalties for white-collar crime have been clarified and increased, including those for chief executive officers (CEOs). There have been dozens of convictions of CEOs in recent years, from Martha Stewart to WorldCom's Bernie Ebbers, and Enron's Kenneth Lay and Jeffrey Skilling. Their infractions were against the public trust. They were gatekeepers who abrogated their duties for personal gain. All those involved in upholding the parameters of financial reporting set by accounting standards, auditing standards, and standards for each group with responsibilities in the financial reporting process should be on notice that the price is high for failure to carry out legal duties to act in the public interest. In the face of ongoing convictions and tough new laws and standards, greed and the related corruption can nevertheless be expected to remain a human failing. A recent example supporting this expectation is the 2006 inquiry of federal prosecutors into allegations that a personal fortune was built by UnitedHealth Groups' CEO William McGuire through backdating stock option grants.

To be sure, the Sarbanes-Oxley Act remains controversial. The act's supporters believe that it has aided the return of public confidence in financial reporting and cite the rising stock market. Opponents point to the higher U.S. regulatory standards and cite the exodus of capital and corporations from U.S. public markets to other world markets. Throughout this book, the Sarbanes-Oxley Act and its effects upon corporate financial reporting will be analyzed. The next two chapters will consider first accounting standards, and next auditing standards in a global versus a nation-state context. These two sets of promulgated standards in effect set the parameters of financial reporting for corporations and for the accounting profession. The prospects for improved financial reporting in world markets are hinged on improvements in these standards on a global basis.

2

Overview of Accounting Standards in the Global Economy

As capital increasingly seeks its best uses regardless of national borders, the divergent accounting standards of individual nation-state jurisdictions are proving to be inefficient at best. Accounting standards are within the legal province of nation-states and will likely remain under the ultimate control of individual nations or groups of nations. Yet the huge volume of international business transactions and the ever-more complex interconnected global markets make movement toward global standards recognized among all nations evermore imperative. There is general consensus that global market participants would benefit from the adoption of a single set of required accounting standards that would be consistent, comparable, and relevant across the world-spanning environment of finance and commerce.

Both national and international financial reporting authorities continue to work toward improving and converging their standards toward this goal. These actions, it is hoped, will best facilitate the objectives of both capital owners and capital users in their search for optimum return in the world's liquid markets. World standards, it seems certain, will aid in better allocation of economic resources, which will in turn enhance the world's economic performance.

National standards by their very nature vary in quality and purpose. As one would expect, standards in industrialized countries have become highly developed and are viewed as better in quality than in less-developed economies where the needs of financial reporting may be less complex.

Many in the United States hold the opinion that U.S. standards are the premier of the world. Not surprisingly, citizens of other nations often hold a different opinion. In other parts of the world, the U.S. Securities and Exchange Commission's (SEC's) refusal to accept other than U.S. standards within U.S. markets is often viewed as a form of U.S. hegemony.

In a 2002 McKinsey Global Investor Opinion Survey on Corporate Governance, 90 percent of responders supported a single set of accounting standards. But 78 percent of responders from Western Europe thought that the single standard should be the International Financial Reporting Standards (IFRS), while 76 percent of those from North America thought that the single standard should be U.S. generally accepted accounting principles (GAAP; Task Force on Rebuilding Public Confidence in Financial Reporting, 2003, 20).

The U.S. House of Representatives Subcommittee on Capital Markets held hearings in 2001 to review "the efforts to harmonize international accounting standards, given the nature of the changing world economy" (Baker, 2001, 2). Subcommittee Chairman Richard H. Baker stated that "The United States capital markets are the deepest and most complex in the world. And while there are very legitimate concerns about the rules, the markets consider the Generally Accepted Accounting Principles, or GAAP, the most comprehensive standards in the world" (Ibid.).

Baker's statement is supported by the fact that U.S. GAAP are predominantly used in more stock markets than any other standard when market capitalization is considered. Capitalization in the world's capital markets totaled approximately US$36 trillion in December 2005, of which US$17 trillion was in markets where U.S. GAAP were predominant as compared to US$11 trillion in markets where IFRS were predominant and US$4 trillion where Japanese standards prevailed (Prada, 2006, 4).

As a witness before the U.S. House of Representatives Subcommittee on Capital Markets, Paul Volcker, in his role as chairman of the Trustees, International Accounting Standards Board Foundation, pointed out: "I think traditionally the United States has taken the attitude we have the best standards. That's good enough. The rest of the world can come and join us if they're interested in approaching the big American markets" (Baker, 2001, 16). He observed, however, that he believed that American regulators and the Financial Accounting Standards Board (FASB) have come to agree that input from the rest of the world is beneficial. A truly international standard, which is an improvement on American standards, not a diminution, is the objective (Ibid.).

Volcker indicated that he believed that the SEC and FASB both recognize that "these are very contentious matters that in some cases have attracted political interest, and that indeed, advancing the platform to an international level may provide a more appropriate perspective than a purely national level" (Ibid.).

The case for international standards was succinctly put by Volcker in his later remarks before the Northwestern University Conference on Credible Financial Disclosures in 2002. He said: "In a world of global finance, we have a strong interest in encouraging high quality standards every place our companies do business" (Volcker, 2002, 1). Further, for foreign-based corporations to participate in our developed market, investor needs dictate adequate information. Lack of information, inconsistent information, or misinformation leads to "distortions in the international flow of capital" (Ibid.). In Volker's view, the costs of compliance with financial reporting laws and regulations will be lowered when a single set of standards is achieved (Ibid.).

The Economist agrees that the goal of global generally accepted accounting principles is worth attaining. In its words: "It will be a struggle. But if the standard-setters are successful in their quest, there could be a double pay-off: greater clarity and transparency for investors everywhere and cheaper capital for the companies they invest in" (*The Economist,* 2004b, 3).

The dimensions of incompatible accounting standards are significant and can perhaps be better appreciated by concrete examples. In commenting upon the problem in his 2002 *Forbes* article titled "Tower of Babel," Michael Maiello advised investors, "If you want to invest abroad, know the local accounting rules—or stick to buying shares in giant multinational corporations that also report financial results according to US generally accepted accounting principles" (Maiello, 2002, 1). He noted that there were at least twenty-six different accounting standards used by the Forbes International 500 Companies and all were different in some respects from U.S. GAAP.

In Maiello's view, corporations also "pay a high price" to reconcile even within their own companies. He cited Thomas Jones, former principal financial officer at Citigroup, who said that Citigroup had subsidiaries in 101 countries reporting under various standards. This causes substantial problems in understanding and preparing the financial reports of the corporation (Ibid.).

In 2001, Novartis, the Swiss pharmaceutical company, reported under the International Accounting Standards (IAS) and U.S. standards. Earnings under IAS were reported as $4.1 billion, whereas under U.S. GAAP they were $2.8 billion (Ibid.). This was a substantial difference in any language. Maiello indicates that the causes were mainly from two differences in the standards. Under IAS, development costs for drugs were capitalized, while they were expensed under U.S. GAAP. Investment portfolio decreases were included in income under U.S. GAAP but not under IAS (Ibid.).

Many European companies were using their home country standards at the time of the Maiello article. Volkswagen earnings for 2000 using German standards were 28 percent below earnings reported under IAS. Development costs for new cars were capitalized under IAS, creating a 10 percent difference, and car leases were treated as receivables, creating another 18 percent difference (Ibid.).

Maiello noted that, up to 2001, European firms that used IAS were in a minority. However, Maiello believes that by 2010 one standard will prevail in the world even if called by different names. He cited the fact that the European Union (EU) countries were scheduled to convert to IAS from their own country standards by 2005 and that IAS, in his view, are meant to resemble U.S. GAAP (Ibid.).

Regardless of whether IAS are designed to resemble U.S. GAAP or not, it is clear that the U.S. FASB is committed to closing differences in standards. The international section of the FASB Web site states that the board is obligated and engaged in narrowing the differences between other countries' standards and U.S. standards. "The FASB's objective for participating in international activities is to increase the international comparability and the quality of standards used in the United States" (FASB, 2006b, Overview of FASB's International Activities). The board notes that there remains no one set of standards acceptable in all world capital markets.

International Accounting Standards in Transition

Indeed, this remains true even though international standards have been in existence and in transition for some time. Prior to 2000, developments in international accounting standard setting had the goal of harmonization of country standards. With the advent of the International Accounting Standards Board (IASB) in 2001, the time was right to change the goal to convergence of country standards. In both the harmonization and now the convergence era, progress has been made in moving accounting standards toward comparability and mutual agreement and toward the eventual goal of development and adoption of one set of global accounting standards.

In 1973, national accounting authorities recognized the need for improved cross-border reporting and formed the International Accounting Standards Committee (IASC). The effort began with membership consisting of the national accounting authorities from Australia, Canada, France, Germany, Japan, Mexico, the Netherlands, the United Kingdom (UK) and Ireland, and the United States. From these original nine national accounting bodies as its membership, IASC grew to eighty-nine, representing sixty countries, by 1985 (McKee and Garner, 1992, 38).

The IASC created an IASC Board to issue accounting standards. Resulting IAS were descriptive in nature and did improve financial reporting on the margins, particularly so when adopted in countries that did not have their own national standards. Yet the standards contained far too many options to make financial reports comparable across companies and across countries (Ibid.). Over time, IAS were revised but remained a loose set of standards unable to produce reliably comparable financial statements because of the many optional treatments (for further discussion, see McKee and Garner, 1996, 32–35).

In order to create a clearer perspective, the goal of one set of standards for GAAP for all uses was revised in the 1990s to one of development of a set of standards that could be used by entities listed on the world's stock exchanges. In 1995, the IASC and the International Organization of Securities Commissions (IOSCO) and similar agencies agreed upon a work schedule to develop a core set of international standards useful for preparing comparable financial statements for multinational offerings and cross-border stock exchange listings. The IASC Board developed the standards with content and suggestions provided by IOSCO. In 2000, IOSCO endorsed the standards, then known as IASC 2000 Standards, as acceptable to IOSCO for use in multinational offerings and cross-border listings, but revisions were recommended (McKee, Garner, and McKee, 2002, 161).

The time was right for a major organizational change. The consensus appeared to be that the IASC Board had moved the cause forward but the board had problems that prevented its ultimate success in producing a single set of standards acceptable for use in all world stock exchanges. In 2001, the IASC created a successor organization with a new standards board, the International Accounting Standards Board.

The IASC Board structure had been a large body with representatives from the various member countries, which in its earlier years tended to seek compromise in order to establish standards. IASC Board members devoted their efforts on only a part-time basis. Accounting and report-ing issues, it was thought, were not posed before the board as sharply as needed, and the board's pronouncements allowed too many alternative treatments. These factors, it was thought, weakened the intellectual in-tegrity of the board's pronouncements as compared to British, Canadian, American, or other standards set in industrialized countries.

The goals of the IASC, as noted above, had been in transition for some time. Early on, the emphasis was to describe existing practices and allow numerous alternative treatments. The board moved to a period in which the goal was to harmonize differing country standards as opposed to standardize accounting practices across the world. Beginning in 1987, the IASC began its Comparability and Improvements Project in which the goal was "to reduce or eliminate alternatives and make standards more detailed and prescriptive rather than flexible and descriptive of current practice" (Deloitte IAS Plus, 2006b, 1987).

In the reorganization, the IASC and its member nations agreed upon a smaller board consisting of twelve full-time and two part-time members. A structure for board operations similar to the U.S. FASB organization was chosen. In 2001, the International Accounting Standards Committee Foundation began operations as a not-for-profit corporation incorporated in the State of Delaware (International Accounting Standards Board, 2001, 1).

The IASC Foundation is an independent organization under control of the IASC Foundation Trustees. It has two main bodies, the Trustees and the IASB. There are also a Standards Advisory Council and the International Financial Reporting Interpretations Committee. The IASC Foundation Trustees appoint IASB members, who have the sole respon-sibility for setting accounting standards (Ibid.).

The IASB procedures ensure that, like the FASB, their meetings are open to public observation and disclosure. Proposals for new or revised standards are first presented in public discussion documents. This is fol-lowed by an exposure draft. The IASB determines whether public hear-ings should be held on the topic prior to adoption of a new standard. The title for new standards was changed to International Financial Reporting Standards (Ibid.).

The stated objectives of the IASB organization are to develop in the public interest a set of global accounting standards that will be under-standable, transparent, and comparable for use in world capital markets. The global standards must be of such quality that they will be enforceable

by the countries of the world. In the public interest, the board is committed to seeking convergence of national standards with IFRS by working
with national standard-setters. It also seeks to promote the rigorous use
of these standards throughout the world (Ibid.). The IFRS are meant to
be used as general-purpose standards for financial statements of entities
that are profit oriented without regard to their legal makeup and without
regard to stock market or cross-border listings (Ibid.).

The prior International Accounting Standards will be in force until
changed or withdrawn by the IASB. In order to be considered as complying with IFRS, financial statements must meet all of the requirements set forth by each standard and interpretation that is applicable to
those statements (Ibid.). Through 2005, seven IFRS had been issued.
The board has updated, superseded, or withdrawn a number of existing IAS.

Convergence to International Accounting Standards

Acceptance of IFRS as the one world standard remains a work in progress. There are many aspects to setting the global standard, which will
require nations to adjust their current reporting standards and their ways
of doing business. An important consideration is that the proposed world
standards are now predicated largely on information needs of U.S.- and
British-style securities markets. In a number of countries, accounting
standards in use have been geared to other types of capital markets. In
continental Europe, for example, financing is often dependent on banking
sources for capital funds, or combines in the case of Germany, rather than
capital markets. In the Japanese system, capital funds are geared to the
banking system. Financial reporting systems required in those countries
have been geared to the needs of the sources of capital funds. The accounting and reporting systems, as one would expect, were dependent
upon who provided capital and what information capital providers needed.
Clearly, in centrally planned economies information requirements have
been handled differently.

Another aspect to the convergence problem is that current IAS and
U.S. standards provide one standard for all entities regardless of size.
To receive an unqualified auditor's opinion on financial statements, the
full set of rules must be complied with in detail. Unlisted companies
must follow the same prescribed standards as listed companies. A lively
debate has been ongoing in the United States for many years, sometimes

called Big GAAP versus Little GAAP. Should there be two or perhaps more sets of standards that would be better suited to the size and needs of the particular company in question? Smaller companies are thought by some not to need the full complex array of accounting and reporting required for large companies.

There seems to be merit in these objections. For example, consolidated financial statements are a requirement of GAAP. This essentially means that all businesses and operations under control of the parent entity must be consolidated into one set of financial statements, a relatively costly undertaking.

This procedure and reporting requirement is quite useful and necessary for full disclosure to outsiders of a large company. The consolidated results in a large company should also be quite useful in the internal management of the company. But, for smaller companies, the added expense may exceed the benefit to the company. Consolidated financials may be of limited use in the internal management of a smaller company.

The IASB recognized the small-entity problem and in 2003 established an Agenda Project to study the merits of Accounting Standards for Small and Medium-Sized Entities (SMEs). The project team has been working in conjunction with the IASB to establish what are now named International Reporting Standards for Small and Medium-Sized Entities. At its January 2006 meeting, the board had its initial discussion of a preliminary draft of an Exposure Draft of International Financial Reporting Standards for Small and Medium-Sized Entities. When issued, such standards will not be intended for publicly listed companies, even if national law or regulation were to permit this in some jurisdictions (Deloitte IAS Plus, 2006d, Accounting Standards for Small and Medium-Sized Entities).

The project participants' consensus was to approach the problem from the viewpoint of whether entities have or do not have public accountability. For those entities with public accountability, the thinking is that IFRS requirements should be followed. The project will study whether and how those entities without public accountability may be better served with a separate set of standards. Such SME standards would be general-purpose financial statements prepared for investment or credit decisions and the like, to be made by those without any other access to financial information, that is, those outside the entity (Ibid.).

The study surveyed interested parties and found widespread support for global SME standards. There was much support for special promulgation of the accounting standards for SMEs for such items as eliminating difficult options, making complex judgments, simplifying recognition and measurement criteria, and eliminating guidance that would not be applicable to SMEs (Ibid.).

Separate standards for small entities are available in the United Kingdom where Financial Reporting Standards for Small Entities (FRSSE) are issued by the UK Accounting Standards Board (ASB). These standards have simplified accounting requirements in the areas of disclosure, presentation, recognition, and measurement.

Should a particular issue not be included in the FRSSE, there is no automatic fallback to UK GAAP. Preparers of small entity financial reports are given the following guidelines. Financial statements must give a true and fair view. Where there are no stated requirements, the accounting carried out should be consistent with the requirements of FRSSE and of the UK company's legislation. When choices are allowed, the particular entity must use those policies and techniques most appropriate to its particular circumstances that will result in giving a true and fair view, taking into account that the objectives of accounting and reporting are to be relevance, reliability, comparability, and understandability. When the preparers are in doubt about whether the provisions of the FRSSE would give a true and fair view, full disclosure and explanations should be made in notes to the financial statements concerning the transactions and treatments involved. The concept of principle-based standards is clearly at work in these UK standards (Accounting Standards Board, 2007, 2).

The question of whether standards should be principle based or rule based is another ongoing question with a number of ramifications. The U.S. FASB is thought by many to be overly reliant on detailed, specific rules to promulgate accounting standards. The IASB, on the other hand, is thought to rely more on principles-based logic in its standards. In the litigious U.S. society, compliance with rules-based standards is thought to provide more protection to preparers and auditors from liability litigation. U.S. standards are seen as attempting to minimize professional judgment, thereby assuring comparable financial statements while at the same time reducing preparer and auditor liability. The rules-based approach is seen by some, however, as replete with complexity and details, bright-line tests, multiple exceptions, and internal inconsistencies. These and other problems, it is thought, result in financial statement incompatibility (SEC, 2003, 13).

Some have observed that rules-based systems often have provided a road map for preparers to avoid the intent inherent in standards. Those preparers whose agenda is to manipulate presentations in financial statements, it is said, find it easier to justify desired accounting treatments when rules are specified than they would if broader principles were used. Many of the recent financial scandals, it seems certain, were partly the result of such manipulation. In the Enron case, Mike McNamee observed: "If Andersen couldn't show Enron a specific rule prohibiting what it wanted to do, Enron would do it" (2002, 1). Nor does it seem that Enron was alone in using rule-based standards to nefarious ends.

As part of the effort to improve the corporate financial reporting system, the U.S. Congress in the Sarbanes-Oxley Act of 2002 directed the SEC staff to study adoption of a U.S. principles-based accounting system. The resulting report (SEC, 2003), which is more fully discussed in a later chapter, recommends neither the rules-based nor the principles-based system. The SEC staff envisions an objectives-oriented system in which every standard would define and be framed by specific objectives set for the standard such that the economic substance of transactions and events would be reflected in financial reports without resorting to overreliance on detailed rules (Ibid., 14).

Several problems are seen as arising from a principles-based system. Differing management and auditor judgments in applying standards without specific rules would cause comparability problems in financial reports. Principles-based standards are thought to be more difficult to enforce than rules-based standards because of the leeway afforded for judgments. Corporate preparers and their auditors are also seen as being skeptical that enforcement agencies and the courts will accept good-faith judgments (Ibid.). These objections to the principles-based approach are thought to be mitigated under the SEC report's proposed objectives-based system (Ibid., 13, 14).

The adoption of IFRS as a world standard clearly is more than merely substituting one set of standards for another. The standards, however, do appear to be gaining widespread support and recognition from countries across the globe. Over 100 countries throughout the world now permit or require IFRS for companies listed on stock exchanges within their jurisdictions. To be sure, some of these have used modified versions of the IFRS in their jurisdictions, so that it cannot be said that IFRS have been adopted as a single global standard across all of these countries.

Deloitte IAS Plus reported in 2006 that in seventy-four countries IFRS are required to be followed by all domestic listed companies. To be included in this group by IAS Plus, financial statements in those countries must refer to conformity with IFRS in the basis-of-preparation financial statement footnote and in the accompanying auditor's report (Deloitte IAS Plus, 2006a, 1).

A number of countries are in the process of adapting their standards to converge with IFRS. Japan began an active convergence project with the IASB in 2004. Australia and New Zealand have each adopted national standards that they describe as IFRS equivalents. China has committed to converge its standards with IFRS. Sir David Tweedie, chairman of the IASB, made note of this in his statement at the February 15, 2006, ceremony marking the establishment of China's new accounting and auditing standards. Tweedie indicated that he believes that the new China standards "suit the development of the market economy and convergence with the international practices" (IASB, 2006, 1). The new China standards are effective January 1, 2007, for all listed companies in China (Ibid.).

The U.S. FASB and IASB are pursuing an ongoing convergence project. In September 2002, FASB and IASB issued a joint memorandum that committed the boards to the pursuit of a common set of high-quality accounting standards that could be used both for cross-border reporting and for domestic purposes. In this agreement, referred to as the Norwalk Agreement, both boards pledged their best efforts to make existing standards compatible as soon as practical. Further, they pledged to maintain compatibility once attained through joint projects (Deloitte IAS Plus, 2006c, 1).

These commitments were reaffirmed in February 2006 when, in a joint statement, the two boards set 2008 as the date to reach conclusions about a number of focused areas where their standards diverge. The FASB agreed to examine fair-value options, investment properties, research and development, and subsequent events. The IASB agreed to examine borrowing costs, government grants, joint ventures, and segment reporting. They agreed to jointly examine impairment and income tax accounting (Ibid., 2). The boards have ongoing topics that are already on their active agenda in the areas of business combinations, consolidations, fair-value measurement guidance, liabilities and equity distinction, performance reporting, postretirement benefits, and revenue recognition (Ibid., 3).

Europe Adopts International Standards

As noted above, in June 2000 the European Commission recommended that International Accounting Standards be adopted by January 1, 2005, as mandatory for European Union (EU) stock exchange–listed companies. The commission's recommendations were submitted to the Council and Parliament of the European Union in a report titled *EU Financial Reporting Strategy: The Way Forward.* Member states, it was also recommended, would be permitted to extend this reporting requirement to enterprises not listed on stock exchanges (Commission of the European Communities, 2000, 1). The European Parliament enacted the commission's proposal in March 2002.

The commission estimated that approximately 7,000 companies would be subject to the new rule. In 2001, 275 European-listed companies prepared their consolidated financial statements under IAS, 300 under U.S. GAAP, and the remainder used their own national GAAP. These European Community numbers did not include Switzerland, where most large companies were reported to follow IAS (*The Economist*, 2004b, 1).

These European developments set the large part of the IASB pre-2005 agenda. At its inception, the board had previous IAS as a starting point. Of the existing thirty-four standards, fourteen were not fully acceptable to IOSCO without revisions. David Tweedie indicates that the IASB was faced with the choice of improving these fourteen standards before the EU adoption of IAS in 2005 or having the EU adopt the standards only to contend with later revisions. The board chose to improve the standards before 2005 and adopted a work program that was dubbed the Improvements Project (Tweedie, 2006b, 2).

By March 2004, following the Improvement Project, the IASB had amended seventeen standards and issued six new ones. By this unusual pace of change, IASB set out to create what it viewed as a "stable platform" for which major changes need not be made before 2006 (Ibid.). This commitment to stability would provide time for proper implementation of and adaptation to the new IFRS system. Changes that were made during that period to the stable platform, in the view of the IASB, were made to deal with implementation concerns raised by preparers, regulators, and auditors (Ibid., 3).

In 2006, members of the European Union and more than seventy other countries throughout the world began financial reporting under the revised IFRS. The board expects that other issues will be raised as the standards are used but hopes that in the near term these will call for minor amendment of the standards and will be relatively infrequent (Ibid.).

The need for stability of standards in the near term was important, the board's chairman indicated, but the board could not put aside the work on convergence with other national standards (Ibid.). In its early agenda, the IASB saw the opportunity to make headway toward convergence of IFRS and U.S. standards. In the aftermath of the Enron and other accounting scandals, it was thought that the United States was more willing to accept international methods and standards. The convergence project with the United States was seen as vital to the effort to bring a single set of world standards to the world's capital markets (Ibid., 2).

The importance of convergence can further be highlighted by a comparison of stock market and company use of IFRS versus U.S. or Japanese GAAP. Capitalization in the world's capital markets totaled approximately US$36 trillion in December 2005. Of this total, US$11 trillion was in markets that used or permitted IFRS. In markets where U.S. GAAP prevailed, market capitalization was US$17 trillion. Of the remainder, Japanese standards were used in markets that totaled US$4 trillion (Prada, 2006, 4). Among Fortune 500 companies, U.S. GAAP are used by 176 companies, compared with 200 companies that use IFRS, and 81 companies that use Japanese GAAP (Ibid., 5).

The work of convergence to one set of standards remains a work in progress. As can be seen from the data in the preceding paragraph, success in the current scheme of things depends in large measure on the conversion of U.S. GAAP and IFRS.

In April 2005, the U.S. SEC and the European Union Internal Market Commission issued a joint memorandum of understanding that set 2009 as the target year for acceptance of IFRS as comparable to U.S. GAAP. In February 2006, a joint memorandum of understanding was issued by the IASB and FASB that also set the goal of 2009 as the latest time to complete the reconciliation to U.S. standards required by the SEC for foreign registrants listed on U.S. exchanges and using IFRS.

Convergence is not a simple matter. With the number and importance of the remaining differences between U.S. GAAP and IFRS, as enumerated above, this is an ambitious goal. The U.S. system of rule-based standards has been in use for over seventy years, and many believe that it has been time-tested in a litigious environment. IFRS have been designed to be more principles based, which brings its own set of problems. IFRS are widely used but quite new in their present form and have not stood the test of time.

The political aspects of standard setting will continue to be problematic. Governments fully intend to have their say. The European Commissioner for the Internal Market and Services, Charlie McCreevy, opposes the use of the convergence period to make new accounting advances. He stated: "I will not take on board any revolutionary new standards" (Woolfe, 2006, 1). In his view, the exercise of convergence is to narrow the existing differences.

Political aspects of standard setting are well known in the United States with the interplay of the U.S. Congress with the SEC and the FASB. In the United States, political influence is frequently brought to bear by various interested parties. The European Community displayed similar attributes in the run up to 2005. The 2005 conversion from national standards to IFRS was approved by the EU Accounting Regulatory Committee and the European Parliament Economic and Monetary Affairs Committee in October 2004 with a "carve-out" of seventeen paragraphs from IAS 39. The carve-out allowed fair-value hedge accounting for bank core deposits on a portfolio basis and prohibited the use of fair value for liabilities (Woolfe, 2004b, 1).

The convergence of IFRS with U.S. GAAP does appear to be important for European industry's cost of capital. GDP growth in the EU has been substantially below U.S. growth since the 1980s by approximately 30 percent. The higher cost of capital in Europe's fragmented capital markets is thought to be one of the major causes (Ibid.). Further, as Kevin Stevenson, a member of the IASB, indicated: "European companies cannot fall back on EU funds because the financial markets are just not there" (Woolfe, 2004a, 2). With the convergence in place, a large barrier for European companies in raising capital in the U.S. market would disappear.

At the same time, the U.S. securities industry should also be finding that convergence is important. The industry has felt the negative competitive effects of IFRS versus the more rigorous U.S. standards, including the SEC reconciliation requirement for foreign companies listing in U.S. markets, as well as the negative impact of Sarbanes-Oxley rules that call for foreign companies listed on U.S. exchanges to meet the same standards as domestic companies.

Initial public offerings in 2005 raised $9.5 billion on the London and Luxembourg exchanges versus $1.3 billion on the New York Stock Exchange (Karmin and Lucchetti, 2006, 3). This was reported as the biggest spread between the two markets favoring the London market since 1990. To be sure, the negative effects caused by the more rigorous U.S. requirements are mitigated when the U.S. market is advancing. In the 2000 to 2005 period, the U.S. stock market was outperforming the home markets of foreign companies. Citigroup reported that in that period 87 percent of capital raised by foreign companies was raised using U.S. American Depository Receipts. In periods when the local markets were doing better, 64 percent of the capital raised by foreign companies was in international Global Depository Receipts.

So, for a variety of reasons, national standard-setters and market participants alike seem to have come to a consensus that global markets and economies would benefit from recognition and enforcement of one set of standards for all global markets. A number of aspects of this movement will be discussed in subsequent chapters. The next chapter will discuss the enforcement issues, particularly those arising from auditing financial reports on a global basis.

3

The Role of
Auditing Standards

Since the dawn of organized human existence, auditors have been needed within their societies to attest to the accuracy and fairness of accounting and financial reports, however rudimentary or complex. Audit activities are both formed by and limited by the scope of economic activities of the times. Auditors, because of their attestation responsibilities, have occupied a pivotal position in society. The history of auditors has been traced to ancient China in the Zhou Dynasty (circa 1122 B.C.E.–256 B.C.E.), where elaborate systems of government budgets and accountability were audited. In ancient Egypt (circa 3000 B.C.E.), scribes performed auditlike service and were highly esteemed. In the English-speaking world, the history of auditing goes as far back as 1130 C.E. (Hayes et al., 2005, 3.)

With the Industrial Revolution and the advent of corporate structures, modern independent auditing had its beginnings. As ownership and management of wealth became more widely separated, the need for independent audit grew. By 1853, the Society of Accountants had been founded in Edinburgh, Scotland. The British Companies Acts from 1845 to 1862 contained the essential requirements for modern auditing (Ibid., 2, 3). Several accountants' institutes that had formed in Great Britain merged in 1880 to become the Institute of Chartered Accountants in England and Wales. These institutes served as the predecessors to professional accounting institutes and organizations throughout the Western world and beyond.

The need for effective independent audit grows and evolves as economic activities expand in volume, scope, and complexity. Today, securities markets cannot properly function without effective independent audit. This is especially so in the international arena.

As discussed in the previous chapter, accounting standards, whether used for domestic or for cross-border corporate financial reporting, are vital to market-based economic systems. Auditing standards are no less important. In fact, the soundness of standards and practices followed by all parties in the financial reporting process is essential to the credibility of corporate financial reports and to investors' decisions. Absentee owners require information upon which to base decisions about performance of existing investments and about future allocations of capital to best uses. The functioning of market-based financing for public corporations, in particular, depends upon the reliability and fairness of financial reporting in all its phases. Appropriate audit standards appropriately applied are at the heart of this process.

Auditing standards, like accounting standards, are today the province of nation-states. And, just as the global marketplace and world economies would benefit from one set of global accounting standards, they would benefit from one set of global auditing standards that are consistent, comparable, and relevant in the world-spanning environment of finance and commerce.

Differences among the various countries' auditing requirements and standards have been much less pronounced than have differences with respect to countries' accounting standards. An analysis by McKee and Garner found that, of forty-five countries studied, thirty-three were thought to have audit standards comparable to those of the United States in 1986 (McKee and Garner, 1992, 31–33).

As capital has increasingly sought its best uses across the globe, national audit standards promulgated by individual nation-state jurisdictions and international audit standards alike have proven to be inadequate and insufficient for international use. National standards differing in scope and coverage cause inconsistencies and incompatibilities when used for audit of cross-border transactions and financial reporting. Further, both the national and international audit standards in use prior to 2002 were shown to be insufficient by failing to prevent the widespread accounting and auditing debacles that occurred in many countries in the final decades of the twentieth century.

Audit standards and practices in many market-based countries had long been delegated to private-sector professional organizations. These private-sector standard-setters were usually controlled or heavily influenced by the accounting professionals in the country in question. Not surprisingly, audit failures of the recent past have led governments to review and change their laws in regard to audit standards and other regulatory practices.

Improved Audit Standards Needed
to Restore Public Confidence

The emphasis of recent national legislation has been to move away from private-sector self-regulation to more direct government regulation through the use of governmental or quasi-governmental regulatory bodies. Intensified government regulations have not been directed solely at auditing standards and practice. Those who have a public duty to be fair and honest have also seen stricter regulation of their activities. In the process, national authorities have expanded the explicit standards, which previously seemed to be set for auditors alone, to include not just auditors but the wider range of those who have roles in full, fair, and true public disclosure of corporate financial information. These circumstances may make the attainment of one set of world auditing standards even more difficult to attain as more and divergent national standards are adopted.

In the United States, for example, self-regulation of the accounting profession in its modern form dates to the passage of the Securities Act of 1933 and the Securities Exchange Act of 1934, which established the U.S. Securities and Exchange Commission (SEC). These laws were passed in response to the stock market crash of 1929 and the financial depression that followed. Although serious consideration was given at that time to federal direct regulation of public company financial and auditing standards, the SEC was given statutory authority for these duties and, in effect, delegated them to the accounting profession through the American Institute of Accountants, which later became the American Institute of Certified Public Accountants (AICPA). The AICPA's *A Brief History of Self-Regulation* (2002) describes self-regulation in the United States from the outset of the SEC era in the 1930s through 2002.

In the international arena, the International Federation of Accountants (IFAC) is open to national and international accountancy organizations that are devoted to improving world accounting. Member organizations total in excess of 160 from 120 countries. An affiliated organization, the International Auditing Practices Committee (IAPC), promulgated standards designed to improve auditing and reporting since 1977. The Council of the IFAC in November 2003 approved a series of reforms that had been developed by the IFAC in conjunction with regulators from its member countries. The reforms were designed to strengthen international audit standard-setting and to converge national standards with international standards. Among the reforms was to replace the IAPC with the International Auditing and Assurance Standards Board (IAASB). This board now has the responsibility of an independent auditing standard-setting body and has instituted several new series of directives, including International Standards on Auditing (ISA).

In October 2002, as part of the response to the Enron-Andersen auditing debacle, the IFAC appointed the Task Force on Rebuilding Public Confidence in Financial Reporting to examine avenues to restore credibility to international financial reporting and corporate disclosure. Members of the task force, each highly qualified, were drawn from six countries: Australia, Canada, France, Japan, the United Kingdom, and the United States. The group devoted considerable time and effort to analysis of the causes of the substantial decline in credibility and prepared a report with recommendations for improvement. The task force members saw their job as one of identifying real causes and recommending appropriate solutions. They studied, in particular, recent aspects of the credibility problem in Australia, Canada, France, Japan, the United Kingdom, and the United States. They also studied recent international developments from the IFAC, International Organization of Securities Commissions (IOSCO), the European Commission, and the International Accounting Standards Board (IASB) (Task Force, 2003, 1).

One of the major outcomes of the report involved recommendations for improvements in the standards and practices of auditing. The report, however, goes well beyond accountants and auditors to cover the many parties involved in financial reporting processes. The task force did its work at the beginning of a time of substantial transition and its study bears on matters that remain very much a work in progress.

The task force concluded that the low credibility of financial reporting constituted a serious problem. Recent scandals were symptomatic of larger problems but were not the primary cause of the credibility problem. The loss of credibility in capital markets had occurred across the globe. This loss, the task force believed, occurred over many years beginning in the 1980s. During much of this period, the fact that many securities markets operated at historically high prices contributed to the problem, as maintaining company security price levels became a top management goal. This desire to keep security prices up contributed to some corporations reporting earnings that were not consistent with economic substance. When this became known in the market, the fall in prices spread through international markets generally. Problems in one industry or country quickly spread to other areas and countries.

The resulting loss in public confidence in financial statements, the group concluded, had been cumulative. The credibility loss extended to those who prepared and issued financial statements. A spectrum of perceived causes was found. The task force report detailed recommendations for courses of action and best practices in the areas of financial and business reporting, corporate governance, and auditor performance.

The task force concluded that restoring integrity to the system must be the major contributor to the problem's solution. Actions to restore credibility to financial reporting were needed on a country by country basis as well as on an international level. If changes made at the national level were to result in consistent and permanent improvements, international changes would be needed as well (Ibid., 24).

In the task force's view, all participants in the financial reporting process need to take actions to improve and to return integrity to financial reporting. Those involved include independent auditors, standard-setters, and regulators, as well as lawyers, investment bankers, analysts, and credit-rating agencies (Ibid., 1). Integrity must be returned to all points on the information supply chain that delivers financial reports. Primary responsibility must, however, be with boards of directors and corporate managements (Ibid., 1).

The task force report was clearly based on considerable effort and study by well-qualified members. The report and its recommendations should provide a useful gauge in the analysis of both what went wrong with auditing and audit firms and what actions will be needed to restore credibility to financial reporting. The detailed report is analyzed here with a view to understanding changes needed in corporate management and governance, in the audit function and in regulation of other private-sector participants.

The report was based on the view that public reporting is a public-interest activity that places responsibilities on all of the participants. The primacy of this public duty needs to be recognized by all who undertake public reporting responsibilities inside and outside the company in question. The lack of integrity by individuals and institutions producing and using financial reports in the public interest has been a major cause of the recent financial scandals. Actions at both national and international levels are necessary to ensure reporting that is credible, comparable, and consistent.

Structural Weaknesses in Financial Reporting

Improvements, the task force indicated, are needed throughout the entire supply line of corporate reporting. This must include corporate managements, boards of directors, auditors, standard-setters, regulators, lawyers, investment bankers, analysts, and credit-rating agencies. All of these groups must improve their practices and procedures, and all must recognize the primacy of their public-interest duty (Ibid., 1).

The task force found that business failures, governance failures, and reporting failures were at the heart of most of the high-profile corporate reporting problems. Business information that should have been disclosed was not properly reported. The corporate and audit structures designed to detect such misinformation did not, resulting in misinformation provided to public users (Ibid., 5). The decades of the 1980s and 1990s saw large numbers of such reporting failures, which led to a steady loss in the credibility of both financial reports and those producing them.

Although widely accepted as being the cause, the collapse of Enron was not the cause but the confirmation of long-standing reliability problems in financial reports (Ibid., 7). The task force report provides a long list of reporting failures caused by failures of corporate governance, many with attendant fraud involved and many with flawed audit performances (Ibid., 7). The list comes from most of the developed world.

As an important example, a 1999 United Nations Conference on Trade and Development report on the East Asian financial crisis of 1997 indicated that disclosure deficiencies were a crucial factor in the East Asian market collapse. There was a lack of required disclosure requirements and internal controls that contributed to problems of imprudent risk taking by managements and banks (Ibid., 6). At the time, these problems were not seen as ones that would occur in the United States and other Western markets, but only in some Asian countries (Ibid.). Subsequent events were to prove this view wrong.

The task force report cites a large number of specific structural weaknesses in the chain of financial reporting. These are seen to have resulted from the relationships between market participants, the range of pressures placed on participants, and the sheer number of participants in the process. Incentives given to management often produced undesirable results. Senior management remuneration often has been linked to share price, creating pressure to manage the price of company stock in the short run.

The focus on short-term share prices has often led to neglect of effective internal controls. Internal audit has often been neglected or overlooked. Chief financial officers have been more involved with strategic planning for corporations than they have in operations and controls over financial functions needed in preparing fair financial statements. Thus, basic accounting, internal controls, and internal audit have been neglected in some companies, the task force indicates (Ibid., 12).

Boards of directors have not fulfilled their responsibilities for oversight of management, particularly in the area of financial reporting. Audit committees of the boards of directors have not functioned properly in regard to financial reporting, often lacking the time, skills, experience, independence, or resources.

In the view of the task force, auditors being paid by the corporations they audit cannot be independent in the strict sense. The main responsibility and allegiance of auditors have been to management rather than to shareholders, with management in effect hiring the auditors and setting their fees. Auditors have been under pressure from their own organizations to sell other services than attestation, with resultant independence problems. The wide range of services provided to audit clients appears to be a major independence problem, the task force concludes. The closeness of the auditor to corporate management, and increased reliance by the auditor and the audit firm on management, have negative implications for independence (Ibid., 13).

Further, the auditing profession and the audit firms have not maintained an effective quality control apparatus, in the view of the task force. There have been ineffective consultative practices within the audit firms, including weak independent partner reviews of audits and override of the firm's technical arm for business reasons. Further, even though the market expects that audits can detect material fraud, auditors maintain that not all fraud, even if material, can be detected where collusion exists, particularly among senior management (Ibid.).

Accounting standards in various countries have been deficient, and varying country standards have caused problems in comparisons among companies and countries. Corporations have had to deal with multiple sets of standards in the preparation of their reports. Some of the problems seen by the task force in national standards are that the standards may not be grounded in underlying principles, may not be issued on a timely basis, may be weak rather than appropriate to the situation, may fail to consider intangibles or off-balance-sheet financing, may have inappropriate emphasis on forward-looking information, or may fail to take proper account of risks (Ibid.).

The task force notes that regulation of corporations and the financial reporting process has been less than fruitful in many jurisdictions.

Whether professional organizations perform self-regulatory duties or whether a government agency is the regulator, often the skills needed are lacking. Resources devoted to regulation are frequently inadequate. Regulators are subject to political pressures to do too little in some cases and too much in others. If the self-regulating bodies are not adequately and independently monitored, perceptions are often that the system lacks effectiveness.

In some cases, managements whose objective is the manipulation and misstatement of financial reports have been aided and abetted by investment bankers and lawyers. Products that were clearly designed to further corporate managers' misstatement of financial reports have been sold to corporations by investment banks. Loans that are structured as sales, off-balance-sheet financing that does not represent economic reality, and the use of special purpose entities are examples of such manipulation. Lawyers, among others, have produced opinions that were based on technicalities without regard to fair presentation of the economic substance of the transactions.

In far too many cases, the task force indicates, boards of directors have failed to adequately carry out their duties. Audit committees of the boards of directors have been used for a number of years and have been charged with a central role in governing the financial reports of most public companies. The task force concludes that many of the failures have been caused by poorly defined committees that did not understand or devote adequate time to committee responsibilities. Committee agendas were often controlled by senior management. Committee members lacked the knowledge or courage to challenge management (Ibid., 29).

Ethical behavior has been sorely lacking among many participants. The task force's list of such unethical actions includes auditors who misled, auditors who looked the other way, transactions that were disguised to hide economic substance, withholding of necessary information, abuse of trust, misuse of insider information, and providing advice that was not balanced (Ibid., 15).

Improving Systemic Weaknesses

With the many systemic weaknesses in mind, the task force sets forth detailed conclusions and recommendations for returning credibility to financial reporting (Ibid., 24–45). The recommendations for corporate management and governance are by far the largest group. The task force indicates that the board of directors has a central oversight role in company governance that is shared by each of its members. The board and its committees must ensure that management does not dominate them. Adequate time must be devoted to board duties. Skepticism and the courage to challenge decisions and judgments of management are essential to an effective board (Ibid., 28).

Primary responsibility for corporate financial reporting does rest with the chief executive officer (CEO) and to a lesser extent with the chief financial officer (CFO). In many countries, the board of directors must approve financial and other reports to shareholders before issuance. These responsibilities of the chief executive and the board of directors need to be emphasized explicitly in shareholder reports. Since the duties of the CFO require that reporting and controls are a core competency, the CEO and audit committee should include this competency in their assessment of candidates before CFO appointment. Regular annual reports should be made to shareholders on management's evaluation of the condition of company internal controls together with an attendant report from the independent auditor expressing an opinion on management's evaluation (Ibid., 25).

Company internal auditing should focus on adequate and effective internal controls, the task force recommends. The internal auditor should report directly to the CEO and have complete access to the audit committee. The audit committee should have significant involvement with the internal audit function, including assessing the level of resources devoted by the internal auditor to ensure internal control adequacy and effectiveness.

The board of directors audit committee should oversee the charter of the internal auditor. The audit committee should be consulted when an internal auditor is employed and approve any termination of the internal audit chief. The internal auditor should have access to any information needed to perform the internal audit. Regular reports should be made by the internal auditor to the audit committee on his or her work so that the committee can assess management's responses to internal audit recommendations and assess internal audit effectiveness (Ibid., 25).

In the area of reducing incentives to misstate earnings, the task force indicates that companies should not provide short-term forecasts of earnings, which assume an unrealistic precision. Forecasts could of course continue to be made by analysts and others outside the company. The task force recommends that the costs of stock options should be expensed, with clear disclosures including detailed terms of options granted (Ibid., 26). Such stock option expensing with appropriate disclosures will likely encourage the board to require appropriate hurdles for the granting of options. The linkage of executive compensation to short-term goals for share prices needs to be reduced because it provides an incentive to misstate financial results (Ibid., 26).

The form and level of senior management compensation and employment conditions and terms should be set by the board of directors or a committee of the board made up of independent members of the board. Incentive arrangements should be long term in nature. A detailed report of the setting and review of senior management compensation should be made to shareholders (Ibid., 27).

An important duty of the board of directors should be to ensure that management creates an open and transparent environment that will promote ethical behavior throughout the organization. A well-monitored code of ethical conduct appropriate to the circumstances and applicable to everyone in the company, including senior management and directors, should be widely distributed and provide for such matters as conflicts of interest, confidentiality, compliance with all laws and other regulations, and protection of company assets. The code should encourage all employees to report illegal or unethical behavior. A strong monitoring system needs to be established. The internal audit function should operate the monitoring system, with the board or an independent committee of the board maintaining a key role in evaluating compliance, handling complaints, and reporting to shareholders any serious breaches of the code. Ethics training and support are recommended throughout the organization to help all employees face difficult ethical questions (Ibid.).

The board of directors needs to perform its oversight of management effectively. The appointment and evaluation of the CEO is among the most important duties of the board. The board should regularly evaluate the CEO's performance in the areas of ethics, governance, and financial reporting in addition to performance of the company. The board should also regularly evaluate its own effectiveness and the effectiveness of individual members of the board in performing corporate governance responsibilities (Ibid., 28).

Each company should have an audit committee, or similar governance body, of the board of directors that should meet regularly and report regularly to the full board with adequate time to discuss the committee reports, including concerns that the committee may have about financial information, internal controls, or audit matters. The committee should regularly monitor and review entity financial reporting, the internal financial control and risk-management systems, internal auditing, and the appointment and performance of the external auditor (Ibid.).

The committee should be responsible for monitoring the integrity of financial reporting; the effectiveness of the internal audit function; and the effectiveness, independence, and objectivity of the external independent auditor. This governance body should recommend the external auditor for appointment, along with the audit firm's terms of engagement and remuneration. Audit committee responsibilities should be agreed to by the full board of directors and a copy of the committee charter should be provided to company shareholders (Ibid., 29, 32).

The audit committee should be independent and competent. It should have access to adequate outside advice and the power to seek additional information if needed for its decisions. The committee should receive from both management and external auditor reports that set out areas where judgments have been made or where disputes occurred, including alternatives considered and reasons for conclusions drawn. These reports to the committee are especially important where a departure from best financial reporting practice is contemplated for the company (Ibid., 29).

The audit committee should normally function from an oversight position but needs to become closely involved when proposed financial reporting runs contrary to the committee's independent judgment or where management proposals are inappropriate (Ibid., 30). The committee should conduct a regular in-depth review of the audit relationship, which should consider the quality aspects of the audit relationship as well as audit costs. This review should include auditor independence and objectivity issues (Ibid., 35).

The audit committee should be made up of board members who are independent from management, are financially literate, and, for at least the majority, have substantial financial experience. The task force feels strongly that members of the audit committee should be independent from management. While not thinking it appropriate to set forth a detailed international definition of independence, the task force states that a principles-based approach to determining independence is more appropriate. They suggest transparency be attained by public disclosure of board members' experience, background, remuneration, and shareholdings. The task force also indicates that boards of directors should consider the potential for non-independence from management of any board member who holds company share options, receives remuneration related to company profitability, or holds an amount of company shares that is material in relation to either the company itself or the board member's total wealth (Ibid., 31).

To help prepare the audit committee to be effective, members should receive training on their responsibilities as well as on company business issues, financial reporting, control systems, and risk-management matters (Ibid., 30).

The task force recommends that the audit committee should control which members of management are to be present in committee meetings. Private sessions should regularly be held with the internal auditor and the external auditor without management being present. Private sessions should also be held with the CFO and other financial personnel (Ibid.).

Turning to the audit function, the task force believes that the competence and independence of the outside auditor is critical to ensuring credible financial reports. The task force recommended that the IFAC Code of Ethics be used as the basis for national ethics codes. This would provide a principles-based framework of acceptability of non-audit services. While that code makes the auditor responsible for assessment of independence, the task force recommends that decisions about auditor independence should also be the responsibility of company officials who are independent of management (Ibid., 32).

To help ensure auditor independence and objectivity, the audit committee should construct procedures for non-audit services based on the nature of the service. The task force did not see the necessity for audit committee approval in advance but rather believed that procedures and policy should be established to guide decisions. Audit and non-audit fees should be publicly disclosed and broken into categories with major individual engagements specified (Ibid., 33).

Excessive familiarity is a problem for auditor independence. Key audit personnel who would include the engagement partner and the independent review partner should be rotated off a given company audit at least every seven years. Former auditors who occupied key positions on a company audit should not be hired in key company positions until two years after having left the audit team. Any such hiring should be approved by the audit committee with full disclosure if the company position is that of a director (Ibid., 34).

To avoid inappropriate pressure on individual members of the audit team from the client or from within the audit firm itself, both the company and the audit firm need to have safeguards in effect. The audit committee should monitor audit firm policies on consultation within the audit firm, remuneration of partners, and firm quality control. Within the audit firm, consultation procedures should ensure sufficient support be given as needed by individual partners. Such consultations should ensure that decisions on the audit are the firm's decisions and not those of individual partners on their own. The procedures should ensure that audit decisions that have negative impact on an audit firm's short-term income are not affected by the individual partner's concerns about the effect on his or her income (Ibid.).

Audit firms should not, in the view of the task force, base remuneration of partners who can influence the audit opinion on sales of non-audit services to an audit client (Ibid., 35).

The task force concludes that, in many cases of audit failure, auditors failed to follow audit standards or the policies of their own audit firm. Quality control procedures within audit firms and within the total audit profession need to be more effective. Policies and procedures for client retention should be more rigorous and skeptical. Many of the client companies where audit failures occurred had been identified as high risk by their audit firms but were nonetheless retained as clients. The assumption should be made that some current clients will not be retained by the audit firm (Ibid., 36).

In the firm's audit consultative process, technical advice given to the audit team should be in writing. Any disagreements between the engagement team and technical team should be documented. Such disagreements should be referred to a sufficiently high level within the audit firm such that client pressure does not dominate the process. Where the engagement partner's position is followed versus the technical advice, the audit committee should be apprised of it, including the rationale for the decision (Ibid., 37).

In addition to independent partner review of the audit prior to issuance, the task force recommends that independent review take place at interim dates as well. This review should focus on audit risks, areas where the accounting treatments are not in accordance with best practices, and any areas of dispute with company management. Independent partner review should be performed by partners who have not worked on the audit in prior years and have the same reporting line as the engagement partner within the audit firm. Post-audit reviews should be made, which cover compliance with firm policies and procedures including recruiting, training, and consultation, in addition to the quality of the individual audit approach (Ibid., 36).

Audit firms need to increase transparency in regard to the degree of independence the firm has from a given client company. The task force indicates that the relevant information is the profit-sharing unit for partners who receive remuneration on the basis of major audits. If a partner is shown to be reliant on one or a small number of clients, the firm should disclose the special quality control processes that have been put it place to ensure partner and firm objectivity and independence.

Details of the firm's quality control processes and the firm's procedures for ensuring that the processes are effective should be publicly disclosed, including results of internal inspection programs and external reviews conducted on any of its worldwide units (Ibid., 37, 38). The task force recommends that firms publish financial information and disclose the financial relationships among the firm's network of members and its coordinating unit.

In turning to other private-sector participants in the financial reporting process, the task force cites the near $1.4 billion settlement by U.S. regulators with eleven investment banks for issuing research reports not based on the facts but upon exaggerated claims (Ibid., 38). This large settlement is indicative of the problems caused by other private-sector participants in the financial reporting process. The task force recommends that a publicly disclosed code of conduct for investment bankers be issued that covers advice investment banks give to companies. There should be a monitoring system within the investment banks and externally to ensure compliance with the code of conduct (Ibid.).

Financial analysts should also have a code of conduct covering the operation of financial analysis, which should be made public and monitored externally, as well as within financial analysts' employing firms. The code should prohibit monetary payments to analysts based on stock sales or on products in other parts of the firm (Ibid.).

A code of conduct should be developed for lawyers who provide clients advice on financial reporting matters, the task force recommends. The code should be publicly available and monitored within the law firm as well as externally. Such a code of conduct should recognize that the company and not its management is the client, and that advice on financial reporting must uphold a public-interest standard. Should the advice given not be for best practices, the lawyer should summarize best practice and indicate reasons for not following such best practice. When lawyers give advice on financial reporting from a position of advocacy, alternatives including best practices should be summarized for evaluation by the board. Details of lawyer's fees paid in relation to financial reporting and the fee basis should be disclosed to the board and the audit committee (Ibid.).

Finally, credit-rating agencies need to establish greater transparency for their ratings by public disclosure of criteria, evaluation processes, and related quality control mechanisms used (Ibid.).

The task force indicates its support for International Standards on Auditing as the worldwide standard for all audit and related matters. A significant number of IFAC members currently use the ISA as a basis for developing their own national standards. They noted that ISA development needs to be accelerated to be more acceptable as a global standard, which will require substantial additional resources for the IAASB (Ibid., 40). There needs to be a process for convergence of auditing standards that is similar to the process now under way for convergence of national accounting standards to International Financial Reporting Standards.

Changes are taking place, but it is difficult to judge how rapidly. However, some knowledgeable observers feel that worldwide audit standards may come to pass rather quickly. O. Ray Whittington and Kurt Pany indicate that in view of the rapid progress in setting international auditing standards, "It is likely that within five years an audit in conformity with IASSB standards will be acceptable for multinational securities offerings in virtually all countries" (Whittington and Pany, 2006, 48). Others are not so sure. These and other matters will be further examined in the next chapter and in a later chapter devoted to considerations of worldwide audit standard convergence.

The next chapter, which contains detailed consideration of the requirements of the Sarbanes-Oxley Act, also offers the comparative view of the U.S. Congress in setting required actions for improvements to the financial reporting system. Many of the recommendations made in the report of the Task Force on Rebuilding Public Confidence in Financial Reporting are in fact legislated into law by the Sarbanes-Oxley Act.

4

Changing Realities in the Sarbanes-Oxley Era

Self-regulation of public company auditors in the United States came to an inglorious end as the Sarbanes-Oxley Act was passed by Congress and signed into law on July 30, 2002. In the wake of the reform actions of the United States, legislated reforms spread to virtually every developed and most of the developing countries in the world. There seems to have been general worldwide recognition that financial reporting and all those who have roles in financial reporting processes must improve significantly. In this chapter, the reforms legislated in the United States will be analyzed in some detail, followed by consideration of the reforms in the major jurisdictions of the United Kingdom (UK), France, Japan, and the European Union (EU).

In the United States, the newly created Public Company Accounting Oversight Board (PCAOB) moved to organize and begin operations under its Sarbanes-Oxley legislated mandate. By April 25, 2003, the Securities and Exchange Commission (SEC) announced that it was satisfied that the board had been properly organized with the capacity to carry out the requirements of the Sarbanes-Oxley Act (PCAOB, 2003, 1). A new era of greater government regulation and oversight for U.S. auditors, and indeed for auditors around the world, had begun. A new era for public corporations had also begun with the passage of the act, which strengthened government regulations over issuers of financial securities, their affiliated support companies, and all those involved in the processes of financial reporting.

The U.S. Congress was stirred to act by public outrage over the collapse of world-spanning public corporations and the attendant unprecedented losses to stakeholders' and public interests. In many cases, criminal behavior on the part of corporate officials, affiliated organizations, and gatekeepers alike had occurred. Congress responded by revising the SEC laws to bolster the perceived problems in regulation of these public-interest groups. The Sarbanes-Oxley Act (U.S. Congress, 2003) was designed to restore public confidence in the vital market for corporate securities by making reforms and revisions in the problem areas of existing SEC law that were thought responsible for giving rise to the debacles.

Sarbanes-Oxley Act Provisions

A reading of the Sarbanes-Oxley Act, which is organized into Title I through Title XI, indicates that the act can best be analyzed according to major problem areas. The act addresses problems in the following areas: financial accounting standard-setting, corporate boards of directors, corporate management, public company internal controls, public company auditing, auditor independence, other parties involved in the financial reporting process and penalties for noncompliance.

Financial Accounting Standard-Setting

The act authorizes the SEC to recognize accounting principles as generally accepted so long as they are established by a standard-setting body that meets the act's criteria. The requirements include that the body be a private entity funded in a manner similar to the PCAOB and be governed by a board of trustees or equivalent body, the majority of whose members are not or have not been associated in the prior two years with a public accounting firm. The standard-setting body must have adopted procedures to ensure prompt consideration of changes to accounting principles. Decisions by the standard-setting organization should be determined by majority vote. The body is required by the act to consider, when adopting standards, the need to keep them current and the extent to which international convergence of standards is necessary or appropriate. The current Financial Accounting Standards Board (FASB) was accepted by the SEC as such a body, so long as the added congressional provisions are met (Section 108).

Corporate Boards of Directors

As indicated in chapter 3 of this volume, a public company board of directors should be in ultimate control of the corporation, independent of corporate management. Changes made by the Sarbanes-Oxley Act are designed to bolster audit committee independence as well as auditor independence from corporate management. Corporate audit committees and their public corporations must meet a number of new standards.

Each audit committee must be provided by its corporation with funds to properly carry out its functions, including the funds and authority to engage independent counsel or other advisers, as the audit committee determines necessary to carry out its duties (Section 301).

Only independent board members are permitted to be part of the audit committee. The company must disclose whether at least one member of the audit committee is expert in financial matters. Procedures must be established by the audit committee for the receipt, retention, and treatment of complaints received by the corporation that concern the areas of accounting, internal controls, and auditing.

The audit committee is to be directly responsible for appointment, compensation, and oversight of the corporation's auditor. Auditors must report to corporate audit committees all critical accounting policies and practices used by the client corporation. They must report alternative treatments of generally accepted accounting principles (GAAP) that have been discussed with corporate management, together with the ramifications of each alternative. The accounting treatment alternative preferred by the audit firm must also be reported to the audit committee in question (Section 301).

Corporate Management

Corporate responsibilities are covered throughout the act. Each corporation issuing securities to the public must disclose whether it has adopted a code of ethics for its senior financial officers. The contents of the code must be disclosed. Prompt disclosure on SEC Form 8-K is required for changes in, or waivers to, the corporate code of ethics (Section 406).

The corporate chief executive officer (CEO) and chief financial officer (CFO) must certify in each shareholder annual and quarterly report that, based on their knowledge, the corporate financial statements, together with disclosures, present fairly the operations and financial condition of the corporation in all material respects. The certification must state that the financial statements and disclosures fully comply with provisions of the Securities Exchange Act. They must certify that they have read the report and that it does not contain an untrue statement or have a material omission. The certifications also must state that the officers are responsible for establishing and maintaining internal controls that they have evaluated for effectiveness.

Financial reports in accordance with GAAP must include required disclosures, including all material off-balance-sheet transactions as well as other relationships with unconsolidated entities that may have a material current or future effect on the financial condition of the corporation. For pro forma financial information, the SEC is required to issue rules providing that pro forma financial information must not contain an untrue statement or omit a material fact necessary to make the pro forma financial information not misleading (Section 401).

Penalties for willful and knowing violations of this section are fines of not more than $500,000 and/or imprisonment of up to five years. Improperly influencing the conduct of audits is specifically made unlawful. All corporate officers and directors are expressly prohibited from taking any action that would mislead any auditor or fraudulently influence, coerce, or manipulate the audit of financial statements for the purpose of making the statements misleading. The SEC may prohibit a person from serving as an officer or director of a public company if the person has committed securities fraud (Section 1105).

The act also contains a sense of the Senate declaration that the corporate federal income tax return should be signed by the corporation's CEO (Section 1001). Since a sense of the Senate declaration does not make law, the Congress seems to have indicated a preference for the CEO to take personal responsibility for the annual corporate federal income tax return.

The act prohibits corporations from extending credit to any director or executive officer, except that companies may make home improvement and consumer credit loans and issue credit cards to its directors and executive officers if it is done in the ordinary course of business on the same terms and conditions made to the general public (Section 402).

Directors, officers, and owners of 10 percent or more of the company stock must report to the SEC transactions in company securities by the end of the second business day following the day on which the transaction was executed (Section 403).

Officers, directors, and other insiders of a corporation are prohibited from either the purchase or sale of company stock during blackout periods for other holders of the stock such as employee pension funds. Profits that resulted from sales that violate this provision can be recovered by the corporation, or, should the corporation fail to bring suit or prosecute diligently, a suit to recover such profit may be instituted by the owner of any security of the corporation (Section 306).

The government's ability to recover assets from corporate officers was enhanced by the act. If the corporation issues a restatement of financial reports because of material noncompliance with financial reporting requirements, the CEO and the CFO are required to pay back any bonus or other incentive-based or equity-based compensation received in the twelve months following the original issue date. Profits realized from the sale of securities of the issuer during that period must also be paid to the corporation. Further, the act authorizes federal courts to grant equitable relief that may be deemed appropriate or necessary for the benefit of the investors in actions brought by the SEC for violation of securities laws (Section 305). The SEC was authorized to freeze an extraordinary payment to any director, officer, partner, controlling person, agent, or employee of a company during an investigation of possible violations of securities laws (Section 1103).

Public Company Internal Control

There are substantial requirements that will improve internal control over corporate financial affairs and reports. Future annual reports to the SEC and shareholders must contain a statement that corporate management is responsible for establishing and maintaining both an adequate internal control structure and adequate procedures to ensure proper financial reporting. A management-prepared report on internal control must either be part of the annual corporate financial statement or made in an accompanying separate report referenced in the annual financial statement. The annual internal control report must contain management's assessment, as of the end of the issuer's fiscal year, of the effectiveness of the internal control structure and the effectiveness of the corporation's procedures for financial reporting. Auditors are required to prepare a report on internal control and attest to management's internal control assessment. PCAOB-established standards for internal control attestation engagements must be followed (Section 404).

The CEO and CFO must certify that they have disclosed to the auditors and to the audit committee all significant deficiencies in the design and operations of internal controls and any material or immaterial fraud that involved management or other employees who have a significant role in internal control. Any significant changes made to internal control after their evaluation must also be disclosed.

Public Company Auditing

The audit provisions of the act make extensive changes in the environment of public accounting, which, as noted above, had previously been self-regulating. The PCAOB was created as a private-sector nonprofit corporation with responsibility and authority to protect the interest of investors and further the public's interest in the preparation of informative, fair, and independent audit reports by overseeing the auditors of public companies. All CPA firms that audit U.S. public companies are required to register with the PCAOB, whether the audit firms in question are U.S. or foreign based (Section 103).

A code of ethics for the board itself was adopted in June 2003, designed to ensure the highest standards of ethical conduct and to provide the public with confidence in the objectivity of board decisions and actions. As noted previously, the board began to carry out its responsibility to register audit firms and by October 2003 had reviewed and approved the registrations of 598 public accounting firms. To facilitate mandated inspections of registered firms, the PCAOB announced plans to establish regional offices in Atlanta, Dallas, and San Francisco, in addition to its offices in Washington, DC, and New York City.

Creation and provisions for the PCAOB are primarily contained in Title I. The PCAOB shall consist of five financially literate members to be appointed for five-year staggered terms on a full-time basis. Members of the board are appointed by the SEC commissioners, in consultation with the chairman of the Federal Reserve Board and the secretary of the Treasury. Three board members must not have been certified public accountants (CPAs). The remaining two members must hold or have held the CPA designation. A CPA board member may be the board chair so long as such member has not engaged in practicing public accounting in the past five years (Section 301). Clearly, this board is not meant to be a professional self-regulation entity.

A PCAOB member is prohibited while on the board to share in profits of, or receive payments from, a public accounting firm, except for fixed continuing payments, such as retirement payments. The salary of board members is $452,000 per annum. The chairman receives a salary of $556,000.

Fees to pay for the board's annual budget approximating $100 million are levied by the board on companies that issue securities to the public. The budget must be approved by the SEC annually (Section 109). The board's staff of over 300 has its headquarters in Washington, DC.

The PCAOB is subject to complete oversight and approval by the SEC. The board must report on its standard-setting activity to the commission on an annual basis. Appeals from the board may be taken to the SEC, which can modify or reverse PCAOB decisions. The board is subject also to SEC inspections and enforcement.

The responsibilities and authority of PCAOB are contained in Section 101 of the act. These include performing duties and functions that the board determines necessary to promote high professional standards for registered public accounting firms and their employees and to improve audit services quality of these firms.

The powers of the board include enforcing compliance with the act, the rules of the board, professional standards, and the securities laws relating to the preparation and issuance of audit reports and the obligations and liabilities of accountants with respect thereto. The board has broad authority to set and enforce standards of auditing, quality control, ethics, independence, and other necessary standards that relate to preparation of public company audit reports. Part of the PCAOB's power to set standards for the auditing industry includes the power to regulate the non-audit services audit firms may offer their audit clients, such as consulting or tax services.

Section 103 directs the PCAOB to establish a standard requiring a registered accounting firm to prepare proper work papers and other information related to any audit report that will provide sufficient detail to support conclusions reached. This documentation must be maintained for no less than seven years. The board must require that, prior to issuance of audit reports, second partner reviews and approvals are conducted.

The PCAOB is also required by Title I to adopt an audit standard that implements the auditor internal control review required by Section 404(b) of the act. The standard must require auditors to evaluate whether the internal control structure and internal control procedures encompass records that accurately and fairly reflect the transactions of the company under audit, provide reasonable assurance that the transactions are recorded in a manner that will permit the preparation of financial statements in accordance with GAAP, and provide descriptions of internal control material weaknesses.

To carry out its responsibilities, the board is empowered to register public accounting firms that intend to prepare public company audit reports, to conduct inspections of registered accounting firms, to conduct proceedings of an investigatory and disciplinary nature concerning registered accounting firms and all those associated with these firms, and to impose appropriate sanctions, including fines of up to $100,000 on individuals or $2 million on accounting firms.

Disciplinary hearings of the board will be closed unless the board orders that they be public, for good cause, and with the consent of the parties. The board may sanction a registered accounting firm or the supervisory personnel of a firm if a registered firm fails. Reports of any sanctions will be made public only after any pending appeal has been lifted (Section 105).

Any information or documents received or prepared by the board shall be confidential and privileged as evidentiary matter. Such information and documents shall not be subject to civil discovery or other legal process in federal court, state court, or administrative agency unless and until presented in connection with a public proceeding. Such materials can be released, however, in connection with a disciplinary action and can be made available to the SEC, the U.S. attorney general, and other federal and appropriate state agencies (Section 105).

The board may require audit firms and those associated with them to provide testimony and documents that may be in their possession. Individuals or firms that refuse to provide such testimony and documents can be subject to being suspended or barred by the board from audit of public companies (Section 105).

Accounting firms that audit public companies are required to follow the standards for auditing, attestation, quality control, and ethics established by the PCAOB. These standards, plus all SEC rules, must be followed by registered firms in their work to prepare and to issue audit reports for SEC-listed companies. A violation of PCAOB rules may be viewed and treated as a violation of the Securities Exchange Act of 1934 and can incur the same penalties imposed for violations of that act.

For accounting firms that audit more than 100 public companies, an annual quality control inspection by the PCAOB is required. All other registered accounting firms must be inspected at least once each three years. In addition, special inspections as deemed necessary by the SEC or the PCAOB may also be conducted.

The board, as noted above, was granted the ability to impose sanctions on any registered firm that is determined by the board to have engaged in violations of the Sarbanes-Oxley Act, the PCAOB rules, or any securities laws pertaining to the issuance of audit reports. Sanctions available to the board include temporary or permanent revocation of registration, monetary penalties, censure, requirements for additional education or training, or others that may be included in board rules (Section 105).

When it sanctions a registered accounting firm or associated person, the board must notify the SEC. The findings and sanctions may be reviewed by the SEC, which may enhance, modify, cancel, reduce, or require remission of such sanction.

Auditor Independence

Title II of the act deals with auditor independence issues. The lead audit or coordinating partner as well as reviewing partner is required to rotate off of the audit every five years. The CEO, controller, CFO, chief accounting officer, or persons in equivalent positions with the audited corporation may not have been employed by the company's audit firm during the one-year period preceding the audit (Section 105).

Accounting registrants are prohibited from providing the following non-audit services to a public corporation audit client: bookkeeping or the like; financial information systems design and implementation; appraisal or valuation services, fairness opinion or contribution-in-kind reports; actuarial services; internal audit services; management functions or human resources; broker or dealer, investment adviser, or investment banking services; legal services and expert services unrelated to the audit; or any other service that the board determines, by regulation, is not permitted. The board may permit exemptions on a case-by-case basis, subject to review by the commission (Section 201).

Except for the above listed prohibitions, other non-audit services may be provided to the audit client if they are preapproved by the corporate audit committee. Such services must be disclosed to investors in periodic reports. The authority to preapprove services can be delegated to one or more members of the audit committee, but any decisions must be presented to the full audit committee (Section 202).

The Government Accountability Office (GAO), formerly named the General Accounting Office, was directed in the act to perform a study to determine whether mandatory rotation of audit firms is beneficial. Both the lead audit partner and reviewing audit partner are required, as noted above, to be replaced at least every five years.

The act directed that several other studies be conducted. In addition to the GAO-required study on auditor rotation, noted above, the act directs the GAO to conduct a study on causal factors of consolidation of accounting firms since 1989, the impact of this consolidation on capital formation and securities markets, and solutions to problems identified. Such solutions should include recommendations for increasing competition, that is, for increasing the number of audit firms capable of providing audit service to large business organizations subject to the securities laws (Section 701). Subtitled section Concentration of the Market for Large Company Audits in chapter 10 includes discussion of the resulting GAO report (USGAO, 2003).

Other Parties Involved in the Financial Reporting Process

Among its provisions for others involved in the financial reporting process, the act directed national securities exchanges and registered securities associations to adopt conflict-of-interest rules for research analysts who recommend equities in research reports. The SEC was directed to establish rules setting minimum standards for professional conduct for attorneys practicing before it. The SEC was given the right to censure, temporarily bar, or deny the right to practice before the SEC to those who lack the requisite qualifications to represent others, who lack character or integrity, or who have willfully violated federal securities laws (Section 602).

SEC is also directed to conduct a study of securities professionals, such as public accountants, public accounting firms, investment bankers, investment advisors, brokers, dealers, and attorneys who have been found to have aided and abetted a violation of federal securities laws in calendar years 1998–2001 (Section 703).

This study indicated the SEC brought actions against 1,596 securities professionals found to have violated, or aided and abetted violation of, federal securities laws. A further 117 were found to have engaged in improper professional conduct or had failed to reasonably supervise their employees who had violated securities laws. Of the total 1,596 violators only 13 were charged with aiding and abetting alone, while 1,299 were found to be principal violators. Those found to be aiding and abetting violations who were also principal violators numbered 284. Sanctions ordered by the SEC for the infractions included 782 permanent injunctions, 730 civil monetary penalties, 673 disgorgements, 613 permanent cease-and-desist orders, and 434 bars from association with broker-dealers (SEC, 2002).

Penalties for Noncompliance

Criminal penalties were increased in a number of additional ways. The statute of limitations on securities fraud claims was extended to the earlier of five years from the fraud, or two years after the fraud was discovered.

Knowingly destroying or creating to impede, obstruct, or influence any existing or contemplated federal investigation was made a felony. The maximum penalty for mail and wire fraud was increased to ten years.

Section 1102 of the act establishes a penalty of up to twenty years in prison for corruptly altering, destroying, mutilating, or concealing any document with the intent to impair the object's integrity or availability for use in an official proceeding or to otherwise obstruct, influence, or impede any official proceeding.

Corporate and accounting firm employees were given whistle-blower protection that prohibits their employer from discharging, demoting, suspending, threatening, harassing, or in any other manner discriminating against employees who lawfully disclose private employer information to parties in a judicial proceeding involving a securities-related fraud claim. Whistle-blowers are given a remedy of special damages and the payment of their attorney fees (Section 806).

Benefits and Costs of Sarbanes-Oxley Compliance

The act increased SEC appropriations for 2003 to $776 million, and it directed that $98 million of the funds be used to hire an additional 200 employees to provide increased oversight for auditors and audit services as required by the federal securities laws (Section 601).

There has been a great deal of private expenditure, as well, to comply with the Sarbanes-Oxley requirements since 2002. Some corporations thought that the compliance expense would be a one-time charge. But many expenditures now appear to be ongoing. Some corporate executives have asserted that the costs of the changes required are too high for benefits received, particularly for smaller businesses. A movement to create new exemptions appears to be gaining support in Washington (Labaton, 2006, 4). Others believe that the results of changes made have been beneficial and more than worth the costs, particularly in restoring confidence in the securities markets and lowering the cost of corporate capital.

Costs for Sarbanes-Oxley compliance were reported to average $16 million per company in 2004, which was a jump of 77 percent in average costs from 2003 (RHR International, 2004). A study by AMR Research in 2004 estimated that corporations will spend a total of $5.8 billion on Sarbanes-Oxley requirements in 2005. Thirty-six percent of responding companies planned to increase spending, 52 percent planned to maintain the spending at 2004 levels, and 12 percent planned to decrease such spending. Ninety-eight percent of the responding 200 companies indicated that spending on Sarbanes-Oxley requirements was higher than or at the level that was anticipated. Eighty-one percent of the companies that had an operational solution to the Sarbanes-Oxley requirements in place indicate that they plan, nonetheless, to improve or add to their procedures (AMR Research, 2004).

The requirements of Section 404 on internal control are in large measure the center of the cost problems as some businesses see it. Section 404 in this view is a large cost expenditure that has little real return. It has been called a compliance tax levied on public companies (Committee for Economic Development, 2006, 2).

Jack T. Ciesielski, author of a Baltimore-based accounting newsletter, believes, to the contrary, that costs of implementing the 404 requirements of Sarbanes-Oxley have been heavy because corporations are having to repair infrastructures after years of neglect (Johnson, 2005, E01).

Stephen Labaton, in a January 1, 2006, *New York Times* article reported that America's top executives would just as soon see the Enron debacle, with all its attendant changes and costs, disappear. Despite the high-profile trials and the reform legislation that have turned out to be expensive for corporations, changes in corporate behavior have proven to be more muted than anticipated by many observers. Moreover, adding to the evidence that Sarbanes-Oxley was needed, public corporations continue to have serious accounting problems, Labaton reports (Labaton, 2006, 1).

Restatements of earnings by public companies in 2005 increased by 50 percent over 2004. By October, restatements totaled 1,031 for 2005, whereas in all of 2004 there were 650 restatements, and in 2001, 270. Much of this increase would seem to be the result of better audit coverage and vigilance. In the internal control area, out of 15,000 corporations reporting through October 2005, 1,250 reported material internal control weaknesses and 232 companies reported significant but less material internal control weaknesses (Ibid., 2).

The four years since adoption of Sarbanes-Oxley have seen varying improvements in boards of directors according to some observers. Mark Van Clieaf, the managing director of consulting firm MVC Associates International, is of the opinion that more has happened in the past four years than in the last thirty years as corporate boards have begun to realize that the job of the board of directors is not just ceremonial (Ibid., 3). Van Clieaf thinks that boards are in denial concerning the demand, especially from large shareholders, that corporate executive compensation reflect performance. He suggests that this is because low corporate performance reflects back on the board (Ibid.).

Underperforming companies are continuing to pay their executives outsized amounts, which do not appear to be tied to corporate performance. Mark Van Clieaf and Janet Langford Kelly, a law professor at Northwestern University, reported in their study of sixty corporations that were in the bottom 10 percent of the Russell 3000 Index, that although the market value of these firms had decreased by $769 billion over the five-year period ending in 2004, their highest five executives were paid over $12 billion for this same period (Ibid.). Likewise, a study by Lucian A. Bebchuk of Harvard and Yaniv Grinstein of Cornell disclosed that the compensations for the top five corporate executives as a percentage of corporate earnings increased from 5 percent in 1993 to over 10 percent in 2003, even though no associated increase in managements' incentives was found, resulting in substantial decline in company values (Ibid.).

Christopher Cox, chairman of the SEC, declared that the reform legislation has produced a number of benefits and, even given the recent backlash from some corporate interests, he did not favor rewriting major parts of the Sarbanes-Oxley Act. He thought, however, that in some areas change may be appropriate. In his view, the new regulations are meant to improve market competitiveness and might do the opposite without ongoing careful consideration. Cox asserted that corporate directors could not fail to take account of the lessons from the corporate scandals and the reform legislation. He indicated that the commission would hold proceedings in 2006 to ensure that disclosure rules make executive compensation more transparent (Ibid., 3, 4).

The Committee for Economic Development, in its *Private Enterprise, Public Trust: The State of Corporate America After Sarbanes-Oxley,* sees Section 404 as providing a way to make the external audit more valuable as a management tool. The report points to an increasing number of corporations as well as their auditors that indicate that fulfilling the requirements of Section 404 has resulted in more and better financial information and an improved understanding of a wide range of functions in the corporation (Committee for Economic Development, 2006, 2).

According to an Associated Press report by Rachel Beck, the costs of Sarbanes-Oxley compliance, which involves review of accounting procedures, should be considered well spent if an environment is created in which financial fraud becomes harder to get away with (Beck, 2005,

D-3). Corporate America, according to Beck, complains that the costs to assess accounting procedures are a waste of money that could be spent on productive uses. She asserts that corporations say that any problems found through the required, expensive, and labor-intensive process will not be material in nature, by which they mean that any problems discovered will not be likely to affect company stock prices or investors' opinions about the company.

Costs have been exceeding what was expected, it seems clear. The government had estimated that each company would spend $91,000 to comply with the internal control aspects of the bill, an estimate that businesses say has been far exceeded. The Beck article cited a Financial Executives International survey that found that companies were on average spending $4.36 million each. This was 39 percent higher than the per company average planned of $3.14 million. Nonetheless, Beck states that, in her view, even these costs are worth it to boost investor confidence (Ibid.).

Beck reports that, of the 2,600 companies filing required reports with the SEC by March 16, 2005, 11 percent reported warnings of material weaknesses in internal control. Several examples of companies reporting internal control weaknesses were cited by Beck, including Cray Inc., whose stock had dropped 20 percent when the company announced that it could not complete its review on time. Eastman Kodak reported that it had material weaknesses that involved retirement benefits and income tax accounting and restated earnings for both 2004 and 2005. MCI cited a material weakness in control over income tax accounting and reported a restatement for 2004 that deepened its previously reported loss. Three areas of material weakness in internal control, which included recognition of vaccine sales, were reported by Chiron (Ibid.).

An online, by-invitation survey of U.S. corporate financial executives was conducted by Oversight Systems Inc. (2004). Financial executives from 222 companies participated. Of these, 25 percent indicated that their companies had annual sales of more than $5 billion. Twenty-three percent had annual sales of $1 billion to $5 billion. Twenty-two percent had annual sales between $999 million and $251 million. Thirty percent were from companies where annual sales were $250 million or less (Ibid., 4).

Costs of compliance were deemed a good investment by 57 percent of responding financial executives, while 79 percent said that their company's internal control was stronger after implementing the compliance requirements of the Sarbanes-Oxley Act. Only 16 percent thought that their company's internal controls were sufficient and adequately documented before Sarbanes-Oxley implementation. Another 24 percent indicated that their companies had needed no change in actual controls, but completion of documentation had been needed (Ibid., 6).

Seventy-four percent of responding financial executives indicated that Sarbanes-Oxley compliance benefited their companies. Listed among the benefits attained were strengthening of the accountability of individuals who carry out financial operations and reporting, decreasing financial fraud risks, reducing errors in financial operations, improving the accuracy of financial reports, providing deeper information to the audit committee of the board of directors, and strengthening the opinion of the company in the view of investors (Ibid., 1).

In the same survey, 54 percent of responding financial executives indicated that their companies spent greater amounts in the first year of compliance than originally projected. Another 40 percent indicated that they spent the expected amounts, and 7 percent spent less than had been expected (Ibid.). Implementation within their companies was described as either difficult or very difficult by 63 percent of responding executives. Second-year costs for 2005 were expected to be more than first-year costs by only 3 percent of respondents. The remainder thought that costs would decrease by various percentages (Ibid., 2).

As a result of Sarbanes-Oxley compliance, 37 percent of respondents to the Oversight Systems Inc. survey indicated that their interaction with their CEO had increased (Ibid., 7). As to audit committee involvement in Sarbanes-Oxley compliance issues, 19 percent reported that their audit committee was highly active and interested in the details. Forty-five percent of the executives reported that their audit committee was active. Twenty-eight percent reported their audit committee to be interested but relatively passive, while 8 percent reported their audit committee to be disinterested and relatively passive (Ibid., 4).

The financial executives' opinions toward the Sarbanes-Oxley Act were mixed. Fifty-two percent of the executives believed that the legislation resulted from good intentions in Congress but without full consideration of related costs. Congress was overreacting to the unethical behavior of a few executives in the view of 38 percent of the respondents. A minority of 13 percent held the view that the benefits outweighed the costs, while 25 percent believed that the costs outweighed the benefits of the legislation (Ibid., 1).

Eighty-one percent thought that Congress should revisit the legislation. However, 87 percent thought that the requirement to have CFO and CEO sign-offs on both financial reports and control effectiveness should be included in the bill's requirements. Seventy-five percent indicated that they would vote to include the section requiring internal control documentation, monitoring, reporting, and attestation. Eighty-five percent would vote to require timely disclosure of material changes affecting financial operations or conditions (Ibid., 7).

In a 2003 survey by Chicago law firm Foley & Lardner, the costs of being a small to midcapitalization public company were estimated to have increased from about $1.3 million to $2.5 million as a result of new Sarbanes-Oxley and SEC compliance and disclosure requirements. About 13 percent of the respondents surveyed indicated that their companies were considering reverting to private company, nonlisted status as a result of the more costly requirements (Scott, 2003, 13, 14).

Opposition to Sarbanes-Oxley

In a prelude to opposition to the Sarbanes-Oxley Act, the *Wall Street Journal* reported in 2004 that the ouster of then SEC chairman William H. Donaldson was being sought in a quiet campaign by groups that had played a critical role in the reelection of President George W. Bush. The groups identified in the December 13, 2004, article were the Business Roundtable, the U.S. Chamber of Commerce, and the National Association of Wholesaler-Distributors. The groups reportedly held the view that the reform efforts had gone too far and were hampering corporate risk taking. Further, in this view, the increased authority given the SEC in the post-Enron reforms was detrimental to the business environment. The *Wall Street Journal* predicted the departure of Donaldson in early 2005 (Accountingweb, 2004d, 1). Donaldson had sided with the two democratic members of the SEC in seeking reforms that, allegedly, had incited opposition from those whose interests were served by the status quo (Smartpros, 2004a, 1).

A constitutional challenge to the PCAOB was filed in U.S. District Court in Washington, DC, in February 2006 by the Free Enterprise Fund and Beckstead & Watts, an accounting firm. The challenge alleged that the PCAOB had been given wide government powers with insufficient oversight, thereby violating the separation of powers provided in the

Constitution. Further, plaintiffs asserted, procedures whereby PCAOB appointments are made by the SEC violates the appointments clause of the Constitution, which requires top federal officers to be appointed by the president and confirmed by the Senate. Further, lower-level officials are required to be appointed by the president, the courts, or a department head (Accountingweb, 2006a, 1).

Because the Sarbanes-Oxley Act does not have a severability clause, the plaintiffs alleged that the entire law must be invalidated if the courts hold for the plaintiffs (Ibid.). *BusinessWeek* reported that if the outcome of the lawsuit was in favor of the plaintiffs, the U.S. Congress would need to act to correct the legislation. Legal experts indicate that it is likely that much of the act would survive any reopening by Congress (Ibid.).

Unexpected Benefits for Accountants

Some in the business of providing accounting and auditing services at first thought that the Enron-Andersen affair would spell the end of their profession. It now seems that the reforms made following the profession's failures have unleashed new and varied engagement opportunities to a much wider range of firms of varying sizes. Because of the prohibitions and requirements of Sarbanes-Oxley, many corporations' accounting needs cannot all be handled by the same Big Four accounting firms. The next tier of large accounting firms, as well as regional firms, have been in a good position to provide both the attestation and the professional non-attestation work needed by corporations in this new environment (Wolosky, 2004, 1). These aspects and other adjustments to a new reality will be discussed in chapter 9.

Clearly, internal auditing has experienced a resurgence as a result of the Sarbanes-Oxley reform legislation. Internal auditors have taken on a more prominent role in their corporations. In many companies, internal audit now reports directly to the CEO or the board of directors. The New York Stock Exchange adopted requirements that all listed companies have an internal audit function. Membership in the Institute of Internal Auditors has more than doubled in the last ten years, according to Trish Harris, director of communications for the institute. Since 2000, membership has grown 38 percent. The number of auditors sitting for the Certified Internal Auditor examination has risen from about 30,000 in 2000 to 38,000 in 2005 (Accountingweb, 2006b, 1).

Worldwide Reforms

Although U.S. reforms received the greatest visibility in the international arena, similar significant financial reporting, corporate governance, and audit reforms were taking place across the globe in countries, associations of countries, and international organizations. Some of these reforms pre-date the Enron-Andersen debacle, while others appear to be in response to the period of mounting accounting and corporate scandals in which public confidence was lost as well as to the reforms set in motion by the U.S. Congress.

United Kingdom

In the United Kingdom, a number of reviews had been taking place since 1992 aimed at improving financial reporting in its many aspects. These led to major changes in UK corporate governance requirements and in the regulations of auditors (Task Force, 2003, 53). The Cadbury Report in 1992 had the objective of strengthening corporate governance. The UK Code of Best Practice, which resulted from the Cadbury Report, has since been expanded in scope, although it remains voluntary. The UK regulatory authority does require companies that do not comply with the Code of Best Practice to explain such noncompliance (Ibid., 54).

The areas included in the Code of Best Practice include the composition of the board of directors and the responsibilities of the board of directors and audit committees, as well as relationships with auditors. Listed companies in the United Kingdom following the Turnbull Report of 1999 have been required to report their processes for identification, evaluation, and management of significant risks facing the corporation. The UK Auditing Practices Board (APB) is-sued a paper in 2001 discussing aggressive earnings management by corporations (Ibid., 54).

These UK auditing and auditor reviews set in motion a reordering of UK standard-setting and regulatory bodies. The government believed that there are strong connections between corporate reporting, auditing, cor-porate governance, and the professionalism of accountants. Accordingly, the Financial Reporting Council (FRC) was restructured to incorporate under one agency responsibilities for all of these functions. The FRC chair and deputy chair are appointed by the government (Ibid., 59).

The FRC was given statutory authority for setting, monitoring, and enforcing accounting and auditing standards, overseeing and regulating auditors, setting actuarial standards, operating an independent investigation and discipline scheme for public-interest cases, overseeing the regulatory activities of the professional accountancy and actuarial bodies, and promoting high standards of corporate governance.

The Accounting Standards Board, previously independent, was placed under FRC jurisdiction but otherwise continues to operate as before the reorganization. The Auditing Practices Board, a private company limited by guarantee, was also placed under the FRC and given added responsibilities for auditor ethics and independence. The Financial Reporting Review Panel is charged with taking a more proactive role in cases of failure to comply with accounting standards. The Investigations and Discipline Board was added to the FRC to consider serious public-interest cases of alleged audit failure. A Professional Oversight Board now has responsibility for the quality inspection process of auditors of public-interest entities (Ibid.).

Audit firm mandatory rotation was rejected, but the rotation of the lead partner on an audit was reduced to five years. The United Kingdom followed the EU restrictions on non-audit services, using the threats and safeguards approach. Greater transparency is now required on the part of audit firms. Firms with listed audit clients are required to annually provide financial and firm management information as well as information on policies and procedures related to audit quality and the management of threats to the auditor's independence (Ibid.).

Starting in January 2005, group accounts for UK-listed companies, with the exception of smaller companies, were required to follow International Accounting Standards (IAS) for group accounts, that is, consolidated financial statements. The current intentions of the government in the United Kingdom are to permit individual companies and nonlisted groups to choose to use the International Accounting Standards Board (IASB) standards.

The APB issues Statements of Auditing Standards (SAS), Practice Notes, Bulletins, and Statements of Investment Reporting Circular Standards. APB members are appointed by the Nomination Committee of the FRC for three-year terms. The membership of APB is required to be made up of 40 percent members who are eligible for appointment as company auditors under companies legislation and the remainder, if they are accountants, are not permitted to be officers or to be involved in the governance of an accounting body and may not be accounting firm partners authorized to conduct audits. APB meetings are private but are open to nonvoting representatives of the Financial Services Authority, the Department of Trade and Enterprise in the Republic of Ireland, the Accountancy Foundation, and the Department of Trade and Industry, who may attend and speak at APB meetings.

Prior to amending or issuing a new SAS, the APB publishes on its Web site an exposure draft and circulates hard copies to accountancy bodies and other interested parties. Usually three months, unless a shorter exposure period is required by circumstances, are allowed for parties to contribute their representations on the exposure draft. A Technical Advisory Group was established by the APB. A review of the group's activities is published annually.

A majority of all voting members, present at a meeting or not, is required to establish, publish, amend, or withdraw a SAS or exposure draft. A simple majority of members present at a meeting at which a quorum is in attendance is required to establish, publish, amend, or withdraw nonmandatory guidance, notes, or other materials relevant to auditing. Only a majority of votes actually cast at such a meeting is required for other decisions.

The practice of accountancy per se in the United Kingdom is not legally restricted. However, company auditing is regulated. To practice company auditing, an individual must be a registered auditor who holds recognized audit qualifications under the Companies Act of 1989. Education requirements for auditors is set by the Department of Trade and Industry, a major government department that is under a cabinet minister, the secretary of state. Requirements to obtain a license to audit companies include academic study specific for obtaining a license, practical experience, and a licensing examination.

Licensing requirements come from the European Union (Eighth Company Law Directive), the UK Companies Act of 1989, and the regulations of recognized qualifying and supervisory bodies, such as the Institute of Chartered Accountants in England and Wales (ICAEW). ICAEW grants licenses to qualifying individuals.

A recognized university degree, although not compulsory, is sufficient to meet minimum entry standards to train for ICAEW qualifications. ICAEW has two stages of professional examination: the Professional Stage, comprised of six papers, and the Advanced Stage, comprised of the Test of Advanced Technical Competence and the Advanced Case Study. Candidates must gain a place with an authorized firm and complete a period, normally three years, of approved training and work-based learning requirements.

France

France has also made significant corporate structural and financial reporting reforms. The Bouton Report was published in September 2002 to review aspects of corporate governance (Ibid., 53). This was preceded by the Le Portz Reports in 1992 and 1999. One of the results of these reviews was that the Financial Markets Authority was set up to improve protection of investors and savers. The authority instituted the Council of Statutory Auditors as an audit oversight body. This council is required to assure the strict separation of audit and non-audit services to audit clients, among other matters. With the exception of ancillary work, auditors are not permitted to carry out other than audit work for the client companies. The Bouton Report reasserted the French system of joint audits, which is thought to reinforce auditor independence because the process should ensure that key issues are considered twice. Also reasserted was the requirement that auditors have a fixed term of six years. Compulsory firm rotation was rejected but partner rotation was supported. The audit committee of the board of directors is required to oversee a tendering process at the end of the auditor's term (Ibid., 59).

A new legal framework in France allows companies to separate the functions of the chairman and chief executive for the first time. Provisions were made in the law for shareholder rights improvement, prevention of conflicts of interest, rules for share option allotment and disclosure, as well as the enumeration of board of directors responsibilities and duties (Ibid., 54). Boards of directors' effectiveness was strengthened by providing an evaluation process for boards; defining the meaning of independence for board members; strengthening the processes for the audit, compensation, and nominating committees; and delineating the relations between the board and company auditors (Ibid., 56).

Japan

The Japanese passed legislation after a December 2002 report of a subcommittee of the Financial System Council. The law covers matters similar to those put in place in other countries. The focus is on auditor independence, with rules relating to non-audit services prohibitions, engagement and review partner rotation, restriction on employment by corporations of former audit engagement partners, and required public disclosure of audit and non-audit fees. The Japanese are in the process of increasing the number of practicing CPAs in order to have greater capacity for quality auditing. Japanese auditor oversight has been enhanced by creation of the CPA and Auditing Oversight Board, which is charged with monitoring the Japanese Institute of Certified Public Accountants' quality control system. The Financial System Council has been assigned the general right to inspect audit firms. The council can also require improvements at audit firms as well as the Japanese Institute of Certified Public Accountants (Ibid., 60).

The corporate governance structure in Japan was also strengthened. This was after questions had been raised by the public about the adequacy of the Japanese system of corporate checks and balances (Sheard, 2006, 1). The board of statutory auditor system used in Japan has been strengthened by increasing the number of independent statutory board members required. At least half of the board must be outsiders with no director or employee relationship with the company. In addition, starting in April 2003 there is an additional option for Japan's listed companies under which they may have a board and committee structure similar to Anglo-American systems. In this system, the corporate structure would include a board of directors with audit and compensation committees. Under this option, a majority of the members of each committee needs to be independent of the company (Task Force, 2003, 56).

International Organizations

Reforms have taken place in literally every developed and most of the developing countries in the world. Most have not risen to the level of the reforms in the United States. But, there seems to have been general worldwide recognition that financial reporting and all those who have roles in financial reporting must improve significantly. Reviews in the various countries of accounting standards and standard-setting have generally confirmed existing structures while making strengthening improvements. Countries have also supported the role of the IASB and the need to converge on one set of accounting standards (Ibid., 56). In the United Kingdom, existing processes were confirmed, especially as they relate to setting accounting standards that are based on principles rather than detailed rules, as has been the U.S. approach (Ibid., 57).

The review conducted in France included suggestions for assessing material risks, providing more specific information disclosures, and including in reports a summarization of the company process for identifying off-balance-sheet commitments. The French review supported the convergence of national and international accounting standard, but found fault with IASB approaches to transparency in the standard-setting processes in general and IASB moves to impose fair-value accounting for derivatives (Ibid.).

International organizations have also recognized and acted to make improvements. To improve international financial architecture, the G7 finance ministers established the Financial Stability Forum in 1999 in response to the East Asian financial crisis. Forum members are representatives from national finance departments and ministries, central banks, and other regulatory and government agencies, as well as international institutions.

The forum concluded that stability and responses to financial crises would be enhanced if all nations would construct strong market foundations that used best regulatory practices in the areas of securities, banks, and insurance. The forum reported that there were twelve sets of international standards that together could constitute best practices. The list includes IASB International Financial Reporting Standards, International Auditing and Assurance Standards Board International Standards on Auditing, OECD Principles of Corporate Governance, and International Organization of Securities Commissions Objectives and Principles of Securities Regulation. Others on the list are in the areas of banking, insurance, insolvency, transparency of monetary and fiscal policies, data dissemination, settlement systems, and money laundering. The World Bank and the International Monetary Fund took on the duty of assessing individual countries for compliance. Their reports indicated a wide gap in many countries between standards and actual practices. The World Bank, in order to develop plans and actions to upgrade actual practices and existing standards, has facilitated forum meetings around the world. The forum, in its twice-a-year meeting, as well as in regional meetings, encourages international organizations to continue to improve standards in light of current events and to increase the rate at which change is made toward the desired international standards (Ibid., 49).

The European Union has been quite active in moving toward the adoption of standards favored by the forum. After the less-than-successful Fourth, Seventh, and Eighth Company Law Directives, the European Union adopted for all member countries the use of IASB International Financial Reporting Standards effective in 2005 for consolidated financial statements of listed companies. Convergence with attendant improvements in financial reporting appears to be moving forward in the European Union.

EU auditing standards have been slower to evolve, with most responsibility for audit delegated to member states prior to 2005. Through discussions in the EU Committee on Auditing, composed of representatives from each EU state government and from the accounting profession, recommendations on external audit quality control and auditor independence have been issued. European Commission proposals for extensive changes in corporate governance and auditing were proposed in May 2003 and passed in 2006 in the form of revisions to the Eighth Directive, including annual statements of corporate governance, minimum standards for hiring and remuneration of auditors, improved transparency and shareholder input to directors' remunerations, adoption of International Auditing Standards, improved audit profession public oversight, and strengthened regulatory infrastructures (Ibid., 51).

The revisions of the Eighth Directive included more comprehensive regulations for statutory audits. Statutory audits are required by law when a company listed on a public stock exchange prepares an annual consolidated financial statement. The update was in response to the corporate scandals in the United States and the Parmalat scandal in Italy, which showed the existing audit regulations were ineffective in preventing large-scale corporate fraud. The revision is designed to improve transparency and reliability of audits by enacting legislated controls over public-interest entities and audit firms.

The revised directive requires EU states to establish audit oversight boards responsible for approval and registration of audit firms, adoption of national standards on audit ethics, quality control of audit firms and auditors, continuous education of auditors, and investigative and necessary disciplinary actions against audit firms.

The firms that perform statutory audits must have approval from the state's oversight board and must be included in public national registers of statutory auditors. The audit firms are to maintain an internal quality control system that is subject to public oversight. Firms that audit public-interest entities must be reviewed by an oversight authority every three years. EU member states must provide civil, administrative, and criminal sanctions and penalties for improper conduct of a statutory audit. Documentation and information obtained in the pursuit of a statutory audit must be kept confidential and rules to that effect must be drawn up. Such rules must provide, however, that confidentiality cannot impede oversight investigations.

Audit committees responsible for appointing and dismissing statutory auditors must be established by each public-interest entity. The auditor is required to report to the audit committee on key matters of the statutory audit, including any material weaknesses in internal controls in the financial reporting process. The audit committee must be made up of non-executive members of the board of directors. The committee must have at least one financial expert. The committee is responsible to ensure that entity financial statements are consistent with international accounting standards and that the fees paid to the audit firm are fair.

Public-interest entities are required to disclose fees paid to the audit firm for both audit services as well as fees for non-audit services. EU member states are required to ensure that statutory audit fees are adequate to allow a proper audit, and that these fees are not influenced by fees for additional services.

To provide greater transparency of statutory audits, audit firms must publish an annual transparency report in which disclosure must be made of the legal structure and ownership of the firm, the firm's internal quality control system, the date of the firm's last quality assurance review, a listing of public-interest entities for which statutory audits were conducted in the past year, a breakdown of fees charged by the firm, and partner compensation structure information.

The revised directive contains provisions designed to ensure that statutory auditors are independent of their clients. Non-audit work for audit clients is restricted if such work would compromise the audit firm's independence from the client entity. The auditor should not carry out the statutory audit if there are any financial, business, employment, or other compromising connections with the client entity. The audit firm must confirm its independence in writing each year and disclose any threats to its independence. Periodic rotation of audit partners or audit firms is recommended.

Auditors are required by the revisions to follow specified international auditing standards and to use a common standard audit report that is consistent with international accounting standards. Audit firms must maintain professional ethics. Established educational standards must be met by auditors. Such responsibility includes the work of other auditors, who may be in another jurisdiction. Copies of the other firms' audit working papers for the group audit should be retained (Ernst & Young, 2005, 1). Shared audit opinion responsibility as seen in the United States is not permitted.

As discussed in chapter 2, IAS have been adopted by more than seventy countries, including those of the EU. Some observers believe that IAS are on a fast track to adoption as the world standard. The International Federation of Accountants (IFAC), through its various task forces and committees, following the lead of the Anglo-Saxon model, had been promoting convergence of these audit standards in a self-regulatory pre–Enron-Andersen environment. Seeking world acceptance of IAS, the IFAC also reorganized its audit standard-setting organization to follow the model of the U.S. self-regulating structure. The reasons seen for this emulation were that the U.S. markets represent more than half of the world equity market capitalization. It is also the most regulated market in the world.

The U.S. SEC had indicated as late as 2000 that self-regulation of the auditing profession was still the order of the day. The Sarbanes-Oxley Act caused an SEC reversal on both public and private standard-setting arrangements, increasing governmental regulation. The IFAC needed to respond in kind if it was to continue its convergence to IAS. In 2003, new reforms were set in motion to adapt to the changed U.S. model.

The Public Interest Oversight Board (PIOB) was created with an objective of overseeing the IFAC's standard-setting activities, including those in the areas of auditing, assurance, ethics, and independence (Giles, Venuti, and Jones, 2004, 3). It is hoped that this oversight organization can move the IFAC away from professional self-regulation and closer to the new U.S. model.

The position of the PCAOB on convergence to IAS rather than establishing its own standards was for a time an open question. The PCAOB is not prohibited by the Sarbanes-Oxley Act from the convergence route of acceptance of IAS. U.S. accounting standards are set by the private-sector FASB, which is moving to converge with IASB's International Financial Reporting Standards. It does not appear, however, that the PCAOB will delegate its responsibilities any time soon.

Quite the contrary, in April 2003 the PCAOB indicated in establishing interim professional auditing standards that existing American Institute of Certified Public Accountants standards for auditing, attestation, quality control, independence, and ethics would be accepted as the PCAOB standards until PCAOB can issue its own standards in these areas. This was followed in November 2003 by the issuance of a proposal titled *Proposed Auditing Standards on Audit Documentation and Proposed Amendment to Interim Standards on Auditing,* which was heavily prescriptive and confirmed that PCAOB would be issuing its own standards.

Subsequently, after approval by the SEC, the board began issuing its audit standards, and, by February 6, 2006, four PCAOB Auditing Standards had been issued (Public Company Accounting Oversight Board, 2006a, Auditing Standard No. 4).

The PCAOB standard-setting does appear to be a problem for the global convergence effort for auditing standards, at least for public companies. It does not seem that the PCAOB will accept IAS in place of its own standards any time soon. The differences in approach to standards would seem to be a major hurdle. The more detailed and proscriptive U.S. approach to standards, which is embedded in the Sarbanes-Oxley Act, severely limits the freedom of choice available to the accounting profession and corporate managements. These and other matters relating to convergence of national auditing standards to one world standard will be discussed at length in the next chapter.

Part II

Some Specific Issues Facing Accounting and Auditing Practice

5

The Harmonization of Auditing Standards

With a convergence road map for accounting standards agreed to by accounting standard-setters, the time may be nearer when global powers will turn greater attention to integrating, harmonizing, and converging national audit and assurance standards into one set of international standards that will be generally accepted worldwide. However, the world accounting environment has changed radically since 2000, and changed in ways that may not bode well for the movement toward one set of auditing standards. In the years since the Enron Andersen debacle, very significant changes have occurred in auditing and financial reporting standards in a great many countries in the world.

As a result of the passage of the Sarbanes-Oxley Act, the United States now has a set of American Institute of Certified Public Accountants (AICPA)-sponsored auditing standards that apply to nonpublic entities and a set of Securities and Exchange Commission (SEC) standards that apply to public companies. The SEC standards are in the process of rather rapid redevelopment by the Public Company Accounting Oversight Board (PCAOB). In the international arena, reforms in many jurisdictions of the world have taken, at least partially, the lead set by the U.S. Congress.

Recent changes made in the International Federation of Accountants (IFAC) structure and in the IFAC-sponsored international standard-setting processes have been designed to adjust to the new U.S. system of government regulation of public company auditors. The IFAC standard-setting body for auditing, the International Auditing and Assurance Standards Board (IAASB), has been updated in an attempt to adapt to the U.S. change from a self-regulated public accounting profession. Both the IFAC and IAASB have made changes to allow for greater direct public input, more transparency, more rigorous processes, and independent international oversight of their operations. The IFAC Ethics

Committee has also been updated and has been renamed the International Ethics Standards Board for Accountants. This board now is overseen by the newly created IFAC Public Interest Oversight Board (PIOB).

The IFAC has been quite responsive to changing conditions in the United States. The IFAC organization, headquartered in New York, seems fully appreciative of the fact that the SEC regulates in excess of half of all world securities trading. The IFAC, in the years just prior to the Sarbanes-Oxley Act, had restructured its organization to reflect the U.S. self-regulatory model for the accounting profession. At that time and in response to SEC suggestions, membership in the audit standard-setting IAASB was broadened and strengthened. A program to monitor compliance with IFAC standards by member bodies was initiated. The Forum of Firms was initiated as an organization of large public accounting firms that performed or intended to perform international audits and that agreed to comply with forum quality control standards, including accepting quality control reviews performed by other forum member firms.

After the enactment of the Sarbanes-Oxley Act, the IFAC changed course in an attempt to accommodate the changing U.S. regulations. In November 2003, the IFAC Council announced structural and other revisions designed to again align the international standard-setting processes to the U.S. lead and to move toward the goal of harmonization and convergence of national standards with IFAC's international standards (Giles, Venuti, and Jones, 2004).

The latest revisions moved the IFAC from the self-regulatory model to a more public-private-partnership approach that it viewed as more adaptable to the current U.S. regulatory situation. A large part of the IFAC effort was the formation of the Public Interest Oversight Board (PIOB). The was designed to oversee IFAC's standard-setting activities, particularly with respect to auditing, assurance, ethics, and independence. By having the PIOB as an oversight body, public confidence, it was thought, should be enhanced. The IFAC structure would be more responsive to public interests. The changes would foster the establishment of high-quality auditing and assurance standards and practices; and, it was envisioned, the PIOB would move the IFAC away from its self-regulatory structure toward a more public-private partnership that would in turn facilitate the movement toward global acceptance of IFAC-sponsored IAASB international standards (Ibid.).

The mission statement of the IFAC commits the organization to contributing to the development of strong international economies by establishing and promoting adherence to high-quality professional standards and furthering the international convergence of such standards (IFAC, 2004, 1).

According to James Sylph, IAASB technical director, the three main activities of the IAASB center first and most importantly on developing international standards. The second activity is to communicate the board's work to its various constituencies, and the third is to gain global acceptance of and convergence to international standards (Sylph, 2005, 1).

Increasingly, as more countries converge national standards with International Standards on Auditing (ISA) and International Financial Reporting Standards (IFRS), Sylph sees the need for systematic and consistent convergence approaches across all jurisdictions. The IFAC, national and international standard-setters, and regulators all need to understand the challenges of adopting and implementing convergence in a systematic and consistent way to make the processes more efficient at earlier stages (Ibid.).

Sylph believes that the benefits of convergence to a commonly understood financial reporting framework include greater financial information comparability for investors, increased investment across borders, lower cost of capital, more efficient allocation of resources, and increased economic growth (Ibid.).

In a major effort to assist member organizations toward convergence, the IFAC Board in March 2004 approved a series of seven Statements of Membership Obligations (SMOs) designed to clarify and strengthen these obligations by providing clear benchmarks to current and prospective IFAC members. These statements are titled: 1. Quality Assurance, 2. International Education Standards for Professional Accountants, 3. International Standards Related Practice Statements and Other Papers issued by the IAASB, 4. IFAC Code of Ethics for Professional Accountants, 5. International Public Sector Accounting Standards, 6. Investigation and Discipline, and 7. International Financial Reporting Standards (IFAC, 2004).

The SMOs serve as the basis for IFAC's Member Body Compliance Program, which is designed to assist IFAC and its member organizations in identifying successes and challenges in the convergence process to international standards and regulation (Ibid., ii). As part of this compliance program, IFAC collects information from member bodies describing their regulatory and standard-setting frameworks. This is done through a fact-based questionnaire, Assessment of the Regulatory and Standard-Setting Framework. A second Self-Assessment Questionnaire is also completed by member bodies (IFAC, 2006b).

Information from the questionnaires will be used as a basis to evaluate members' uses of best endeavors to maintain their memberships in good standing as well as making progress in complying with each of the SMOs (IFAC, 2006b). The compliance program is a work-in-progress, but has already provided much information from the Assessment of the Regulatory and Standard-Setting Framework questionnaires, which are available in detail on the IFAC Web site. The program should assist the IFAC toward successful convergence of members' national standards with international standards.

For some member bodies, such as the AICPA, the conversion path may be less than obvious. The AICPA, a founding member of IFAC, has supported the global convergence effort and the common goal of developing one set of high-quality auditing and assurance standards. Prior to the Sarbanes-Oxley Act, conversations had begun about shortening the time frame for reaching this common goal. The act appears to have made a great deal of difference, however, since the PCAOB is now responsible for regulation and oversight of public company auditing. The convergence of U.S. auditing standards for public companies seems problematic at best.

The PCAOB has assumed a leadership role in the Consultative Advisory Group of the IAASB and, as a nonvoting observer at IAASB meetings, PCAOB has provided input directly. Likewise, the IAASB, as well as the UK ASB, have observer nonvoting status on the PCAOB's Standing Advisory Group. AICPA leaders in the audit area as well as the independence standards area actively participate on the IAASB and IFA Ethics Committee. The U.S. Auditing Standards Board has committed to convergence to ISA (Horstmann, 2005,1); but such convergence remains to be seen.

International Self-Regulation by Large Firms

The IFAC's Forum of Firms was inaugurated in 2001 as part of the reform actions being taken at that time. The forum is open to international public accounting firms that audit financial statements used across national borders. The stated purpose of the organization is to raise standards of international auditing practices in the interests of users of accounting services. Members voluntarily agree to meet requirements set out in the forum's constitution. The organization is in its initial stages, and all members have been classified as provisional. Provisional members must complete reporting requirements in 2007 to remain in the organization and to move to full membership. Membership of the forum in March 2006 was twenty-three large public accounting firms. This number included all of the Big Four accounting firms and most of the second-tier firms (IFAC, 2006a).

The Transnational Auditors Committee (TAC) conducts most of the business of the forum. This executive-type committee's stated major role is to encourage member firms to meet high standards of international auditing practice. The TAC role includes providing a forum for firms to discuss best practices in quality control, auditing, independence, and training and development; acting as a conduit between international accounting firms, regulators, and financial institutions on matters of audit quality, quality control, and international network transparency; identifying issues involving international audit practice and making recommendations for review to appropriate IFAC standards boards; and identifying individuals to serve on standards boards and on the IFAC Regulatory Liaison Group (IFAC, 2006a).

One of the requirements for membership is that members promote the use of ISA and support the convergence of national audit standards with ISA. It is safe to assume that the major accounting firms are in favor of adoption of ISA as the single standard for auditors around the world. In fact, the Forum of Firms appears to be an organization for large-firm professional self-regulation in the international environment. It is fairly clear that the PCAOB will have difficulty accepting such an arrangement.

The future of this pre–Enron-Andersen debacle Forum of Firms remains to be seen. The organization may become successful in becoming a self-regulating professional body, albeit with PIOB oversight. There does not appear to be an international equivalent to the U.S. SEC with legislative authority to impose regulations in another fashion. The creation of the PIOB as a response to the Sarbanes-Oxley Act appears to be another piece to a self-regulating international accounting profession. This board may prove to be similar to the U.S. Public Oversight Board, which could not impose proper authority over the large accounting firms, resulting in disaster.

Even Without the United States, More Countries Adopt International Audit Standards

More countries, however, have been adopting the international standards promulgated by the IAASB. In the European Union (EU), the Eighth

Directive has been revised, including the requirement for EU member countries to adopt ISA for companies listed on securities exchanges by 2005. In Europe, there are an estimated 7,000 public-interest entities and more than 1 million private entities. The additional nonlisted companies may be required to come under the ISA by 2007. For nonlisted companies, the EU currently allows individual member countries to decide whether to require or permit the use of international standards or to use national standards.

The IFAC indicates that over seventy countries have adopted the auditing standards promulgated by the IAASB and its predecessor body. This count is apparently the total number of countries that have either adopted ISA in whole or have declared that their national auditing standards contained the equivalent content as the ISA (Giles, Venuti, and Jones, 2004).

Many of these countries have adopted the ISA with changes or additions because of local conditions or legal requirements. Some countries may have adopted the quality control and the international code of ethics standards as well. But by 2006, the situation had become rather murky. That is, which countries could claim and should claim that they were following ISA? Could the adoption of ISA issued by the IAASB but with substantial revisions be considered adopting the ISA? Is it enough to have adopted the ISA or should the country also be following the code of ethics and quality control standards of the IFAC?

Various arms of the IFAC, in fact, issue a suite of standards. These are similar in makeup and purpose to the AICPA U.S. standards that cover audit, attestation, and other assurance work as well as quality control and professional ethics. Under the IFAC umbrella, the following authoritative pronouncement series are available. International Standards on Auditing are designed for use in the audit of historical financial information. International Standards on Review Engagements (ISRE) are designed for review engagements of historical financial information. International Standards on Assurance Engagements (ISAE) deal with subject matter that is not in the form of historical financial information. International Standards on Related Services (ISRS) are designed for compilation engagements, agreed-upon procedures engagements, and other related services specified by the IAASB. International Standards on Quality Control (ISOC) are applicable for all services that fall within the ISA, ISAE, and ISRS. The Code of Ethics for Professional Accountants is applicable to all professional accountants. Would it not seem that the entire series of standards would need to be globally accepted as the one series of standards for international auditing and assurance services?

In July 2006, the IAASB issued a clarifying Policy Position Statement (IAASB, 2006). The board indicates that its statement of policy is not to be viewed as an authoritative promulgation. But the board believes that it is appropriate to state its position in the interest of seeking common understanding among standard-setters, regulators, and the public. Circumstances that the board believes should exist before a country's national standard-setter may assert that the country's auditing standards are in conformity with IAASB's international standards are spelled out in the position statement (Ibid., 1).

The board emphasizes that it does not endorse terms such as "based on," "in substantial compliance with," or "in compliance with the principles of" in conjunction with ISA. Further it does not rule out the possibility that a different approach from that taken in the position paper could create national standards that are equivalent to the ISA (Ibid., 3).

Meaning of Adoption of International Auditing Standards

When a country's national standard-setters adopt the ISA series completely with little or no changes or amendments, that country is likely to assert that its standards conform to ISA. However, the board indicates that to be viewed as in conformity with its international standards, one of which is ISA, national standards must meet a number of conditions (Ibid.).

The country's professional accountants must be required to adhere to a national standard that conforms to the International Standards on Quality Control (IFAC, 2006a). The quality control standards require all professionals to uphold the independence requirements of a national ethics code and the IFAC Code of Ethics for Professional Accountants (Ibid., 18). In effect, the board seems to be indicating that to be in conformity with any of its international standards the subject country standards must include quality control and independence standards that are at least at the level of IFAC promulgations (IAASB, 2006, 3).

Further, the board indicates, the county's standards must include all requirements and guidance of the international standard in question to be considered in conformity. Requirements and guidance in the national standard must carry the same intention as to their meaning and effect as the international pronouncement in question. Accountants of the country in question must be required to consider all of the international guidance in order to apply and understand the international requirements.

Additions to an international standard should be limited to national legal and regulatory requirements. Additional requirements and guidance that are not inconsistent with the international standards are permitted. Deletions should only be made to eliminate options provided in the international standards or to eliminate requirements or guidance in the international standards that are not permitted by national laws or regulations or that are recognized in the international standards as not being applicable in some jurisdictions, one of which is the country in question. Any modifications made to the international standards should be afforded proper due process and be publicly disclosed (Ibid., 3–5). This position paper appears logical and should explain and clarify what adopting international standards entail.

U.S. and International Auditing Standards

Acceptance by the United States of international standards must occur if there is to be one world set of generally accepted auditing standards. U.S. Generally Accepted Auditing Standards (GAAS), which do not purport to be in conformity with ISA, are different in form from the ISA. U.S. GAAS consist of ten standards developed by the AICPA and grouped into general standards, standards of fieldwork, and standards of reporting. The standards were first developed in 1947. Minor changes have been made since.

The general standards are three in number. The audit is to be performed by a person or persons having adequate technical training and proficiency as an auditor; in all matters relating to the assignment, an independence in mental attitude is to be maintained by the auditor or auditors; and due professional care is to be exercised in the planning and performance of the audit and the preparation of the report.

The standards of fieldwork are three in number. The work is to be adequately planned and assistants, if any, are to be properly supervised; a sufficient understanding of internal control is to be obtained to plan the audit and to determine the nature, timing, and extent of tests to be performed; and sufficient competent evidential matter is to be obtained through inspection, observation, inquiries, and confirmations to afford a reasonable basis for an opinion regarding the financial statements under audit.

The standards of reporting are four in number. The report shall state whether the financial statements are presented in accordance with generally accepted accounting principles; the report shall identify those circumstances in which such principles have not been consistently observed in the current period in relation to the preceding period; informative disclosures in the financial statements are to be regarded as reasonably adequate unless otherwise stated in the report; and the report shall either contain an expression of opinion regarding the financial statements, taken as a whole, or an assertion to the effect that an opinion cannot be expressed. When an overall opinion cannot be expressed, the reasons therefore should be stated. In all cases where an auditor's name is associated with financial statements, the report should contain a clear-cut indication of the character of the auditor's work, if any, and the degree of responsibility the auditor is taking (AICPA, 2007).

Statements on Auditing Standards (SAS) are serially numbered pronouncements promulgated by the AICPA Auditing Standards Board that provide specific and practical guidance to carry out generally accepted auditing standards. SAS are codified within the framework of the ten generally accepted accounting principles and are the highest authoritative pronouncements that U.S. auditors can use when problems are encountered in the audit of nonpublic entities. In practice, the terms "U.S. auditing standards" or "GAAS" often refer to the SAS or the ten GAAS, or both. In order to carry out the GAAS and the SAS appropriately, the AICPA Code of Conduct must be adhered to, which includes the AICPA independence requirements. There is a separate series of Statements on Quality Control, which is meant to guide firms when performing auditing or other attestation and accounting service engagements for which professional standards have been established by the AICPA.

As noted earlier in this volume, the SAS and other associated existing pronouncements were accepted as interim PCAOB auditing standards until the new board could issue its own standards, which it is proceeding to do. The PCAOB standards apply only to public company audits just as did the SEC rulings before them. The SAS and independence standards issued by the AICPA have differed in some respects over the years. So, while the United States finds itself with two sets of auditing pronouncements, this is not a new development. The AICPA Auditing Standards Board, if it survives, can be expected to issue standards quite similar to the SEC/PCAOB pronouncements or vice versa.

For other attestation services, such as reviews of nonpublic companies, the AICPA has issued a separate though similar set of AICPA Attestation Standards, with broader application than audits of financial statements. These standards apply to all attestation engagements including audits since they are inclusive in nature. Statements on Standards for Attestation Services are issued by the AICPA to serve as a framework and to set boundaries for attestation services that do not rise to the level of financial statement audits.

The standards of the IAASB are not structured as are the AICPA standards. The IAASB uses a framework that defines and describes elements and objectives of assurance engagements. It provides a frame of reference for the various types of engagements and identifies the engagements to which ISA, International Standards on Review Engagements, and International Standards on Assurance Engagements apply. The framework does not contain procedural requirements or establish standards. These are codified in the ISA, ISRE, and ISAE, which describe basic principles, essential procedures, and guidance consistent with the framework for each type of engagement.

Practitioners who accept any assurance engagements are also governed by International Standards on Quality Control, which contain quality control standards and guidance for the practitioner firm's quality control, and the IFAC Code of Ethics for Professional Accountants, which contains ethical principles fundamental to professional accountants.

The first part of the Code of Ethics applies to all accountants and contains such fundamental principles as integrity, objectivity, professional competence, due professional care, confidentiality, and professional behavior.

The second part of the code, applying to accountants in public practice, contains a conceptual approach to independence that discusses public-interest obligations and, for each assurance engagement, threats to independence and proper safeguards against these threats, as was discussed elsewhere in this volume. Public accounting firms and assurance team practitioners are required to identify and evaluate relationships and circumstances that could impair independence and to eliminate such threats to independence or to reduce the threats to an acceptable level by employing appropriate safeguards (IFAC, 2006a, 281–83).

The approaches used by the United States and the IFAC for the standards differ, but the content of the two sets of standards is not substantially different and there would not appear to be major problems in converging the two standards sets, except that the approach taken by the

United States is proscriptive, with detailed specific requirements, whereas the international standards take a principles, threats, and safeguards approach. This is of major concern, as the U.S. approach was designed to nail down legally permitted or prohibited actions so that violators can be prosecuted. There are, of course, other substantial problems that must be dealt with before convergence into one worldwide set of standards can be achieved.

Problems on the Convergence Path

There are any number of differences of some substance that need to be resolved in the movement to create worldwide auditing standards. Many of these will be fairly easy to resolve but many will not. For example, to determine whether an entity is a going concern at any date, U.S. audit standards require the auditor to estimate whether the entity will remain a going concern for one year in the future. The ISA use a longer time horizon. In the U.S. standards, the detection of illegal acts is the responsibility of the auditor only for illegal acts having a direct and material effect on the financial statements. The ISA approach has a wider dimension. As mentioned earlier, the U.S. standards allow shared-responsibility audit opinions, whereas the ISA do not.

The IFAC in November 2003 commissioned Peter Wong, a former IFAC Board of Directors member and an experienced international accountant, to head up a study of the problems and the pathways to convergence of national standards with IFAC standards. The results of his study were published by the IFAC in 2004 in *Challenges and Successes in Implementing International Standards: Achieving Convergence to IFRSS and ISAS* (Wong, 2004). The methods used for the study were to collect a cross section of views from the international financial reporting community, from regional and national accounting organizations, national standard-setters, financial statement users, regulators, and accountants who had a variety of backgrounds (Ibid., 2).

To gather facts, focus group meetings were held with regional and national accountancy organizations' members. Interviews were conducted with representatives of national standard-setters, financial statement preparers, auditors, financial statement users, and regulators. IFAC member bodies were requested to send written responses. There were nine focus groups held, approximately twenty interviews conducted, and twenty-nine written responses received. Those who participated in the study came from a wide international range of organizations with one notable exception. The United States did not appear to be among the participants listed.

There were a number of topics about which participants were asked to respond. Some of these were: factors that might encourage or discourage national decision makers to converge; regulatory challenges to convergence; cultural barriers to adopting and implementing convergence; cost problems, particularly for small- and medium-sized firms; complexity and structural issues; resources and problems with translation of standards; and education of accountants and students about international standards.

The evidence collected by the study is by its nature anecdotal. However, the diversity of the participants and the consistency of their responses leads to the conclusion that the results provide clear indications of the challenges that must be overcome if adoption and implementation of international standards is to be facilitated (Ibid., 5).

Study participants agreed that the International Accounting Standards Board (IASB) and the IAASB should be the organizations for international standard-setting. They expressed positive attitudes toward adoption and implementation of international standards. Similar challenges to both IFRS and ISA adoption and implementation were expected. The participants spent more time discussing the international accounting standards than the international auditing standards. An industry participant gave what seems a plausible reason. The accounting standards more directly affect many more people than do the auditing standards. Auditors must deal with the auditing standards. Everybody else has to deal, or is effected more directly, by the accounting standards (Ibid., 6).

Responses from participants raised the following question: What do we mean when we say that international standards have been adopted by a country? There seemed to be no accepted definition of adoption of the standards. Such terms as "harmonization," "transformation," "based on," and the like were used by participants. Some referred to their national standards as being 80 percent identical or 95 percent identical to international standards. Peter Wong's view was that convergence is a process, with adoption being the end result. The progress toward adoption is difficult to measure without a clearer idea of what can be counted as adoption (Ibid., 7).

The World Bank, in its *Reports on the Observance of Standards and Codes,* indicates that the adoption of IFRS has been described as "full adoption," "full adoption but with time lags," "selective adoption," and "national standards based on IFRS." Peter Wong indicates that these categories could be used for the adoption of ISA as well, with one added item: "adoption of a summarized version of ISA." And, in the case of ISA adoptions, each category could be labeled with the phrase "contains added national requirements" (Ibid., 7).

The time lags between issuance of an international standard and implementation by a country can be long and are caused in large measure by the problems of translating the standard into the country's language. In one country, a five-year lag was experienced because of translation problems. The selective adoption of international standards is in general caused by the complexity of the standards and incompatible national requirements. The ISAs were summarized in thirty-three pages in one country because the complete standards were viewed as too overwhelming. This particular country is now in its sixth year in this temporary phase of initial adoption of international standards (Ibid., 7).

The IAASB position statement discussed above should clarify what is meant by adoption of IAASB-promulgated international standards. Further, in the revision to ISA 700, *The Independent Auditor's Report on a Complete Set of General Purpose Financial Statements* limits auditor reports that refer to the audit being conducted in accordance with ISA to those in which all of the ISA have been fully complied with on the audit in question (IAASB, 2007, 36). It seems clear that the IAASB position paper must be complied with if nations want their financial audits to be in compliance with ISA. The position statement clears up the problems, found in the Wong study, of defining what adoption of international standards means.

Another problem area found in the study was the adding or deleting of matters from the international standards because of requirements and laws of the country in question. The international standards are, of course, adopted and implemented in the unique environment of the particular country. Existing political, economic, and legal regulations as well as cultural aspects are all present. Study participants cited various of these factors as causing the partial adoption or additions to international standards. Several other studies had found the same conditions, causing partial or amended adoptions of international standards (Wong, 2004, 8).

Hopefully, the IAASB position paper will be followed in the future. As discussed above, the IAASB would limit additions to an international standard to cases where necessary to comply with national legal and regulatory requirements and additions that are not inconsistent with the international standard. In countries where the audit and accounting systems have been traditionally used for taxation purposes, the vital need to adopt international standards, which will serve the needs of the capital markets and investors, should be apparent and should certainly not be the basis for partial adoption or augmentations. Nevertheless, such country specificities may act as a barrier to international standard adoption, unfortunately to the detriment of the countries in question.

If countries need to add national requirements to use international standards, the question becomes how this should be carried out. Participants in the Wong study reported various approaches. The United Kingdom has chosen to differentiate the additions in a clear manner from the ISA content. France and Germany have chosen not to differentiate the additions. The Wong report indicates that clearly differentiating the additional material is to be preferred because it allows auditors and financial statement preparers to readily distinguish between the two, particularly when they wish to comply with international standards. The differentiation approach also facilitates standards maintenance and updating (Ibid., 10).

A major challenge to adoption, implementation, and maintenance of international standards is the need to translate standards and standards revisions into the appropriate language of the country in question. Standards written in English are often difficult to translate. Study participants cited these problems: lengthy English sentences, terminology that is used inconsistently, and terminology that is incapable of translation. The study cited the English words "shall" and "should," which are not capable of translation in many languages. The concepts of "significant" and "material" might have different nuances or have cultural connotations making translation difficult or impossible. Most of the study participants indicated that writing in simple English would be a great benefit and that professional accountants' involvement in the translation process is important (Ibid., 11).

Funding for translations may be difficult for some countries, particularly when standards are updated frequently. The volume of updates to international standards is high, making the maintenance of conforming with standards especially difficult. Further, the timetables allowed between issuance and required implementation need to be extended to allow for translations to be completed. This is particularly acute for exposure drafts for proposed standards, which often have short deadlines for comments. The European Commission indicated that the time between publication of an international standard and the availability of the translation in its *Official Journal of the Commission* may take nine months (Ibid., 11).

The Wong study made a number of recommendations to provide effective translations. A formal translation plan for international standards is needed, which would include having accounting professionals on translation teams and providing for a process for early translation of proposed and final standards. Consistent use of terminology needs to be followed in international standards. This should include a list of key words that are translated. Input should be obtained from translators from other countries where the same language is spoken. Donors for funding would cover the costs of translation of the initial standard and revisions should be actively pursued (Ibid., 12).

Study participants thought that the principles-based approach to standards was preferable, since the standards are complex and long. They thought that rules-based standards are more difficult to implement and encouraged a compliance and avoidance attitude. Some countries must incorporate the standards into national law or regulation. And, the participants did not think that standard-setters made allowances for the fact that standards that are not written in legal form must be transformed before enactment into law (Ibid., 13).

The frequency, volume, and complexity of changes to international standards present a difficult challenge to preparers, auditors, and users of financial statements alike. Participants questioned whether the cumulative effects were worth the efforts and whether those who set the standards monitor these effects. This a particular problem in countries where each change must be transformed into changes in laws and regulations. They cited the example of the revision to the ISA on auditor responsibility to consider fraud issued in 2004. The previous revision of the same standard had become effective for periods ending on or after June 30, 2002. The participants thought that a balance needs to be struck between the need to improve standards on a priority basis with the need to have enough time to properly implement the standards (Ibid., 14).

Despite the many challenges that his study indicates must be surmounted, Peter Wong's judgment, based on the study, is that the goal of international conversion to one set of standards is achievable over time (Ibid., 1).

Study participants, none of whom were from the United States, strongly favored the principles approach to standards (Ibid., 13). As is discussed elsewhere, the U.S. approach to standards is detailed, proscriptive, and prescriptive. This may be one of the main stumbling blocks to convergence of U.S. standards to ISA and is typified by the approach taken by each in their respective ethical codes. The international code follows a threats and safeguards approach, which is thought to be based on principles, with a large number of specific nonrule examples that the auditor is expected to follow if he or she believes that the example is applicable to a situation at hand. Decisions are left to the auditor's judgment.

For each nonrule deemed applicable, which in the code is referred to as an example, appropriate safeguards are listed that may be used to bring a perceived threat to auditor independence within acceptable limits. The subject matter of the examples covered, in fact, appears basically to be the same list of items contained in the U.S. ethics codes. The difference is that the United States takes a rule-based, prescriptive, and proscriptive approach. Such an approach seems to be required by the Sarbanes-Oxley Act. The U.S. Congress, it would appear, would have to legislate another approach, such as the principles-based approach of the European Union, in order to achieve convergence with ISA.

The U.S. PCAOB, some point out, may not be overly interested in convergence to international standards or have a vested interest in doing so. This reasoning is backed up by the fact that the board has the authority to register all accounting firms that desire to audit public companies registered with the SEC, meaning all companies listed on U.S. securities exchanges. The board has the authority to require both U.S. and foreign firms to participate in its quality control and quality review programs. Thus, it can regulate a very large portion of the world's public companies and their auditors.

Earlier U.S. securities laws had exempted foreign issuers of securities and their auditors. The Sarbanes-Oxley Act, however, declared that a non-U.S. public accounting firm must abide by the same rules and legislation as U.S. public accounting firms in the same manner and to the same extent. The PCAOB system of rule making and oversight, including inspections, investigations, and penalties, applies to U.S. and foreign firms alike when their client public companies are listed on United States stock exchanges.

A number of objections to the PCAOB oversight of foreign accounting firms were raised "throughout the international accounting community"

(Rankin, 2004, 1). After consultation and discussions with regulators in other countries, particularly in the European Union and Japan, the PCAOB proposed and the SEC approved a rule under which the board would rely on the oversight systems in foreign countries to the extent that the foreign oversight system was deemed as rigorous and independent as the PCAOB itself (SEC, 2004, II).

As was discussed above, a great many countries have passed securities legislation reforms in recent years, primarily in response to the accounting debacles and the U.S. Sarbanes-Oxley Act. As these reforms take effect in other countries, it seems likely that the PCAOB will be able to rely on more foreign country oversight because the countries' rules will have been reformed along lines similar to the reforms in the United States.

There was no mandate given to the PCAOB to harmonize, converge, or in any other way allow its powers to be transferred to an international organization. In the U.S. political environment, such a change of legislative intent seems unlikely. The board's every decision and action was made subject to SEC approval. The SEC has proven itself over the years to be highly political and responsive to the executive and legislative branches of government. The U.S. Congress in the past has viewed itself as the final arbiter of accounting standards. The Congress now must be presumed to view itself as the final arbiter for regulation of auditors. To relinquish this power would be contrary to the nature of the political realities in the United States and probably in the world. The world may be heading for an accounting standard bifurcated future with two sets of standards, international and United States.

In the next three chapters, other specific problems facing the global accounting profession are examined in some detail. In chapter 6, the hurdle of independence of auditor from client is considered. In chapter 7, we analyze the locational adjustments taking place first competitively in the market for large corporate audit clients, and then geographically as the global financial system expands. Consideration of the impact of improving computers and communications in the form of the Internet, electronic commerce, and Extensible Markup Language on the accounting profession are the subjects of chapter 8.

6

Independence as a Growing Problem for Accounting Firms

Prior to U.S. federal securities legislation in the 1930s, the accounting profession's American Institute of Accountants, through a special committee on cooperation with stock exchanges chaired by George O. May, worked with the New York Stock Exchange (NYSE) to increase the use of independent audit of listed companies. Their success was evident in that, reportedly, over 80 percent of NYSE-listed companies issued financial statements that were audited by independent accountants before the enactment of federal securities legislation in 1933 (Brewster, 2003, 9).

Market forces were at work. To further their business interests, corporations listed on exchanges or those seeking capital through securities markets hired competent third-party independent accounting firms to audit corporate financial statements in order to add to the creditability that the statements were prepared fairly in accordance with generally accepted accounting principles. George O. May was a leading advocate of this approach and testified in numerous court cases and hearings, particularly as to what generally accepted accounting principles were, because no codification existed in those years before the Great Depression. Even though such audits and audit reports were not required by government, the corporate objective was to make company securities more attractive to investors in order to lower the costs of capital.

The Securities Act of 1933 did require that financial reports of public companies that issued securities in the United States be audited by independent accountants. The independent accountant was seen as a better choice than a corps of federal auditors. This was the consensus in both government and private circles (Ibid., 80). Accounting professor G.A. Swanson believes that the consensus of opinion at that time was that power centralization in a government unit would bring with it corruption and stagnation in what was then a vigorous, productive private business environment (Ibid.). Certainly it was not the objective of the securities legislation to bring on corruption and stagnation of economic development. During 1933, the Federal Trade Commission, which had responsibility under the 1933 Securities Act, directed the independent accountants in creating a formal yet general series of regulations that would be used by independent accountants in their task of performing independent audits (Ibid.).

With the enactment of the Securities Exchange Act of 1934, authority over accounting and auditing was transferred to the Securities and Exchange Commission (SEC). The SEC continued the delegation of responsibility, albeit with SEC oversight, for public company audits to independent accountants through their organization, the American Institute of Accountants, later to become the American Institute of Certified Public Accountants (AICPA). Throughout its existence, the SEC has attempted to enforce the principle that auditor independence from the organizations they audit is essential. This was the case in 1934 and continues to be the case today. The commission indicates that such independence is "crucial to the credibility of financial reporting and, in turn, the capital formation process" (SEC, 1997, 1). This view must surely be shared by reasonable persons everywhere in the world.

Capital formation is greatly facilitated when ownership of capital can be put in the hands of corporate agents who can more effectively and productively use the capital in business pursuits. The separation of ownership from management of resources is fundamental in a market-based economy to using capital to best economic advantage and value.

The separation of ownership from custody and management of capital brings with it the absolute need to have accountability over, and proper reporting of, the uses and management of the capital in question. The first independent auditors in America were sent by English investors whose resources had been put to uses far from England. Adequate financial reports to capital owners were essential then and are essential today so that owners can make informed current and future decisions about the best uses of their funds. Presumably such decisions will lead to allocations of capital toward most productive uses. To be sure, this method of capital allocation, wherever it can be done, is preferable to government control and allocations. And, of course, it is fundamental to market-based economies.

Accountability and proper reporting thereof requires verification through a reliable and effective process of examination and attestation of the results of capital stewardship. The importance of this independent function of examination and attestation can clearly be seen in that the U.S. Congress, in the various securities laws, has repeatedly underscored and reiterated that the function of independent auditors is crucial to protect public investors. Thus, U.S. securities laws require financial statements filed with the commission by public companies and other public-interest entities, such as investment companies, broker-dealers, public utilities, and investment advisers, to be audited by independent public accountants (Ibid., 2).

This suggests that the Congress and the commission rightly view the requirement of auditor independence as absolute. The use of the word "absolute," however, is belied by the problems of definition of independence. What does it take to say that an auditor is independent of the organization audited? Clearly events in the recent past have shown that the mark has often been missed.

SEC's versus Firms' View of Independence

Price Waterhouse and its successor firm PricewaterhouseCoopers flagrantly violated fundamental independence requirements that were in force in 1997. A former employee of Price Waterhouse sent a letter to the SEC in 1997 indicating that the Price Waterhouse Tampa, Florida, office was violating independence rules in that partners and employees of the firm owned stock of audit clients. Upon investigation, the SEC determined that the Tampa office was in violation of independence rules and that violations were widespread within Price Waterhouse.

Further, at the beginning of the SEC investigation, Price Waterhouse was merging to become PricewaterhouseCoopers. After the merger, all partners and staff were required by independence rules to divest all stock of all audit clients of the combined firm. The SEC found that some of these required divestitures never took place (Levitt, 2002, 124–25).

As a result, PricewaterhouseCoopers was required by the SEC to hire an outside counsel to undertake an internal investigation. In his book, *Take on the Street,* then SEC chairman Arthur Levitt expressed the opinion that it seemed as though the partners of PricewaterhouseCoopers viewed compliance with the stock ownership prohibition independence rules as merely optional. He reported that "The investigation uncovered an incredible 8,000 violations, involving half the firm's partners" (Ibid.,

125). The chief executive of Price Waterhouse had continued to own stock of an audit client that he did not sell until February 1999, which was four months after an audit of the company in question had been completed by the firm and seven months after the merger of the firms into PricewaterhouseCoopers took place (Ibid.).

Because of the massive violations of this independence rule at the largest of the then Big Five firms, the SEC sought to have the AICPA-sponsored Public Oversight Board hire outside counsel to make probes of the remaining four firms to investigate this important independence issue. The Public Oversight Board was funded by the AICPA and had been created to carry out accounting profession self-regulatory functions in the aftermath of audit failures in the 1970s. In Levitt's view, this was to forestall even tougher regulations from being imposed at the time (Ibid., 126).

As the oversight board was preparing to hire outside counsel for the probes, the AICPA announced that it would not pay for the probes. After protracted negotiations with the SEC, each of the four firms agreed to hire independent counsel. The counsel was to conduct in-house reviews at each of the firms to ascertain whether similar violations had taken place at the firms in question during the nine-month period ending March 31, 2000. The firms also agreed that the Public Oversight Board would review the firms' efforts to ensure that these kind of problems did not recur. The independent counsel reviews were completed, but the Public Oversight Board was disbanded before it could review the firms' efforts to ensure that no recurrences would take place. In Levitt's view, "self-regulation by the accounting profession is a bad joke" (Ibid., 127). He believes that the firms did not intend to submit to scrutiny except when forced to (Ibid.).

The Institute of Internal Auditors (IIA), in its July 22, 1998, commentary on proposed recommendations of the Independence Standards Board, also seemed to be acutely aware of the auditor independence problems in public corporations. The institute's president William G. Bishop III wrote: "The Board's objective of improving auditor independence requirements is of urgent importance to the IIA and all professional financial organizations" (Bishop, 1998, 1). The IIA, it would seem, was in a good position to know of outside auditor independence problems. The IIA was established in 1941 as a professional organization of primarily U.S. internal auditors. By 2000, the institute had approximately 70,000 members, most working in corporate internal audit departments.

It had become a worldwide organization with more than 100 countries represented in its ranks (Ibid.).

Members of the Public Oversight Board, a private AICPA organization, were selected by the profession itself. Its oversight included the AICPA peer-review system, in which one auditing firm would hire another auditing firm to review the quality control system of the firm in question. Independence review was supposed to be a part of the quality control system in each firm. In the face of mounting criticism of the failures of self-regulation, the entire board resigned en masse after then SEC chairman Harvey Pitt proposed that a new, although still private, oversight body was needed to regulate the accounting and auditing industry. The Pitt proposal eventually evolved into the Public Company Accounting Oversight Board (PCAOB). The Public Oversight Board was formally dissolved on March 31, 2002 (Wikipedia, 2002, 4).

Independence Standards Board Too Late to Avoid Sarbanes-Oxley

Earlier, in 1997, as the accounting profession's independence problems were becoming acute, the SEC by agreement with the AICPA had inaugurated the Independence Standards Board by issuing its "Policy Statement: The Establishment and Improvement of Standards Related to Auditor Independence" (SEC, 1997). The board's charge was to initiate research, develop standards, and engage in public analysis and debate of auditor independence issues.

Arthur Levitt, then SEC chairman, indicated in his book, *Take on the Street,* that negotiation with the AICPA and the Big Five accounting firms took a year before the accountants begrudgingly agreed to the board's formation (Levitt, 2002, 119). Levitt describes how he had become convinced that the accountants were determined to protect their lucrative consulting businesses regardless of the independence problems. He had, as he put it, at the top of his list "new rules which would keep the growth of consulting from compromising audits" (Ibid.).

The need for the new board, the SEC indicated in its policy statement, arose from the more complex situations then being faced by auditors in their ongoing work, which exacerbated independence problems. Auditors had entered and continued to enter into new types of service areas. Technology and business practices had become more sophisticated, creating new situations with attendant independence problems. The operations of auditing firms in general had undergone restructurings and mergers. Further, business operations had become ever-more global in their scope (SEC, 1997, 2).

The Independence Standards Board was expected to provide leadership to improve auditor independence requirements and to establish and maintain a body of independence standards to guide all auditors of companies registered with the commission (Ibid.). Others saw the need for the new board as caused by myriad confusing rules and regulations on independence. Many extant rulings and other pronouncements on independence had been issued over a number of years in which circumstances had been changing. Some of the rules were not up-to-date, it was thought. There were conflicts between some of the rules. And, there was no consistent framework of theory underlying the various independence pronouncements. Many of the pronouncements had been issued as interpretations to guide auditor decisions on independence in specific situations. These were difficult to apply if the facts and circumstances of an auditor's relationship with the client entity in question did not match those in the interpretation (McGrath et al., 2001, 1).

The composition of the Independence Standards Board, however, brought it immediately under suspicion. For example, the Institute of Internal Auditors took exception to the composition of the board as one that was not balanced but was instead heavily weighted with auditing firm and AICPA representation. Of the eight board members, three were representatives of certified public account (CPA) firms and a fourth member was the president of the AICPA.

Since a majority of the board was not from outside the accounting profession, by its very nature it was not independent. Therefore an unbiased perspective on the part of the board would be difficult to achieve. Board members were put in a position where they were asked to set criteria for their own and for their firm's independence. This seemed akin to the fact that auditors lack independence if they audit their own work (Bishop, 2000).

The IIA recommended that the Independence Standards Board membership include a clear majority of members who are independent of the public accounting profession. Further, they suggested that the board staff should also be independent of the public accounting profession. A balanced membership composition for the board was preferable, with representatives from public accounting firms, public accounting firm clients, the investing public, and regulators. Such representation from public accounting and public-interest constituencies would enhance the board's ability to address independence issues from a public-interest point of view. The IIA also pointed out that its positions about how the board should be reconstituted agreed with the position taken on the issue by the Panel on Audit Effectiveness (Ibid.).

The Panel on Audit Effectiveness had been instituted in 1998 at the request of SEC chairman Arthur Levitt. Its mandate was to review and evaluate how independent audits were conducted and how recent trends in the conduct of audits affected the public interest. The Public Oversight Board appointed the eight-member panel, which included two former SEC commissioners as well as representatives from U.S. corporations, the accounting profession, and academia.

In its final report on September 6, 2000, the Panel on Audit Effectiveness indicated, among numerous other recommendations, that the Public Oversight Board needed to be strengthened by reconstituting the board with a majority of its members from outside the public accounting profession. Further, looking to the future, the panel recommended that agreement on a unified system of governance to oversee standard setting for auditing, independence, and quality control should be established by the Public Oversight Board, the AICPA, the SEC Practice Section of the AICPA, and the SEC (Panel on Audit Effectiveness, 2000).

The SEC on November 15, 2000, adopted changes in its independence rules that became effective on February 5, 2001. This first independence rule revision since 1983 was based to a large extent on the Independence Standards Board's recommendations. It included modernization of the commission's rules for determining and ensuring auditor independence in light of the increasing scope of services provided by accounting firms to their audit clients, of investments in audit clients by auditors or their family members, and of employment situations that arise between audit clients and members of audit firms and their families. The revisions significantly reduced the number of family members of auditors whose investments in audit clients could be attributed to the auditor when determining auditor independence from the client. The number of auditor family members and former audit firm personnel whose employment status could be considered to impair auditor independence was also reduced (SEC, 2001, 1).

Specified non-audit services provided by an audit firm to public company clients had been added as being considered to impair auditor independence. There were added requirements for disclosure in annual proxy statements of selected information related to non-audit services during the most recent fiscal year (Ibid.).

The reason cited for the need for the revised rules was the changing environment within which audits were then conducted. Prior independence rules concerning financial and employment relationships of auditors and their families with clients were written in an era when CPA firms were small and less diversified. There were few dual career families then. Accounting firms operate today increasingly on a global basis and provide a wide range of multidisciplinary services. Firms now have offices and staff around the globe. There has been a great increase in the number of professionals employed by CPA firms. Most of the partners in a CPA firm who are not in the office responsible for the audit have no connection to, or influence over, the particular audit.

Prior rules were too restrictive in the current environment and needed to be changed to restrict only the ownership and relationships necessary in order to ensure proper independence of auditors from attestation clients. The revisions allowed CPAs and their staffs and families to take maximum advantage of opportunities available to them that did not impair the CPA's independence from clients.

The nature and extent of non-audit services provided to clients is rightly of concern. A number of types of non-audit services are inherently in conflict with auditor independence and objectivity. The more the auditor has at stake with any given client, the greater would be the cost should the client be lost to another audit firm or should the auditor displease the client. The percentage of total fees earned by auditing firms for accounting and auditing had decreased. In 1999, none of the Big Five firms earned more than 35 percent of its total fees from accounting and auditing. In 1993, four of the Big Six firms earned over 50 percent of revenues from accounting and auditing fees.

The SEC's objective for auditor independence is to ensure that auditors approach each audit with appropriate professional skepticism. Auditors must be willing, if necessary for full and fair financial reporting, to take positions that might be against the interests of client management or against the interests of the accounting firm. Factors that might impair an auditor's objectivity are often subtle. The revisions to the SEC independence rules are thought to help minimize the possibility that external factors will influence the auditor's objective judgment.

The Independence Standards Board discontinued its operations by mutual consent of the board members, the SEC, and the AICPA on July

31, 2001. The SEC stated at that time that the work of the Independence Standards Board laid the groundwork for more consistent auditor independence requirements and indicated that most of the board's recommendations had been included in the SEC auditor independence rules adopted in November 2000.

The AICPA's view was that the existing AICPA Professional Ethics Executive Committee could take over the duties of the Public Company Oversight Board and the Independence Standards Board since the AICPA had recently added independent public members to the committee. But, events were overtaking the AICPA and the public accounting profession. One year later, the Sarbanes-Oxley Act passed the Congress and was signed into law.

SEC Independence Rules After Sarbanes-Oxley

The SEC independence rules were again revised effective May 6, 2003, primarily to adopt changes required by the Sarbanes-Oxley Act. SEC rules apply only to auditors of companies that file financial statements with the SEC, that is, those that issue financial securities to the public. The AICPA ethical rules, including independence, remain applicable to CPAs in engagements with nonpublic entities. It is very clear that both of these sets of rules are prescriptive and detailed in the U.S. standard-setting style and are very close in their content. The SEC rules will be discussed here, followed by consideration of a comparison of the two sets of rules that was made by the AICPA in 2005 (AICPA, 2005).

The SEC rules begin with the definition of a covered person. A covered person is defined in reference to the audit of a specific client. This definition is then used to indicate the responsibilities of this limited class of auditors in reference to the specified audit engagement. A covered person is defined as all audit engagement team members; those in the chain of command or persons who supervise or have direct management responsibility for the audit, including all successively senior levels through the firm's chief executive; persons who evaluate performance or recommend compensation of the audit engagement partner, or persons who provide quality control or other audit oversight; partners or managers who provide ten or more hours of non-audit services to the audit client; as well as all partners or those equivalent to a partner from the "office" of the firm in which the lead audit engagement partner primarily practices in connection with the specified audit (Ibid., 1–3). All others would not be subject to restrictions in regard to the audit client in question.

Covered members or their immediate families impair the covered member's independence and the independence of the audit firm by owning any direct or indirect material financial interest in an audit client; serving as voting trustee of a trust, or executor of an estate, containing the securities of a client, unless they have no authority to make investment decisions for the trust or estate; having any direct or material indirect business relationship with an audit client or with persons associated with the client's officers, directors, or substantial stockholders; making a loan to or accepting a loan from the audit client or a client's officers, directors, or beneficial owners of more than 10 percent of the client's equity securities (Ibid., 5).

Independence of the firm and the covered members is impaired if the accounting firm, any covered member in the firm, or any of the member's immediate family has a direct or material indirect investment in an entity in which the audit client has a material investment and the ability to exercise significant influence; a direct or material indirect investment in an entity that has a material investment in the audit client and that enables that entity to exercise significant influence over the audit client; has a material investment in an entity over which the audit client has the ability to exercise significant influence; or has the ability to exercise significant influence over an entity that has the ability to exercise significant influence over an audit client (Ibid., 6).

The immediate family of a covered person, as defined in the independence rules, includes the member's spouse, spousal equivalent, and dependents. Covered members' immediate family members must comply with the same rules as the covered member. There are two exceptions to this for financial interests held in an employee benefit plan. The immediate family of a partner or manager who is providing non-attest services or the immediate family of other partners in the same office as the lead attest engagement partner's primary office may have a financial interest in a client that resulted as an unavoidable consequence of participation in an employer's compensation or benefits program and is disposed of as soon as practicable, but no later than thirty days after the person has the right to dispose of the financial interest. The immediate family of persons on the audit engagement team or those in a position to influence the engagement may not use the exception (Ibid., 7).

The independence of the firm and the covered members is impaired when any partner or equivalent, professional employee, or his or her immediate family or group of such persons has beneficial ownership of more than 5 percent of an audit client's equity securities (Ibid., 8).

Impairment of independence occurs when a covered person's close family, defined in the independence rules as a parent, a nondependent child, or a sibling, has beneficial ownership of more than 5 percent of a client's equity securities or controls an audit client. It also occurs when any partner's, or equivalent's, close family controls a client (Ibid., 9).

If a current partner, or equivalent, or professional employee is employed by a client or serves as a member of the board of directors or similar management body of the client, independence of the individual and firm are impaired (Ibid., 10).

When a covered person's immediate family is in an accounting role or financial reporting oversight role at a client, or a covered person's parent, nondependent child, or sibling is in an accounting role or financial reporting oversight role at a client, independence is impaired. For this standard, accounting role means a role in which a person is in a position to or does exercise more than minimal influence over the contents of the accounting records or anyone who prepares them. Financial reporting oversight role means a role in which a person is in a position to or does exercise influence over the contents of the financial statements or anyone who prepares them, such as when the person is a member of the board of directors or similar management or governing body, chief executive officer, president, chief financial officer, chief operating officer, general counsel, chief accounting officer, controller, director of internal audit, director of financial reporting, treasurer, or any equivalent position (Ibid., 10, 11).

A former officer, director, or employee of a client who becomes a partner or professional employee of the firm impairs independence unless he or she does not participate in, and is not in a position to influence, the audit of the client's financial statements covering any period during which he or she was employed by or associated with that client (Ibid., 12).

An accounting firm is not independent of the audit client if a former partner, principal, shareholder, or professional employee of the accounting firm is employed by the client in an accounting role or financial reporting oversight role. Independence of the auditing firm is not impaired if said individual (1) does not influence the accounting firm's operations or financial policies; (2) has no capital balances in the accounting firm; and (3) has no financial arrangement with the accounting firm other than one providing for regular payment of a fixed-dollar amount that is not dependent on the revenues, profits, or earnings of the accounting firm, and the regular fixed payments are made pursuant to a fully funded retirement plan, rabbi trust, or, in jurisdictions in which a rabbi trust does not exist, a similar vehicle. Independence is not impaired in the case of a former professional employee who was not a partner, principal, or shareholder of the accounting firm and who has been disassociated from the accounting firm for more than five years, and the regular fixed payment is immaterial to the former professional employee.

An accountant is not independent when a former partner, principal, shareholder, or professional employee of the accounting firm is employed in a financial reporting oversight role at a client if the said individual was a member of the audit engagement team for the client during the one-year period preceding the date that audit procedures commenced for the fiscal period that included the date of initial employment of the audit engagement team member by the issuer (Ibid., 13, 14).

An accountant is not independent if the accountant provides the following proscribed non-audit services to an audit client: acting, temporarily or permanently, as a director, officer, or employee of an audit client or performing any decision-making, supervisory, or ongoing monitoring function for the audit client (Ibid., 16).

Any service is prohibited unless it is reasonable to conclude that the results of such services will not be subject to audit procedures during an audit of the audit client's financial statements. Such services include maintaining or preparing the audit client's accounting records; preparing the audit client's financial statements or preparing or originating source data underlying the audit client's financial statements; directly or indirectly operating, or supervising the operation of, the audit client's information system or managing the audit client's local area network; and designing or implementing a hardware or software system that aggregates source data underlying the financial statements or generates information that is significant to the audit client's financial statements or other financial information systems taken as a whole (Ibid., 19, 20).

Providing human resources services of the following types impairs the firm's independence from the client: searching for or seeking out prospective candidates for managerial, executive, or director positions; engaging in psychological testing or other formal testing or evaluation programs; undertaking reference checks of prospective candidates for an executive or director position; acting as a negotiator on the audit client's behalf, such as determining position, status or title, compensation, fringe benefits, or other conditions of employment; or recommending, or advising, the audit client to hire a specific candidate for a specific job, except that an accounting firm may, upon request by the audit client, interview candidates and advise the audit client on the candidate's competence for financial accounting, administrative, or control positions (Ibid., 21).

Any appraisal service, valuation service, or service involving a fairness opinion or contribution-in-kind report for an audit client impairs independence, unless it is reasonable to conclude that the results of these services will not be subject to audit procedures during an audit of the client's financial statements (Ibid., 22).

Independence is impaired if any actuarially oriented advisory service involving the determination of amounts recorded in the financial statements and related accounts for the audit client is provided, other than assisting a client in understanding the methods, models, assumptions, and inputs used in computing an amount, unless it is reasonable to conclude that the results of these services will not be subject to audit procedures during an audit of the client's financial statements (Ibid.).

Independence is impaired by acting as a broker-dealer (registered or unregistered), promoter, or underwriter on behalf of an audit client; making investment decisions on behalf of the audit client or otherwise having discretionary authority over an audit client's investments; executing a transaction to buy or sell an audit client's investment; or having custody of assets of the audit client, such as taking temporary possession of securities purchased by the audit client (Ibid.).

Independence is impaired by providing any internal audit service that has been outsourced by the audit client that relates to the audit client's internal accounting controls, financial systems, or financial statements, unless it is reasonable to conclude that the results of these services will not be subject to audit procedures during an audit of the client's financial statements (Ibid., 23).

Independence is impaired by providing any service to an audit client that, under circumstances in which the service is provided, could be provided only by someone licensed, admitted, or otherwise qualified to practice law in the jurisdiction in which the service is provided.

Providing an expert opinion or other expert service for an audit client, or an audit client's legal representative, for the purpose of advocating an audit client's interests in litigation or in a regulatory or administrative proceeding or investigation impairs independence. Note that an accountant is permitted to provide factual accounts, including in testimony, of work performed or to explain the positions taken or conclusions reached during the performance of any service provided by the accountant for the audit client (Ibid., 25).

AICPA Compared to SEC Independence Rules

A comparison between the SEC independence rules and the AICPA independence rules discloses a number of minor differences. Often these are matters of clarification in one set of the rules or the other. In general, the two sets of independence rules agree with one another in material aspects except for the matter of preparation of audit client accounting records and financial statements. The SEC rules prohibit auditors from performing accounting work for the audit client. The AICPA rules allow bookkeeping and financial statement preparation services for the audit client so long as the auditor does not act in a management capacity. The client management must approve any changes made in the accounting records or source documents. The CPA may not prepare source documents, authorize payments, sign client checks, maintain client bank accounts or have custody of client funds, sign payroll tax returns on behalf of the client, nor approve vendors' invoices for payment (AICPA, 2005, 18, 19).

This difference is understandable, given the differences in the purposes of the two sets of rules. The SEC rules are meant for public companies, which are in general quite large and should of course have their own accounting staff. For these companies, there should be no need for the same firm to perform the accounting and then audit its own work. The AICPA rules, however, are meant for nonpublic companies, which range from the very small to the very large. Many of the smaller firms do not have the capability to perform their own accounting and preparation of financial statements. The members of the AICPA have many such clients. But, it is clear that the CPAs performing accounting work for nonpublic entities should never cross the line where they are making management decisions and carrying out management responsibilities if they have attestation engagements for the client.

EU Auditor Independence

As opposed to the rule-based, compliance-driven U.S. approach, the European Union (EU) code for auditor independence from assurance clients uses guidance to a far greater extent. A principles-based framework is presented within which the practitioner must use professional judgments about threats to independence. Safeguards against such threats are a matter of practitioner judgment, but rather specific and extensive guidance is provided in the code. The point at which safeguards are not adequate and engagement withdrawal is required is also a matter for practitioner judgment.

The revised EU Eighth Directive includes the requirement for accountants and auditors in all EU countries to meet the standards promulgated in the *Code of Ethics for Professional Accountants* prepared by the International Federation of Accountants Ethics Committee (IFAEC). Section 290 of that ethics code covers independence for assurance engagements. Assurance engagements are considered to always be in the public interest and, therefore, assurance teams, defined as firms and, where applicable, networks of firms, are required to be independent of the assurance clients (IFAEC, 2005, 290.3).

An assurance engagement is defined in the code of ethics as one in which the public practitioner expresses a conclusion designed to enhance the degree of confidence of the intended users, other than the responsible party, about the outcome of the practitioner's evaluation or measurement of the subject matter against appropriate criteria. The intention of the attestation engagement is to enhance intended users' confidence in an assertion or subject matter of the engagement. Accountants, the code of ethics indicates, should use the *International Framework for Assurance Engagements* issued by the International Auditing and Assurance Standards Board (IAASB) for descriptions of the elements and objectives of assurance engagements and to identify the engagements to which International Standards on Auditing (ISAs), International Standards on Review Engagements (ISREs), and International Standards on Assurance Engagements (ISAEs) each apply (Ibid., 290.1–3).

Threats and Safeguards

A public accounting practitioner must always consider, when agreeing to or performing any engagement, whether there are threats to practitioner objectivity and independence that might arise from having interests in or relationships with an engagement client or directors, officers, or employees of the client. The ethics code states that independence of mind and in appearance are both necessary to the expression of a conclusion without bias, conflict of interest, or being under undue influence of others

(Ibid., 280.2). The existence of threats to objectivity and independence depend upon circumstances particular to the engagement and the type of assurance engagement being provided (Ibid., 280.2–3).

Should such threats exist, the practitioner must evaluate their significance. Unless clearly insignificant, safeguards against these threats should be considered and used, if possible, to reduce or eliminate the threats to acceptable levels. Appropriate safeguards include withdrawal from the engagement team; added supervisory procedures; termination of the relationship creating the threat; discussions within the accounting firm at the appropriate level; and discussions with client governance officials (Ibid., 208.4).

Assurance Engagements Defined

Engagements to provide assurance involve, according to the ethics code, a responsible party, intended users, and a public accountant, and the examination may be based on an assertion or on direct reporting. The code defines the term "subject matter information" as the outcome of the evaluation or measurement process from applying appropriate criteria carried out by the responsible party, which is communicated to intended users in appropriate form (Ibid., 290.4–5). For a financial statement audit engagement, for example, the assertion made by the responsible party is the financial statement that resulted from the subject matter being evaluated and measured against generally accepted accounting principles, which are International Financial Reporting Standards in the case of the European Union. The subject matter information is made available to the intended users in the form of financial statements (Ibid., 290.5–6).

The direct reporting assurance engagement is viewed differently in that the public accountant either performs the evaluation or measurement of the subject matter or obtains an assertion from the responsible party who has performed the measurement and evaluation, but the results are not available to the intended users. Instead, the subject matter information is made available to intended users in the accountant's assurance report (Ibid., 290.7).

Independence Needed for Objectivity and Integrity

Independence of mind and independence in appearance are both important to practitioners in performing assurance services. Independence of mind allows conclusions to be made without being influenced by factors that would compromise professional judgment. This state of mind allows the practitioner to exercise appropriate objectivity and professional skepticism and act with integrity (Ibid., 290.8).

Independence in appearance, according to the code of ethics, can be achieved when practitioners avoid significant circumstances and facts that would lead an informed and reasonable person having knowledge of all the relevant facts, including safeguards applied, to conclude that the auditor does not appear to be independent of the client. The practitioner must evaluate financial, economic, and other relationships to determine what an informed and reasonable third party having knowledge of all the facts would decide to be unacceptable. Such decisions must take into consideration that each member of any society has relationships with others and, in the view of the code of ethics, no one can be completely free of all financial, economic, and other relationships. The evaluation must be made consistent with what a reasonable and informed party having knowledge of all relevant information would find to be unacceptable in terms of independence from the client (Ibid., 290.9).

Differing Threats Require Differing Safeguards or Actions

These decisions must be made by practitioners based on the facts and circumstances of the given assurance engagement in which differing threats to independence may be present that will require differing safeguards. The code presents a conceptual framework within which practitioners need to identify, evaluate, and address threats thought to exist in a manner appropriate to the given engagement. This approach, rather than a set of specific rules, is, the code asserts, in the public interest.

Examples given in the code, practitioners are warned, must not be taken as explicit rules because the threats to independence, together with safeguards that might be applicable, depend upon individual engagement characteristics that can differ greatly among engagements. The practitioner must use judgment to arrive at the appropriate course of action using the framework of ethical behavior provided in the code. The decision may be to continue with or accept a new engagement or to reject such work. If the decision is to accept or keep the client, the practitioner must decide the safeguards required, including selecting appropriate members of the assurance team (Ibid., 290.13).

For a financial statement audit, engagement independence in appear-

ance is particularly important because of the public nature and responsibilities of the work. Independence requirements for a financial statement
audit engagement should include considerations of the relationships between the audit team and client directors, officers, and employees who are
in positions to exert direct and significant influence over client financial
statements, financial performance, and cash flows (Ibid., 290.14).

For assurance engagements that do not involve financial statements,
assurance team member relationships need to be evaluated with all parties who may be in positions to exert direct and significant influence over
the engagement subject matter that is before application of appropriate
criteria, or over subject matter information that is after the application
of appropriate criteria. In other words, threats to independence can come
from any of the relationships and interests between the assurance team,
the client firm, a network firm, and the party responsible for the subject
matter or subject matter information, which may not be the client firm
(Ibid., 290.15–17).

Where a nonfinancial statement assurance client engagement will result
in a report restricted for use by identified users, such users can be considered to have knowledge of the purpose, subject matter information. and
limitations of the accountant's report since the users participated in the
assignment of the nature and scope of the accountant's work, including
criteria to be used for subject matter measurement and evaluation. The
accountant is able to communicate directly with the users to evaluate the
threats to accountant independence, which should increase the effectiveness of safeguards to independence in appearance. These facts should
increase the effectiveness of safeguards brought to bear to reduce threats
to an acceptable level. The minimum necessary in these circumstances is
to consider the independence of the members of the assurance team and
their immediate and close family. Of course, if the assurance firm held
a material interest in the client, either direct or indirect, no safeguards
would be sufficient. The self-interest threat would require the engagement be resigned (Ibid., 290.19).

If there is more than one responsible party in a nonfinancial statement
assurance engagement, the relationships between the accountant and each
responsible party should govern whether there is a threat to independence
that is other than clearly inconsequential for each of the responsible parties. In this determination, the practitioner should take into account the
materiality of the subject matter information or subject matter for each
responsible party and the degree of public interest associated with the

engagement. If a particular responsible party is determined not to create a material threat, it may not be necessary to apply safeguard provisions for that individual (Ibid., 290.20).

If a financial statement audit client is listed on a stock market, any client-related entities also need to be considered in the processes of independence threats and safeguards described by the code. Such interests or relationships should be identified before beginning the engagement if possible or at the time during the engagement when the assurance team has reason to believe that a related entity may cause independence threats (Ibid., 290.21).

Evidence as to threats to independence should be revealed and safeguarding actions should be carried out when a member of the assurance team knows or could reasonably be expected to know of the independence threat. Should the practitioner or the assurance team violate these provisions inadvertently and the violation is corrected once discovered, such inadvertent error would not compromise independence so long as the accounting firm maintains appropriate quality control policies and procedures in place to promote firm independence (Ibid., 290.22).

Qualitative and Quantitative Factors Affect Judgment and Action

In carrying out evaluations of independence, qualitative and quantitative factors should both be considered. A particular threat should be considered clearly insignificant only if it is both trivial and inconsequential (Ibid., 290.23). Decisions to accept or continue an engagement where there is a significant independence threat should be documented, including descriptions of the threats and of the safeguards employed to eliminate or reduce the threats to acceptable levels (Ibid., 290.27).

When the independence threat cannot be reduced by safeguards to an insignificant level, the code of ethics indicates that actions must be taken to end the interest or activities creating the threat or the practitioner must refuse to accept or continue the engagement. Practitioners should always consider what a reasonable and informed third party having knowledge of all relevant information would conclude is unacceptable with regard to independent assurances (Ibid., 290.24).

Policies and procedures relating to communications with the client audit committee concerning accountant independence should be established by accounting firms. During audits of listed companies, there should be regular communications between the accounting team and the audit committee on relationships and other matters that are thought to bear on the accountant's independence from the audit client. The accounting firm should orally and in writing communicate at least annually, the ethics code indicates, all relationships and other matters between the firm, network firms, and the audit client that, in the firm's professional judgment, may reasonably be thought to bear on independence (Ibid., 290.29, 30).

Independence is required by the code of ethics for the accounting firm and members of the assurance team during the engagement period, which begins when performance of the services begins and ends at issuance of the assurance report for nonrecurring engagements. For recurring assurance engagements, the engagement period ends when either the assurance firm or the client serves notification that terminates the professional relationship, or with the issuance of the final assurance report, whichever occurs later (Ibid., 290.31).

For financial statement audit engagements, the engagement period includes the period of the financial statements reported on by the auditors. The firm should consider any threats to independence from the client that might arise during or after the period covered by the financial statements. Specifically, the firm must determine whether threats to independence are created by financial or business relationships with the client prior to acceptance of the engagement or from previous service to the audit client. For assurance engagement other than financial statement audits, the firm must consider if financial or business relationships of previous services to the client create independence threats (Ibid., 290.32).

Specific Principles-based Assurance Guidance

The code contains a separate section on applications of the principles-based framework to specific situations that enumerates examples of specific circumstances and relationships that can create impairment of independence threats for accountants and auditors. The section also presents potential safeguards that may be used to reduce or eliminate the potential threats to an acceptable level for each given circumstance. The code cautions that the list is not all inclusive. The examples describe the potential threats created, and practitioners are advised to specifically assess the given situation faced with the circumstances and relationships in the examples to determine which safeguards might be applied to satisfactorily reduce the threats to independence, if any (Ibid., 290.10).

If a particular national authority, in its rules for independence, does not differentiate between listed entities and nonlisted entities, the independence examples given for listed companies' financial statement audit engagements should be used for all entities, according to the ethics code (Ibid., 290.26).

If a member of the assurance team has a financial interest in the assurance client, evaluation of the threat to independence and consideration of appropriate safeguards should include the role of the person owning the financial interest, the materiality of the interest, and the financial interest type, that is, direct or indirect (Ibid., 290.104). The type of financial interest is considered indirect by the code when the holder has no ability to exercise control over the financial interest in the client and direct by the code when control can be exercised by the holder. An indirect example would be interest in a mutual fund, unit trust, or the like (Ibid., 290.105).

A direct financial interest or material indirect financial interest in the assurance client by members of the assurance team or their immediate families is considered a self-interest threat to independence so serious that the only acceptable safeguards are to dispose of the direct financial interest before becoming an assurance team member; dispose of all the material indirect interest or enough of it to make the interest not material before becoming an assurance team member; or removed the assurance team member with the financial interest threat from the assurance engagement (Ibid., 290.106).

A direct financial investment or a material indirect interest in the assurance client by a close family member of which assurance team member is aware creates a self-interest threat to the member's independence. This threat should be evaluated using the nature of the relationship between the member and the close family member as well as the materiality of the financial interest. Safeguards need to be considered and applied to reduce or end the risk. Safeguards suggested in the code of ethics include having the close family member dispose of the interest in the client sufficient to reduce the threat to an acceptable level; removing the member from the assurance engagement; discussing the matter with the audit committee or equivalent governance party; or adding an additional practitioner who did not participate in the assurance engagement review the work of the member in question (Ibid., 290.108).

In the case where an accounting firm or assurance team member holds a direct financial interest in the assurance client as a trustee, a self-interest threat to independence is created because of the possible influence of the trust over the client. This type of interest should not be held, except where the member in question or the member's immediate family members and the accounting firm are not beneficiaries of the trust; the trust's financial interest in the client is immaterial to the trust; the trust is unable to exercise significant influence over the client, or the member in question or the firm has no significant influence concerning the investment decisions involving financial interest in the client (Ibid., 290.109).

Self-interest threats may be created by financial interests in an assurance client held by others not on the assurance team or their immediate and close family members. These might be non-assurance team firm partners and their immediate family members, firm partners and managerial employees providing non-assurance services to the client in question, and persons who have a close personal relationship with an assurance team member. Consideration of whether these interests held in the client create an independence threat should include the accounting firm's organizational, operating, and reporting structure as well as the nature of the relationship of the individual with assurance team members. If the threat is considered significant, safeguards should be considered and applied, such as the accounting firm, when appropriate, restricting the holding of such interests as a matter of policy, holding discussions with the audit committee, or assigning an additional practitioner not involved with the original assurance work to review the work done and advise as necessary (Ibid., 290.110).

When an inadvertent violation of the financial interest rules in the ethics code occurs, independence of the firm, the network firm, or an assurance team member will not be considered impaired under the code of ethics so long as the firm has policies and procedures by which all professionals must promptly report any breaches resulting from purchase, inheritance, or acquisition by other means of interests in assurance clients; the professional is notified that the interest must be disposed of; and the professional is removed from the assurance team if disposal does not occur at the earliest practical date. The accounting firm should also consider adopting safeguards such as review of the work done by the assurance team member in question by a practitioner who did not work on the original assurance engagement or not allowing the member in question to make decisions of substance concerning the assurance engagement (Ibid., 290.111, 112).

Specific Guidance for Audit Engagements

The preceding code of ethics examples were for assurance engagements. The code of ethics contains a number of examples for use in financial statement audits. A direct financial interest in audit clients should not be owned by the audit firm or by other firm partners, or their immediate families, who practice in the same office in which the engagement partner practices, since a threat to independence is created that is so significant that safeguards would not reduce the threat to an acceptable level (Ibid., 290.113, 117).

If the audit firm owns a material indirect financial interest in the audit client or a material financial interest in an entity that has a controlling interest in the audit client, the threat to independence created is so significant that no safeguard would reduce the threat to an acceptable level. To continue with the audit, the firm must dispose of the interest completely or reduce the interest owned to a level that is no longer material (Ibid., 290.114, 115).

The holding of a financial interest in an audit client by the firm's retirement benefit plan may create a self-interest threat. This should be investigated, and, if considered other than an insignificant threat, safeguards should be considered to eliminate the threat or reduce it to an acceptable level (Ibid., 290.116).

Other partners not connected with the audit and managerial employees, and their immediate families, who provide non-assurance services to the audit client should not hold direct or material indirect financial interest in the audit client (Ibid., 290.119).

Nonfinancial Statement Engagements

The code provides examples in cases where engagements involve nonfinancial statement assurance clients. The recommendations are similar to the examples for other assurance engagements and follow the threat and safeguards format (Ibid., 290.122–25). Several examples concern loans, loan guarantees, bank deposits, and brokerage accounts. If a loan or loan guarantee is made to the accounting firm by the assurance client that is a bank or similar institution and the loan is extended under normal lending procedures, terms, and requirements, no threat to independence is created so long as the loan or guarantee is immaterial to both the client and the accounting firm. In the case where the loan is material to either, the ethics code indicates, safeguards may possibly reduce the threat to acceptable levels. Safeguards, it is suggested, might include having the assurance work reviewed by a professional accountant from outside the firm (Ibid., 290.126). Such loans made in the course of normal lending practices to an assurance team member, or immediate family members, would not be viewed, according to the code, as a threat to independence. Examples of such loans are home mortgages, car loans, credit card balances, and bank overdrafts (Ibid., 290.127). Bank deposits or brokerage accounts under normal commercial terms of the firm or an assurance team member would create no threat to independence (Ibid., 290.128).

On the other hand, should the accounting firm or a member of the assurance team make a loan that is material to either party to an assurance client that is not a banking or similar entity or should the nonbank assurance client make a loan to the accounting firm or member of the assurance team, a self-interest threat would be created so significant that it could not be reduced to acceptable levels (Ibid., 290.129, 130). If the assurance engagement is for audit of financial statements, the provisions for loans and guarantees should be considered for the firm, all network firms, and the audit client (Ibid., 290.132).

Accountant and Client Relationships

A series of examples are given that have to do with close business relationships with assurance clients. There are a number of commercial or common-interest close affiliations between an accounting firm, an assurance team member, and the assurance client or its management, or, in the case of an audit client, between the accounting firm, a network firm, and a financial statement client, which can create self-interest threats. Examples given by the code of ethics include a material financial interest in a joint venture with the assurance client or an individual with senior management functions for the client in question; or marketing that references both the accounting firm and the assurance client of services or products that are a combination of accounting firm and assurance client services or products; or distribution or marketing as a distributor by either the accounting firm and the assurance client of products or services of the other party. The courses of action available would be to terminate the business relationships, reduce the relationship to where it is clearly insignificant and reduce the financial interests to an immaterial level, or refuse to perform the assurance or audit engagement. Where an individual assurance team member is the party in question, the safeguard would be to remove the individual from the engagement (Ibid., 290.132).

In the case of a financial statement audit engagement for a closely held client, business relationships involving the closely held entity in which the firm, network firm, or assurance team member, or immediate family, is holding a financial interest and the audit client, a director or officer of the audit client, or any group thereof, is also holding a financial interest, a threat to independence is not created so long as the interest does not allow the investor or group of investors to control the closely held entity, the relationship is clearly insignificant to the audit firm, or the network firm and the audit client and the interest is not material to the investor or group of investors (Ibid., 290.133). Purchase in the normal course of business in an arm's-length basis of goods or services from an assurance client or audit client by the accounting firm, the network firm, or an assurance team member would not in general create an independence threat. In some cases, the magnitude or nature of the purchases may create a significant self-interest threat and require safeguards that might include eliminating or reducing the purchases, removal from the assurance or audit team when an individual team member is involved, or holding discussions with the client audit committee (Ibid., 290.134).

Accountant Family and Personal Relationships

Family and personal relationships between assurance team members and assurance client personnel may create self-interest, familiarity, or intimidation threats to independence. The significance of the independence threats depends on a multitude of factors in a wide spectrum of circumstances. Evaluation in the individual case must be made to determine the significance of the threat and safeguards that may be appropriate (Ibid., 290.135).

Removal from the assurance or audit team is the only safeguard acceptable, in accordance with the ethics code, when an assurance team member has an immediate family member, a close family member, or other person close to the member who is a director or an officer of the client in a position to exert direct and significant influence over the assurance engagement subject matter information (Ibid., 290.136). When the person in question is an employee of the client, the significance depends on the position the person has with the client and the role of the practitioner within the assurance team. Evaluation should be made to determine what safeguards may be in order if the threat is significant. Safeguards suggested in the code are removal of the practitioner from the assurance team; structuring the assurance work so that the member in question does not have examination duties in the area of responsibility of the immediate family member; or empowering staff of the accounting firm through regular policies and procedures to communicate any independence or objectivity issues to the firm's senior levels (Ibid., 290.137–139).

Threats to independence may be created in the case where a firm partner or employee who is not a member of the assurance team has a family or personal relationship with a client director, officer, or an employee who is in a position to exert direct and significant influence over the assurance engagement subject matter information. The ethics code states that accounting firm partners and employees should identify any such relationships and consult within the firm according to firm procedures. Evaluation of threats of this nature should include closeness of the relationship, interaction of the practitioner in question with the assurance team, his or her position within the accounting firm, and the role within the client firm occupied by the client associate (Ibid., 290.140). Inadvertent violation of the above section would not impair independence if the firm's policies and procedures require all firm professionals to promptly report any violations caused by changes in employment status of family members or in other personal relationships that create independence threats, additional review is carefully made of the practitioner's work, the practitioner's responsibilities on the assurance team are restructured, or, if this cannot be done, the practitioner is promptly removed from service on the assurance team (Ibid., 290.141). The accounting firm should also consider safeguards, such as adding an additional professional who did not work on the engagement to review the practitioner's work, or prohibiting the practitioner in question from substantive decision making in regard to the engagement (Ibid., 290.142).

Client and Accountant Employee Shifts

Threats to independence may also be created when employees of the assurance client become members of the accounting firm, or vice versa. In the case where a member of the assurance team or a firm partner has joined the client in a position from which direct and significant influence can be exerted over engagement subject matter information, or when an assurance team member believes that he or she may join the client in the future, the independence threats would depend upon the position taken at the assurance client, the amount of involvement the former practitioner will have with the assurance team, the time since leaving the assurance team, and the position held on the assurance team. Safeguards against the independence threat could be modifying the assurance plan as necessary; assigning an experienced new assurance team in the subsequent engagement in relation to the person who joined the client; adding a professional accountant not connected with the engagement to review work or advise as necessary; and having a quality control review of the engagement. The ethics code indicates that the following safeguards are mandatory to reduce the threat to an acceptable level: the individual in question should not continue or appear to continue participation in the accounting firm's professional or business affairs. Payments from the firm can only be made for prearranged fixed payments or benefits. Amounts owing to the former firm member must not be so significant as to threaten the firm's independence (Ibid., 290.143, 144).

If an assurance team member participates in the engagement while knowing or having reason to believe he or she will join the client in the future, an independence threat is created that can be reduced to acceptable levels by application of the following safeguards. The accounting firm's policies and procedures should require practitioners to notify the firm when serious employment negotiations begin with clients. The individual in question must be removed from the assurance engagement. Consideration should also be given to performing a review of any significant judgments the individual made on the engagement (Ibid., 290.145).

Former employees, officers, and directors of the client should not be assigned to serve on the assurance team if, during the period covered by the assurance report, they were in a position with the client to exert direct and significant influence over assurance engagement subject matter information. If the period with the client was prior to the period of the assurance engagement and decisions or the work of the individual will be reviewed in the current engagement, significance of the threat to independence depends upon the position held with the client, length of time since leaving the client, and the role the individual has in the assurance team. Safeguards might include discussing the issue with the client audit committee and having a practitioner who did not work on the engagement review and advise as necessary (Ibid., 290.146–48).

If an accounting firm partner or employee serves as an officer or director of the assurance client, safeguards would not reduce the threat to independence to an acceptable level. The accounting firm may not perform the engagement under these conditions (Ibid., 290.149).

The company secretary position should not be held by accounting firm practitioners unless the practice is specifically permitted by local law, professional rules, or practice, and the duties performed are limited to routine and formal administrative matters such as preparing minutes or maintenance of statutory returns. The practitioner must not make client decisions of any kind (Ibid., 290.150–52).

Auditor Rotation

A familiarity threat to independence may be created by assigning the same senior practitioners over a long period of time to an assurance engagement. Significance of the threat will depend on many factors: the length of time served on the team, the role on the team, the structure of the accounting firm, or the nature of the engagement. Possible safeguards would include rotating the senior personnel off the team; making an internal quality control review; or adding a practitioner who had not worked on the engagement to review the work and advise as necessary (Ibid., 290.153).

In the case of a financial statement audit, the code of ethics indicates that long-serving engagement partners or engagement quality control partners may create an independence threat that is particularly relevant if the client is a listed company. Safeguards should be applied as follows: partners serving as an engagement partner or in an engagement quality control review should be rotated off the client after a predetermined period of combined service in these positions, which should be no more than seven years. Individuals rotating off an engagement should not participate in the client engagement until a further period of time has elapsed, normally two years (Ibid., 290.153–54).

The code indicates that some flexibility should be used in the timing of rotation where necessary because of the importance to the audit of the person in question, major restructuring of the client that coincides with timing of the rotation, or size of the accounting firm. Where rotation does not occur on a predefined schedule, safeguards should be applied to reduce the independence threat to acceptable levels (Ibid., 290.156).

In the case where an accounting firm has few people with necessary experience and knowledge to serve as an engagement or quality control review partner, rotation might not be an appropriate safeguard. Other safeguards must be used such as having an additional practitioner not associated with the engagement review the work done or otherwise advise as necessary. Such an individual could be from outside the accounting firm (Ibid., 290.157).

Non-assurance Work

The performance of non-assurance-type client services may cause independence threats to the accounting firm, the network firm, or assurance team members. For assurance clients, financial statement audit clients, and non-assurance clients alike, the threats must be evaluated for significance and appropriate safeguards employed when possible. Some threats to independence from performing non-assurance engagements, the code indicates, are too significant to be reduced to acceptable levels by safeguards. These include authorizing, executing, or consummating transactions or exercising management authority; deciding which recommendation of the accounting firm should be accepted; or reporting to those charged with client governance in the role of management (Ibid., 290.158, 159).

The activities that may create self-review or self-interest-type threats include having the assurance client's assets in custody of the accounting firm; supervising client employees in normal recurring activities; or preparing source documents. Safeguards that may be used are separating personnel who do the assurance work from those who do the non-assurance work; having an added practitioner to advise on potential threats; and following other safeguards that may be contained in particular national regulations (Ibid., 290.160–62).

Threats to independence from performing non-assurance services will arise most often when the engagement is for a financial statement audit. Safeguards that may be effective in reducing the threat to acceptable levels include having policies and procedures to prohibit practitioners from making client management decisions; having client policies requiring client oversight of non-assurance services; holding discussions with the audit committee; involving an added practitioner to advise on the potential impact of the services on independence; involving an additional professional accountant from outside the firm to provide assurance on a discrete aspect of the assurance engagement; and obtaining acknowledgment of client responsibility for the results of the non-assurance work (Ibid., 290.163).

Preparing accounting records or financial statements for financial statement audit clients may create a self-review threat to independence of the audit firm (Ibid., 290.166). Likewise, when accountants develop and prepare accounting products such as prospective financial statements, they may not provide assurance on these products because of the self-review aspects (Ibid., 290.169). Practitioners must not make management decisions such as the determination of or change to journal entries or the classification of accounts or transactions without specific management approvals, preparation of source documents, or making changes to originating data, documents, or data. Any of these actions would create a risk to independence that could not be mitigated by safeguards (Ibid., 290.167).

The normal audit process calls for extensive dialogue between the audit team and client management. Requests are often made for advice from the audit team on matters such as accounting principles, financial statement disclosure, appropriateness of controls, appropriate valuation methods, the resolving of account reconciliation problems, information on regulatory compliance, consolidation techniques, and translation to differing reporting frameworks such as International Accounting Standards. These consultations and advice do not generally create a threat to independence (Ibid., 290.168).

Accounting firms may provide accounting and bookkeeping services for a nonlisted client of routine or mechanical nature so long as the self-review threat is reduced to an insignificant level. Appropriate safeguards include ensuring that members of the assurance or audit team do not provide the accounting services; implementing policies and procedures to ensure that management decisions are not made by practitioners; ensuring that source documents and data are provided by the client; requiring that underlying assumptions be made by the client; and ensuring client approval for proposed journal entries and other changes (Ibid., 290.170).

The code of ethics states that, under normal conditions, such accounting and preparation of financial statement services may not be performed for listed audit clients because it may impair firm independence or give the appearance of impairing independence at the least. In emergency situations where the client cannot make other arrangements and in countries where the services fall within the statutory audit mandate, the services are acceptable provided that adequate safeguards are employed. The audit firm must ensure that the services do not involve management judgment by members of the audit firm, that the services provided collectively to divisions or subsidiaries of the client are collectively immaterial to the division or subsidiary, and that fees for such services are clearly insignificant collectively. Safeguards should also be applied to ensure that the firm does not make managerial decisions or assume the management role; the audit client should accept responsibility; and firm personnel providing the accounting work should not be part of the audit team (Ibid., 290.171, 172).

Valuation Engagements

Valuation services in which a certain value or range of values is computed for assets, liabilities, or for businesses as a whole may create a self-review threat in a financial statement audit when the values are used in the client financial statements and when the valuation amounts are material and involve a significant amount of subjectivity. The threat created in such a case could not be mitigated by safeguards, in the view of the code of ethics. Such valuation services should not be provided for an audit client (Ibid., 290.174–75).

If the valuation services for an audit client are not in the aggregate material to the financial statements or do not require significant subjectivity, the code indicates that the self-review threat can be reduced to acceptable levels by employing appropriate safeguards such as confirming that the audit client understands and approves of the underlying assumptions and methodologies used; getting acknowledgment from the client that it takes responsibility for the valuations; and ensuring that firm members performing the valuations are not members of the audit team.

The firm needs to evaluate whether these safeguards would be effective by determining the reliability of the underlying data and the degree of subjectivity involved in the particular valuation service. The firm needs to determine the degree to which established methods and guidelines were used in the valuation and the extent of the client's knowledge, experience, and ability to evaluate the valuation issues concerned. The extent to which client management was involved in determining and approving significant judgments used in the valuation service, the extent of financial statement disclosures, and the nature of the future events estimated that could cause volatility in the resulting amounts must also be taken into consideration (Ibid., 290.177).

If the valuation services are a tax return or filing with a taxing authority, computing client tax due, or tax planning, a threat is not created, since an outside tax authority generally has review rights (Ibid., 290.178). Where the valuation service is part of an assurance engagement that is not a financial statement audit, safeguards should be considered and applied to reduce the threat to acceptable levels (Ibid., 290.179).

Tax and Internal Control Engagements

The code of ethics does not view the provision of taxation services for financial statement audit clients as a threat to independence generally.

This includes tax services for compliance, planning, assistance in tax disputes, and providing formal tax opinions (Ibid., 290.180).

Internal audit services for a financial statement audit client that are related to internal accounting controls, financial systems, or financial statements may create an independence threat. Services that are an extension of the audit conducted in accordance with International Standards on Auditing would not create a threat, the code indicates, so long as practitioners do not act in a capacity equivalent to management (Ibid., 290.181, 182). Any self-review threats created by providing internal audit services may be reduced to acceptable levels by making management control of the internal audit functions clearly separate from the carrying out of the functions themselves (Ibid., 290.183).

Information Technology and Other Client Services

Providing information technology services to financial statement audit clients that include designing and implementing financial information that is used to prepare any part of the financial statements may create a self-review independence threat, according to the code of ethics (Ibid., 290.187). Safeguards should be used by which the client takes responsibility for preparing and monitoring the system. Management must have a competent employee responsible for making all management decisions in designing and implementing both hardware and software of the system. Client management must make all decisions concerning the system and test the adequacy and results of system design and implementation. Management must also be responsible for operating the system and all data used or generated by the system (Ibid., 290.188). The separation of practitioners who perform the information technology services from the assurance team, with separate reporting lines within the accounting firm, should be considered (Ibid., 290.189).

The code does not consider an impairment of independence for services that assess, design, or implement internal accounting and risk-management controls so long as the accountants do not perform in management capacities (Ibid., 290.191).

Accounting firms may temporarily loan staff to a financial statement audit client but this may create a self-review independence threat if the staff loaned can influence the preparation of client accounts or financial statements. Loaning staff should be with client understanding that the accounting firm personnel will not make management decisions, approve or sign agreements or similar documents, or commit the client by exercising discretionary management authority. Suggested safeguards include the audit client accepting responsibility for directing and supervising the loaned personnel or assuring that staff loaned do not have audit responsibility for client work (Ibid., 290.192).

Firms may provide litigation support services to financial statement audit clients including acting as an expert witness, estimating damages or amounts due or receivable in a legal dispute, and assisting with legal document retrieval and management (Ibid., 290.193). This may create a self-review independence threat for which safeguards should be used to reduce the threat to acceptable levels (Ibid., 290.194).

Providing legal services to an audit client may create self-review and advocacy independence threats the significance of which, according to the code of ethics, depends upon the nature of the services, whether the services are provided by other than audit team members, and the materiality of the legal matter to financial statements. Appropriate safeguards should be used, if needed, to reduce to acceptable levels such threats (Ibid., 290.196, 197).

The code of ethics indicates that recruitment services for assurance clients may create self-interest, familiarity, and intimidation independence threats. The provisions of these services will require safeguards to reduce to acceptable levels such risks. In any event, the firm should not make management decisions, and the client should make the hiring decision (Ibid., 290.203).

Providing an assurance client with corporate finance services, advice, or assistance may also create advocacy and self-review threats. Services such as promoting, dealing in, or underwriting client securities should not be provided, as the threat is not amenable to reduction by safeguards. For other financial services, safeguards may be sufficient to reduce the risk acceptably (Ibid., 290.204, 205).

Fee Arrangements and Self-Interest Threats

In the case where an assurance engagement is agreed to for a significantly lower fee than had been charged by the predecessor firm or quoted by other firms, the self-interest threat cannot be reduced to an acceptable level unless the firm can show that appropriate audit time and qualified staff will be assigned to the engagement and that the firm is complying with all assurance standards, guidelines, and quality control requirements that are applicable (Ibid., 290.209).

If fees from a given assurance client become a large proportion of total firm fees, overdependence on that client may create a self-interest threat because of the possibility of losing the client. Significance of this threat depends upon such factors as firm structure and how well established the firm is. Safeguards needed might include reducing the dependency on the client; having external quality control reviews; or consulting another accountant or a third party such as a regulatory body (Ibid., 290.206). The self-interest threat may also occur when one client represents a large proportion of an individual partner's income. Safeguards against this threat include firm policies and procedures that monitor assurance engagement quality control or having an uninvolved accountant review the work done and advise the firm as needed (Ibid., 290.207). If fees remain unpaid by the client for professional services for a sufficient length of time, and especially if not paid before the following year's report is issued, further assurance services should not be provided (Ibid., 290.208).

Firms should not enter into assurance engagements that are dependent upon contingent fees (Ibid., 290.211). Providing non-assurance services to an assurance client for a contingent fee will create self-interest and advocacy threats, according to the code. Contingent fee arrangements involving an assurance engagement may not be accepted. For other services, the threat depends on the range and variability of contingent fee amounts, the basis upon which the fees will be determined, whether results will be reviewed by a third party, and any affects that the services have on an assurance engagement for the same client. Safeguards that may be applied for the other non-assurance services include determination or review of the fee paid by an unrelated third party; disclosure to the audit committee of the extent and nature of the fees paid by client; and firm quality control procedures (Ibid., 290.212).

Gifts or hospitality should not be accepted from an assurance client because the self-interest and familiarity threats are so significant they cannot be acceptably reduced by safeguards (Ibid., 290.213).

If litigation occurs between the firm or a member of the assurance team and the assurance client, self-interest and intimidation threats may be created. The significance of the threats depends upon the litigation's materiality, the nature of the assurance engagement, and whether any prior assurance engagements are related to the litigation. Safeguards that may be applied to reduce the risk to acceptable levels include disclosing the nature and extent of the litigation to the client audit committee; removal from the assurance team of members who are parties to the litigation; and review by a non-involved accountant in the firm to advise as necessary. The code indicates that the firm should resign the engagement if safeguards do not reduce threats to an acceptable level (Ibid., 290.214).

Comparison of U.S. and EU Approaches

The EU-adopted IFAC Code of Ethics is extensive in its "guidance" but a careful reading suggests that "guidance" is just another way of saying "rules." There appear to be few substantive differences between the two except for the professional judgment approach used by the EU as compared to the compliance approach used by the United States. The end result of the details in the EU guidance can be expected to be very similar to results required under the AICPA and SEC rules. Together the two rubrics constitute standards being widely accepted in many world jurisdictions.

The EU-adopted IFAC Code of Ethics approach of threats and safeguards would appear to be vulnerable to litigation claims, as much as or perhaps more so than the U.S. rules-based approach. A practitioner's judgment about what constitutes a threat requiring safeguards as well as the selection and extent of safeguards used by the practice unit to reduce independence impairment to an acceptable level would appear to offer ample, if not almost unlimited, opportunities for second guessing. The detailed guidelines provided in this codification would seem to provide very ample material for plaintiff claims of negligence.

Public Companies as Owners of Public Accounting Firms

The evolving structures of ownership of CPA firms in recent times are a new development raising concerns about independence to perform attestation services. CPA firm ownership has been assumed to rest with accounting firm partners, who in the past have taken on unlimited liability for their attestation and professional work. In the 1990s, an alternative form of ownership gained ground in the United States. CPA firm partners were bought out by public companies. Non-assurance work of the former CPA firm is integrated into the purchasing corporation's operations as desired, perhaps restructured into subsidiary form. Audits and other attestation work are conducted by CPAs and others, now employees of the corporation, who are leased back to a shell CPA firm that is ostensibly owned by partners, possibly the former partners, who nevertheless have also become employees of the purchasing parent corporation.

This perhaps innovative alternative structure, then, consists of a public accounting shell entity ostensibly owned by partners and the purchasing public company. The public company is often listed on a stock exchange and registered with the SEC. The CPA firm may have only nonpublic companies as clients but it may perform services for public company audit clients, in which case it must be registered with the PCAOB.

CPA firms of various sizes have entered into this alternative form of practice. American Express, for example, purchased the New York City public accounting firm of Goldstein Golub Kessler in 1997. The firm was integrated into American Express Tax and Business Services. American Express has made a large number of such public accounting firm acquisitions.

Mike Brewster, in his book *Unaccountable,* describes how the new arrangements made employees of the accounting firm employees of American Express as well. The attraction of these arrangements allowed partners to cash out of their firms and to have the backing of a cash-rich parent for future operations. Brewster believes that the corporations benefited from adding accounting services to the list of services they can provide (2003, 200). In the case of American Express in particular, the acquisition provided access to small- and medium-sized businesses and affluent business owners, which were added to the American Express customer lists and contacts.

Not only small public accounting firms are involved. H&R Block acquired the Minneapolis-based accounting and consulting firm Mc-Gladrey & Pullen in 1999. McGladrey & Pullen was the seventh-largest U.S. accounting and consulting firm at that time (*New York Times,* 1999, 1). The acquisition announcement indicated that McGladrey & Pullen's auditing business would remain in a partnership owned by McGladrey & Pullen partners. At the date of the acquisition in June 1999, this was the eighth accounting firm acquired by H&R Block since May 1998 (Ibid.). The transaction was reported as the largest accounting firm acquisition to date and the first of this kind of combination between a Top Ten accounting firm and a major financial services company (*The Trusted Professional,* 1999).

These alternative forms of organization call into question the independence of the attesting firms, which appear to be owned in reality by SEC-listed companies. Former SEC commissioner Arthur Levitt was quoted by

Brewster as holding the view that accounting firm independence ceases when the firm is owned by a public company (Brewster, 2003, 200). The effects that this alternative form of ownership may have on the liability of the partners in the shell accounting firms as well as the liability of the public companies involved remains unclear. The partners' liability may be unlimited, but the corporation's liability would not appear to be so.

Litigation of liability claims from clients and users of CPA assurance and audit services has continued to grow. America's public accountants at the beginnings of the SEC era in 1933, reportedly, sought the opportunity to gain lucrative audit engagements without fully realizing that the engagements came with very large potential liability for work not carried out in a duly diligent manner. The privilege of auditing public corporations also comes with the obligation of independence from audit and other assurance clients, which has been a major cause of increased litigation. The operating parameters provided by generally accepted accounting principles and Generally Accepted Auditing Standards serve as both guidance for properly performing the accounting and auditing functions and as protection from unfair legal actions when these standards are fulfilled. The legal liability of accountants and auditors will be discussed more fully in chapter 10.

This chapter has presented the differing standards and requirements for independence in major world jurisdictions. While independence would appear to be a fundamental and easily established condition, some practitioners have had, it seems, more than some amount of difficulty in complying with this ethical prerequisite to auditing. The next chapter will take up matters relating to public accounting firm locational adjustments in an expanding and competitively changing global economy.

7

The Firms and Locational Adjustments in the Global Financial System

The global financial system has been expanding at a remarkable rate for some time. The facilitating services of public accountants are one of the requirements necessary for the global financial system to continue to be successful. Success requires that accounting firms continue to adjust their services to the expanding needs of the system. Adjustments to international accounting services have primarily been made by the large public international accounting firms, but many other firms, regardless of size, have also had to adjust as their clients increase the volume of their international trade and investment.

A number of high-impact events have occurred in recent times that have caused accountants and their firms to adjust to new realities in their place in the global financial system. The first in importance of these events was the extinction of Arthur Andersen Worldwide, one of five global public accounting firms. The competitive situation within the public accounting markets was drastically altered almost overnight. The partners and employees of Arthur Andersen, as well as their client corporations around the world, rapidly made adjustments to the new reality. Competing public accounting firms adjusted as well, seeking their own best interests.

The change from the Big Five firms to the Big Four had been preceded some years before by a period of consolidation during which the Big Eight firms had declined to be the Big Five. The reasons for each of these two decreases in the number of available large accounting firms were completely different. Accountants and their customers are still adjusting to the latest shift downward to the Big Four firms, as well as to the new requirements of the Sarbanes-Oxley Act, which accompanied the Andersen downfall.

This chapter describes and analyzes these locational adjustments, first from the viewpoint of within the public accounting markets, as the firms adjust to changes in competitive factors within their market, and second from a geographical viewpoint, as public accountants adjust to expand their services to accommodate the expanding global financial system. This chapter also addresses the question of whether expansion of the global financial system is likely to continue in the years just ahead.

Adjustments to the Arthur Andersen Collapse

Arthur Andersen Worldwide in all of its myriad parts did not just collapse into nothingness as the debacle of Enron, WorldCom, and numerous other failed audit engagements came to a climax in full public view. The people of Arthur Andersen did not just disappear with their collapsing firm. Many, if not most, partners, individually and in groups, moved with their clients to other surviving accounting firms. These firms added the former Andersen client corporations and former Andersen personnel to their client, partner, and employee rosters.

Grant Thornton, a second-tier firm, reportedly absorbed 60 partners and roughly 500 employees from Andersen (Krell, 2003, 1). Parts of Andersen went to other second-tier or smaller firms. However, the vast majority of moves were made into the surviving Big Four public accounting firms. Andersen practices in 57 countries, totaling 25,000 partners and employees, for example, moved to Ernst & Young. Accounting practices from 20 countries, which employed 23,000, merged into Deloitte & Touche (*Washington Post*, 2005, 1).

One tabulation indicated that 86 percent of Andersen former clients, or 938 in number, went to the surviving Big Four firms; 45 former clients, or 4 percent, transferred to Grant Thornton; 23 former clients, or 2 percent, transferred to BDO Seidman; and 79 former clients, or 6 percent, transferred to other firms (Krell, 2003, 33–38). As would be expected from the expanded customer bases, revenues were up substantially in the surviving firms. For example, Ernst & Young was reported to have had revenues of $13.1 billion in fiscal year 2003, up 30 percent from the prior year. PricewaterhouseCoopers' net revenue for the same year was reported as $14.7 billion—an increase of $1 billion over the prior year (Goff, 2004, 1).

To be sure, a number of Arthur Andersen people chose to leave public accounting or open their own shops. With the background and training of these high-caliber people, success in their endeavors would be expected. Former Andersen employees in Chicago, for example, started Huron Consulting Group Inc. during 2002 as a financial and legal advisory firm specializing in forensic accounting. Huron was founded by a former Andersen partner and now has more than 600 professionals in 8 offices who, by 2004, had conducted in excess of 1,000 engagements. By the end of 2004, the company was set to issue an initial public offering of $115 million in stock (Gullapalli, 2004, 1).

The departure of client corporations from Arthur Andersen was the immediate cause of the firm's collapse. This, it seems reasonable to conclude, was triggered by the conviction of the firm of Arthur Andersen on the charge of obstruction of justice for destroying Enron Corporation documents that were under notice of federal investigation (Beltran, Gering, and Martin, 2002). The verdict was for the firm as a whole, rather than for those individuals from the firm who were responsible. In effect the verdict convicted the approximate 28,000 Arthur Andersen employees. All but a few paid with their Andersen jobs and many paid by losing their investments and anticipated pensions.

The verdict citing the firm as a whole also prohibited attempts to rescue the firm so that it could remain a viable public accounting organization. No less a great public servant than Paul Volcker had been in the process of what some called a takeover of Arthur Andersen. The Volcker survival plan would have changed the Big Five accounting firms across the board. Andersen's internal procedures would have been reformed. An independent board would have monitored the firm. A separate management board headed by Paul Volcker himself would have included other well-respected, principled, and experienced members, including John C. Bogle, former Vanguard head; Roy Vagelos, retired Merck & Co. chief executive officer (CEO); and retired senator John C. Danforth.

Under the plan, Andersen was to be completely out of the business of consulting and would concentrate on auditing duties and services. Unfortunately, neither Andersen executives nor Harvey Pitt, who was then Securities and Exchange Commission (SEC) chairman, endorsed the Volcker plan. Yet it seems as though the stakes of losing one of only five international auditing firms were high stakes indeed. Volcker and others apparently saw the damage the demise of one of these firms would cause in a world already short of firms capable of worldwide audit engagements.

Further, these senior members of the establishment seemed to believe that an Andersen reform could stand as the new industry standard, one in which the fraudulent codependence of an Andersen and Enron could not take place. The plan also would have provided a settlement in the range of $750 million, which could have funded a compensation plan for losses of Enron pension-holders (Kudlow, 2002, 1).

These opportunities were lost, as the indictment and conviction of the firm caused client departures to the surviving public accounting organizations. The reversal of the Andersen firm's conviction by the Supreme Court came too late and could not change the course of these events. The Andersen firm's conviction was unanimously overruled by the U.S. Supreme Court on May 31, 2005, which said instructions to the jury were deficient.

The Volcker plan, had it been implemented, may not have been successful. But, its existence underscores the importance of having a sufficient supply of independent international accounting firms to compete for the business of attesting to international corporation financial reports. Instead, the competitive field was reduced as the surviving Big Four integrated most of the Andersen clients and much of the Andersen personnel into their own operations.

The declining number of firms available to compete for the business of large corporate audits would seem to run counter to the drive for maintaining a competitive environment to ensure efficient market operations. Government regulators, by their subsequent actions to avoid indicting entire public accounting firms, seem to have signaled their awareness that the further loss of one of the Big Four firms would cause further erosion of competition. And, perhaps, the loss would result in an insufficient supply of auditing services for international corporations and investors.

When Fannie Mae dismissed KPMG as its auditor, the fragile state of the accounting market for large corporations was illuminated. In all likelihood, Fannie Mae was left with either Deloitte & Touche or PricewaterhouseCoopers as a replacement. A remaining Big Four firm, Ernst & Young, had been Fannie Mae's audit committee and management adviser in various matters that U.S. government agencies were probing. Deloitte had assisted Fannie Mae's chief regulatory agency, the Office of Federal Housing Enterprise Oversight, in its examination of the corporation's practices. In that role, Deloitte was in conflict with Fannie Mae management. PricewaterhouseCoopers is free of conflicts of interest with Fannie Mae and presumably could be chosen. The firm is, however, the auditor for Freddie Mac, having replaced Arthur Andersen in 2002. From a public-policy view, would both mortgage giants having the same auditor create a problem?

All of the Big Four firms have large litigation cases pending. Since the firms keep their financial statements private, an estimate of their future viability is difficult to make. The firms, generally, have been self-insurers. Therefore a large enough settlement might bring one or more of the firms into bankruptcy, which would seem to negate their ability to back up their assurance work. So, the importance of the Volcker rescue plan for Arthur Andersen, which was aimed at keeping at least the Big Five firms viable, can be appreciated.

The delicate state of the market for large public company audits also highlights the fact that public accounting firms are not just attesters to corporate financial reports but are, of course, profit-seeking entities. The worldwide pattern for Big Four operations in both skill sets and locations is determined today much as it has been determined in the past. That pattern is to seek their own best interests by supplying needed services, primarily to their multinational clients, wherever in the world those clients have needs for their services, so long as the engagements can prove profitable for the accounting firms. Through various affiliations, mergers, purchases, and growth from within, the world-spanning accounting firm networks have carried out their businesses.

Market Changes Caused by Reform Legislation

With the Sarbanes-Oxley Act and similar reforms across the globe, the environment of the firms has been drastically altered. They can perform attestation services for audit clients but cannot engage in a good many other services for audit clients that the Sarbanes-Oxley Act holds would impair their independence from the audit client. This does not mean, of course, that the firms cannot perform non-attestation services for non-audit clients. Quite the contrary, in fact, this area now appears to be the largest area of operations for the firms.

A large corporation in the pre-Sarbanes-Oxley environment could engage a single Big Five firm for all worldwide needs, or at least a large part of those needs. It was convenient and probably more efficient for corporate managers. Unfortunately, from the viewpoint of public interest, one of the disadvantages of the prior arrangement was that it made the certified public accountant (CPA) firm more dependent on the large client. In the Enron-Arthur Andersen case and in a good many others, the auditors' independence was almost nonexistent.

Generally corporations find that, to fill their service needs, they must employ more than one CPA firm: one for attestation and one or more for other non-attestation services. These new arrangements have acted to transform the environment of public accounting and have caused new business models to emerge.

Revenue reports for the Big Four accounting firm affiliates in Great Britain indicate the dimensions of the transformation that has taken place under the revised regulations. *Accountancy Age* reported in February 2005 that the Big Four accounting firms have greater revenues from non-audit services than from auditing services. Further, fees earned by the Big Four from non-audit services to non-audit clients in 2003–2004 were 46 percent of total Big Four revenues. This was an increase from 38 percent of their revenues two years before. The bulk of work at Ernst & Young was reported as coming from non-audit engagements. Deloitte reportedly earned 810.1 million pounds from non-audit client advisory services in the year to May 2004, as compared to 259 million pounds in earnings from audit services during the same period in the prior period (*Accountancy Age*, 2005).

Grant Thornton CEO Ed Nusbaum indicated that as businesses and the Big Four CPA firms moved to ensure that prohibited non-audit work, and in some cases all non-audit work, was not performed for their audit clients, a large opportunity was created for non–Big Four firms such as Grant Thornton. Internal control under Sarbanes-Oxley's Section 404 and tax services were both areas where large corporations were employing the second-tier and smaller accounting firms. In previous times, this work would have been handled by the Big Four firm performing the audit engagement. Further, according to Nusbaum, investment bankers and analysts in the past routinely recommended the Big Four accounting firms to large and midsized corporations. In recent times, he reports that there has been much greater acceptance of Grant Thornton in lieu of the Big Four (Krell, 2003, 1).

The trickle-down effect from Sarbanes-Oxley changes has provided large amounts of additional work for all sizes of firms below the Big Four. But a new twist seems to have emerged in referring such work. Alliances are being formed in which work is referred to firms in alliance with one another. These alliances are sometimes informal, much as in the past, but some have been formalized, particularly where larger-firm resources are shared with alliance members.

Dom Esposito, chief operating officer for J.H. Cohn in Roseland, New Jersey, explained: "For example, an audit client needs some services we can't provide because of the rules, we would suggest to the client that they consider these two firms we're in alliance with" (Wei, 2006, 1). Such alliances have become more numerous in the current environment, where firms cannot offer public company audit clients a wide menu of services because of the Sarbanes-Oxley restrictions. The managing partner of Eisner LLP, Charles Weinstein, agrees that a referral system is being used. His firm was engaged to perform internal control compliance work for "several dozen" companies that are publicly traded. The referral came from the companies' auditors with which Eisner LLP has a relationship (Ibid.).

As discussed later in this chapter, the Big Four firms do have a virtual lock on auditing large public companies. But, of course, the small- to medium-sized public accounting firms remain able to compete with Big Four firms for audits of small- to medium-sized public companies. Further, audits of private companies, and non-audit services, including tax, forensic accounting, and other management consulting engagements, are areas where all firms are competing for business.

However, firms of all sizes also have reasons to cooperate with one another. Resources and expertise are frequently limited within any firm. Alliances with other firms are an effective and efficient way to offer a wide service menu to clients. For example, the accounting firm of J.H. Cohn, which has ninety-five partners, has become a member of Ernst & Young's CPA Connection through which the firm can access Ernst & Young's client-service, research, or training tools. London-based Baker Tilly International maintains an alliance with middle-sized firms in which a participating firm can call on other firms in the alliance to provide local expertise to clients. The firms in the Baker Tilly alliance number over 100 situated around the world. The McGladrey & Pullen Network has over eighty-five, mostly small, member accounting and consulting firms that have access to McGladrey & Pullen's and RSM International's resources (Ibid.).

The trend toward increasing cooperation, while at the same time competing with other firms, is a practical alternative to formal merging with other firms. And it is understandable as firms seek to increase the level and profitability of business "while challenged by the ever-evolving needs of their clients" (Ibid.). The larger firms involved view alliance arrangements as a way to expand their business while sharing the costs of infrastructure. Ernst & Young has operated its CPA Connection for several years and has fifty members who pay fees for using Ernst & Young resources. Linda McKenzie, a partner and national director of the firm, indicated, "For us, alliances can extend our reach in the marketplace" (Ibid.). The RSM McGladrey Network sells memberships to noncompeting smaller firms. The Baker Tilly alliance allows member firms the ability to provide a high degree of cohesive service through its global affiliations. In the view of one Baker Tilly network member, Scott Moss, partner at Cherry Bekaert & Holland in Richmond, Virginia, the network "provides peace of mind for member firms" that clients will be well served wherever in the world they may be located (Ibid.).

Formal mergers, of course, have long been a way to build accounting practices as well as to sell practices for firms of all sizes, but particularly among small- to medium-sized firms. W.M. Lawhon, managing partner and CEO of Weaver and Tidwell LLP in Fort Worth, Texas, in an interview with Accountingweb, indicated that midsized public accounting firms are likely to continue to consolidate. The reasons include objectives such as obtaining geographical coverage in strategic markets; obtaining talent in other firms to build a competitive advantage; straightening out firm succession problems by merging into a larger unit; moving the firm into a culture of more discipline and accountability; and obtaining more sophisticated practice growth techniques, information system infrastructure, or other resources.

The market for accounting and related services is substantial. The U.S. market for tax preparation, accounting, bookkeeping, and payroll services was estimated by IBIS World in 2005 to total $104.8 billion in revenues for an estimated 454,631 establishments employing 1,848,251 Americans. Wages paid were estimated at $49 billion (Accountingweb, 2006c, 1).

Despite the size of the market involved, the advantages that alliances bring, and the possibilities of mergers, the barriers to entry into the market for audits of large public companies remain formidable. It is unlikely that an alliance of firms could mount an audit of a large public corporation. There is still a very large gap between a Big Four firm and a second-tier firm. Even if the top five or so firms were to merge, it is unlikely that they would have sufficient resources to challenge the Big Four.

The barrier to entry into the top tier has, in fact, grown substantially larger since the days of the Big Eight firms in 1988. The U.S. General Accounting Office (GAO), addressing this question, analyzed average firm attributes for two groupings of public accounting firms for 1988 compared to 2002. The first grouping contained the Big Eight firms in 1988 and the Big Four firms in 2002. The second grouping was for second-tier firms. The firms included in the second-tier grouping in 1988 were Laventhol & Horwath, Grant Thornton, BDO Seidman, and McGladrey & Pullen. For 2002, the second-tier firm of Crowe Chizek and Company replaced Laventhol & Horwath since Laventhol & Horwath had gone out of business before 2002 (U.S. General Accounting Office, 2003, Table 3).

Dollar revenue, the first attribute examined, was price-level adjusted for comparison purposes. Average real revenue in 1988 for the then existing Big Eight firms was $1.566 billion per firm compared to the second-tier group, which averaged $288 million, or a gap of $1.278 billion in same purchasing-power dollars. By 2002, the Big Four firms had average real revenue of $4.468 billion compared to the second tier of $290 million, or a gap of $4.178 billion. The average firm revenue gap between the top tier international accounting firms and the second-tier had substantially increased over the period from 1988 to 2002 (Ibid.).

Other comparisons made in the study disclosed a gap between the firm groupings in the average number of partners per firm of 762 in 1988, a gap that increased to 1,736 by 2002. The differences between the two groupings' average number of nonpartners per firm was 8,804 in 1988 increasing to 14,132 in 2003. The gap in the number of each groupings' offices per firm was 48 in 1988 and 54 in 2002. Finally, the gap between the two groupings in numbers of SEC clients per firm was 1,125 in 1988 increasing to 1,811 by 2002 (Ibid.).

Most of the averages for the second-tier grouping actually declined over the period. The average number of partners for the second-tier grouping declined from 364 to 292 per firm over the period studied. Likewise, the average number of nonpartners per firm declined in the second-tier grouping from 2,118 in 1988 to 1,532 in 2002. The average number of offices per firm in the second tier declined from 57 to 47 in 2002. The average number of SEC clients per firm for the second-tier group did increase marginally from 234 to 245 (Ibid.).

Concentration in the Market for Large Public Corporation Audits

The GAO study concluded that only a few large firms have the capability to audit large public companies both in the United States and globally.

The large firm market concentration raises serious potential problems in auditor selection, pricing, and quality. The GAO concluded that there was potential for significant problems because of the significant market power of the very few large auditing service providers.

However, to the date of the report, July 2003, the GAO indicated that it had found no evidence that competition had been impaired. The GAO was careful to warn that these conditions could change. There was evidence that auditing and related services fees were rising. But the GAO report indicated that these increasing fees were not due to competition impairment but were occurring because of the significant changes taking place in the profession's environment, particularly changes in relation to the Sarbanes-Oxley Act requirements. The GAO concluded that continuing study of the situation would be needed to ensure that competition is maintained and to prevent further consolidation of market participants (Ibid., 25).

In the GAO's view, and in the views of most observers, there are very significant barriers for smaller accounting firms to enter the large public company audit market. The barriers to surmount include not having the following: the global reach necessary for firm operations, a reputation as a major firm, sufficient industry and technical expertise, sufficient capital, or sufficient staffing. It is unlikely that market forces will expand the number of firms in the large corporation audit market from the current four because the differences in the wherewithal between the Big Four and the next tier of firms are great indeed. In fact, a further reduction in major accounting firms could occur (Ibid., 45–53).

This market is likely to remain an oligopoly in which the Big Four audit the vast majority of large public companies. These firms now audit 78 percent of U.S. public companies by count. When taken as a percentage of total public company sales, the proportion increases to 99 percent for the Big Four and 1 percent for all others (Ibid., 1).

Starting in 1987, the transformation of the international accounting firms into the Big Five firms from the Big Eight was a consolidation based on the changing, growing needs of global corporations and markets. The firm of Klynveld Main Goerdeler (KMP) merged in 1987 with Peat Marwick Mitchell to become KPMG Peat Marwick. The firm created was the largest public accounting firm in the international arena. Its U.S. operations were the second largest in that country. At the beginning of the consolidation period, the eight global accounting firms were KPMG Peat Marwick, Touche Ross, Deloitte Haskins & Sells, Arthur Young,

Ernst & Whinney, Price Waterhouse, Coopers & Lybrand, and Arthur Andersen. Within two years of the KPMG Peat Marwick merger, Ernst & Whinney and Arthur Young merged to become Ernst & Young. And, Touche Ross and Deloitte Haskins & Sells combined to form Deloitte & Touche. In 1998, Price Waterhouse combined with Coopers & Lybrand to form PricewaterhouseCoopers, and all these consolidated companies, along with Arthur Andersen, made up the Big Five, which continued until the demise of Arthur Andersen (Ibid., 8–10).

In its study of the matter, the GAO found that the accounting firm mergers were for good economic reasons. In the late 1980s, as the large corporations in the world grew larger and their needs for accounting and related services continued to expand, the existing public accounting firms were hard pressed to meet their clients' needs and still remain profitable. The accounting firms adjusted by consolidating to keep pace with the global reach, growing size, and increasing complexity of their customers (Ibid., 13–15).

One of the purposes for merging some of the firms was to maintain or increase their market share in order to remain competitive with the other international accounting and related services providers. The firms' objective was to hold their position among the top firms able to audit and service the largest of clients. There was another protective aspect to the mergers as well. Some firms thought that their foreign affiliates could and would change alliances with other big international accounting firms if the affiliates perceived greater advantage to be had in retaining and securing clients with another public accounting firm's imprimatur (Ibid., 13–15).

The mergers, as they progressed in the 1980s, did create growing disparity among the largest and smallest Big Eight, or later Big Six firms. Merging was viewed as a good alternative to growing the business internally. When seventh-ranked Deloitte Haskins & Sells and eighth-ranked Touche Ross consolidated their operations, they became the third-largest firm. This placed Coopers & Lybrand in the position of being second smallest until it merged with Price Waterhouse in 1998, making PricewaterhouseCoopers the second-largest firm (Ibid., 13–15).

For their various reasons, the merging firms did achieve great economies of scale by combining forces, particularly with firms that complemented existing firm strengths. This allowed a deepening of combined firm resource pools with greater technical expertise and industry-specific capabilities. And, the amounts of capital available to the combined units became much greater, allowing greater expansion and more efficient operations of their businesses.

The consolidations clearly benefited the remaining partners of the combined firms. The merging of the firms also benefited corporate clients with lower costs of services than would otherwise have been possible, while at the same time improving service quality. Competition between the Big Five firms did not seem to be impaired by these mergers. The GAO report indicates that audit and related fees were kept in check.

Until the 1970s, professional codes of ethics for public accountants, just as for other professions, prohibited competitive bidding for client engagements and contained other barriers to competition. There were strict rules of behavior in the ethics codes concerning approaches to clients as well as employees of other firms. Of course, the members of the professions themselves voted on such codes of ethics and any changes thereto. In self-interest, it made sense for those members already in the profession to continue such prohibitions. In the United States, individual states did have separate state codes of ethics. But the states generally followed the profession's lead.

In the 1970s, the U.S Federal Trade Commission, Department of Justice, and some individual professionals brought challenges to the legality of such restrictions on competition. Under pressure, the profession accepted changes to its ethics codes, which reformed most of the competitive behavior restrictions and certainly all of those related to competitive bidding for clients. The revised ethics code did prohibit false, misleading, or deceptive advertising on the part of U.S. public accounting firms. There were other exceptions made because of the public-interest nature of the accountants' attestation work. Subsequent competition for clients was thought to result in fairer pricing. There was increased incentive for firms to charge competitive fees in order to retain their existing clients (Ibid., 8).

The ethical code revisions, it seems certain, had little if any effect on the problems of small firms overcoming the barriers to entry into the market for large corporation audits. As was discussed above, the natural barriers to entry for all but the largest public accounting firms are prohibitive. The GAO in its report stressed that there are formidable problems to overcome for all but the largest firms to enter the large corporation audit market. The fact that the gap between the Big Four and the next tier of firms has widened significantly between 1988 and 2002 should have come as no surprise.

The GAO report indicated that audit fees for large corporations remained flat or decreased slightly between 1989 and the mid-1990s, after adjustment for inflation effects. Since the late 1990s, the GAO found that fees have been increasing slightly. The rise was attributed to the increasing scope of audits since 2000 and not from the consolidation of the market into only four firms. The GAO report, in fact, found that the firms' consolidations did not increase audit fees, decrease auditing firm independence, nor create any direct effects on the securities markets or on capital formation (Ibid., 4,5).

Accounting and auditing fees have increased since implementation of the Sarbanes-Oxley Act, as is discussed more fully in chapter 9. These increases are thought by some to be the result of delayed maintenance for internal control and improved governance over corporation managements and operations. Many, including those who previously indicated that accounting and auditing fees were unjustified, are now agreeing that the benefits being received from the added costs of Sarbanes-Oxley are worth the added costs. The sharp fee increases, reportedly, are starting to abate as initial phases of the new requirements work are completed. The added requirements of the Sarbanes-Oxley Act will continue to add to accounting and audit costs especially, it appears, in the areas of governance, internal control, and internal audit.

An interesting question is whether auditors are in fact overpaid for their services. Rick Antle, Yale University accounting professor, has studied this area for some time. He believes that since audits were treated as a commodity prior to the Sarbanes-Oxley Act, it isn't logical to conclude that accountants are overpaid. It is logical to expect, he indicates, that the added costs of Sarbanes-Oxley requirements will be passed on to client corporations (Krell, 2003, 32). Nevertheless, there does not yet seem to be general agreement on the costs versus benefits question.

There does appear to be general agreement that a move downward to a Big Three would create substantial problems both as to audit-related fees and availability of sufficient audit services for the global economy. In the current environment, any excess capacity that might have been present in the operations of CPA service providers has been taken up by the increased work created by the Sarbanes-Oxley Act. In fact, the auditing off-season seems to have disappeared for most public accounting firms as their resources are strained by the new demands for their services (Ibid.).

Geographical Expansion

In addition to actions taken by the big accounting firms in their traditional markets to adjust to increasing global client demand, to the loss of Arthur Andersen, and to reform legislation around the world, the Big Four firms have continued to make substantial locational adjustments in a more geographical sense. The firms have continued to successfully respond to the opportunities created by economic expansion in various parts of the world. The global network of offices and personnel maintained by each firm has expanded and grown with the needs of the firms' large international clients, as well as with the opportunities to provide their expert services in national and local settings where economic activity is growing.

In recent years, business expansions in several areas of the world in particular have caused the Big Four firms to adjust operations geographically. Such areas as China, India, and Africa have been growth areas for the Big Four firms. Political and economic changes in Eastern and Central Europe, areas formerly within the Soviet Union's sphere, have created the need and the opportunity to grow operations in that region of the world. Countries in which such adjustments were made included Azerbaijan, Georgia, Belarus, Bosnia and Herzegovina, Bulgaria, Croatia, the Czech Republic, Estonia, Kazakhstan, Latvia, Lithuania, Romania, Serbia, Slovakia, Ukraine, Uzbekistan, and, of course, Russia.

All of the firms have continued to compete everywhere in the world where their large corporate clients have needs and where profitable operations can be maintained. Each firm has extended and intensified its operations in the areas cited above. PricewaterhouseCoopers, for example, has, by its own account, a network that is in excess of 140,000 people in its worldwide organization who are situated in 144 countries covering the developed and developing world.

Expansion of public accounting services into new areas is typified by the former Soviet states of Azerbaijan and Georgia. In 2006, the PricewaterhouseCoopers office in Azerbaijan celebrated its tenth year of operations. Azerbaijan declared its independence from the Soviet Union in October 1991 and the country's constitution was adopted in 1995. The PricewaterhouseCoopers operations in the country were, thus, established shortly after the nation's constitution was placed in effect. The Georgian office, which appears to be an outgrowth of the Azerbaijan operations, has been operational for five years (PricewaterhouseCoopers, 2005, 30).

Professional services provided in both countries appear to consist of the full range of the firm's services of assurance, audit, advisory, and tax services (Ibid., 31). The client list in Azerbaijan includes AIG, Azercell, Bank Standard, BS Services, Chevron, ConocoPhillips, Exxon Mobil, Garadagh Cement, General Electric, Gobustan Operating Company, Halliburton, International Bank of Azerbaijan, Inpex, KBR, Maersk Contractors, McDermott, National Oilwell, Procter & Gamble, Ramstone, Rolls-Royce, Schlumberger, Statoil, UniBank, Weatherford, and World Bank. Clients in Georgia were listed as Bank Republic, British American Tobacco, BP, Geocell, Metechi, Reuters, Sheraton Hotel, Statoil, and United Georgian Bank (Ibid., 30).

The office of this Big Four firm is staffed by expatriate and national specialists in all of the service areas of the firm. They offer a broad range of service assistance "on almost any business challenge" (Ibid., 5). The firm declares that it can bring to bear its global resources for client assistance by using its specialists from virtually anywhere in the world to assist clients in this locale. PricewaterhouseCoopers indicates that it has made a substantial investment in Azerbaijan in the past few years and is committed to the area as the business community grows. This commitment includes both the national and international aspects of the Azerbaijan community.

PricewaterhouseCoopers' Azerbaijan operation can be seen by its client list to service international clients, that presumably are firm corporate clients around the world, as well as national clients in the locale that have need for the firm's services and expertise. The local clients in such areas are frequently banking and infrastructure organizations as well as governmental units or quasi-governmental units, such as central banks. There seems no doubt that public accounting service organizations are facilitators of growth not only for their international corporate clients but for local jurisdictions in which their operations appear to flourish.

PricewaterhouseCoopers' efforts are also typical of the other Big Four accounting firms as opportunities for their services and profits develop in the expanding world economy. Deloitte & Touche reports that its worldwide network includes 120,000 people in 150 countries (Deloitte & Touche, 2005a, 1). It seems to have made adjustments in its global network in similar fashion to PricewaterhouseCoopers. There are two Deloitte offices in Azerbaijan (Ibid., 5). Ernst & Young established its practice in Azerbaijan in 1994. It provides services of similar scope to both international and local businesses in the Caspian region from a

Baku office. Clients served are in the oil and gas, telecommunications, manufacturing, utility, and government sectors. The Ernst & Young global network operates in 130 countries with 107,000 professionals (Ernst & Young, 2006a). KPMG, likewise, has operations in Baku in Azerbaijan. The KPMG worldwide network is located in 144 countries. The firm has 6,700 partners, 76,000 client service professionals, and 21,000 administrative staff (KPMG, 2006a).

China is another area of the world where change, although not initiated as recently as in Azerbaijan, is occurring at a rapid pace. Ernst & Young first entered the China market in 1973. In 1981, the Chinese government allowed the firm to open a representative office in Beijing from which it built its practice. In 2006, Ernst & Young had more than 3,000 professionals in China. Offices are maintained in Hong Kong, Beijing, Guangzhou, Shenzhen, Dalian, Wuhan, Chengdu, and Macau. The full range of services applicable to China are offered to multinational companies. The firm also has a large number of mainland China clients and can advise on public securities offerings on the Hong Kong Stock Exchange (Ernst & Young, 2006b, 23).

The difficulties and obstacles that public accounting firms deal with as they push their businesses forward are well documented in the Ernst & Young publication *Cross-Border Transactions: Spotlight on China* (Ibid.). The report indicates that doing business in China is difficult and substantially different from dealings with other countries. There is a constant need to have bureaucratic approvals. Different levels of government have conflicting aims, and the legal system is full of ambiguity. Local interests may be strong enough to thwart the reforms of the central government. To get agreement on transactions is time consuming and it takes great effort to close a deal. Valuations involved are difficult to agree on. Further, in joint-venture situations, the Chinese are quite reluctant to cede control. There are increasing differentials between those in cities compared with those in the countryside. Political pressures are building because of the lack of democracy. Such pressures, according to Ernst & Young, may be difficult to continue to manage in the future (Ibid., 22).

There are, nonetheless, important factors that favor entering the Chinese market. The Chinese people are "natural capitalists," even though the word "capitalist" remains taboo in China (Ibid.). The Chinese overdependence on personal relationships is declining in business. Once economic growth has begun to advance, it is difficult to reverse course. Chinese people now expect the fruits of economic growth. And, the government, in the view of Ernst & Young, has little choice but to proceed on a path of growth. Cross-border investments and alliances are needed to make improvements in the country's state-owned companies and to raise standards of efficiencies to world levels. In the accounting firm's view, China needs the world for technology and know-how. The world needs China for growth (Ibid.).

Foreign business interests should not, however, expect to be able to take control and insist upon all of the rewards from investments. The Chinese will continue to drive hard bargains. In the past, most business-men thought that investing in China was in effect taking a huge leap into darkness. Now, Ernst & Young advise, it is just a matter of time until most large foreign companies will invest in China (Ibid.).

The other Big Four firms are, of course, equally active and growing in the China arena. Each firm appears to deliver the full range of its services in areas where it maintains offices. PricewaterhouseCoopers maintains a China, Hong Kong, and Macau staff of more than 7,000, including over 280 partners. Their mainland China offices are in Beijing, Chongqing, Dalian, Guangzhou, Qingdao, Shanghai, Shenzhen, Suzhou, Tianjin, and Xi'an (PricewaterhouseCoopers, 2006a).

Deloitte & Touche indicates that it is one of the leading service orga-nizations in China. The firm offers services to those who are seeking to develop local businesses, expand into new markets, or make investments in China from a foreign base. The firm opened its first office in Shang-hai in 1917, followed by an office in Hong Kong in 1972. The Deloitte staff in China totals more than 5,000 in ten offices that include Beijing, Dalian, Guangzhou, Hong Kong, Macau, Nanjing, Shanghai, Shenzhen, Suzhou, and Tianjin (Deloitte & Touche, 2006).

KPMG in China has grown to over 4,200 professionals who work from offices in Beijing, Shanghai, Guangzhou, Shenzhen, Hong Kong, and Macau. The firm indicates that its over sixty years in Hong Kong and China are indicative of its long-term commitment to and focus on the China market. Its practice is in tune with the local environment. The KPMG client base in China is extensive. The firm claims to have the largest audit market share, by market capitalization, of both the top 100 Hong Kong–listed companies and the top 100 China A-share-listed companies (KPMG, 2006b).

Judging from the past history and growth of public accounting firms, it seems certain that they will continue to develop their practices in the future, and on a worldwide basis. Facilitating services that the firms offer, now primarily to non-audit clients, seem certain to continue in high demand. Corporations, investors, and affected governments, among others, are likely to continue to need these services as they expand their investments throughout the world. Two groups that specialize in the growth of businesses are venture capitalists and entrepreneurs. Both are likely to continue to be important customers for public accounting firms and, in fact, may be important drivers of future firm growth.

Mark Jensen, Deloitte & Touche national director of the firm's Venture Capital Services Group, believes entrepreneurship is an important U.S. export. Mark Heesen, president of the National Venture Capital Association, agrees: "The United States has been and will continue to be the worldwide leader in entrepreneurship. It is critical that we continue to foster an environment that protects innovators, encourages risk takers, and allows the best companies to enter the public markets when ready" (Deloitte & Touche, 2005b, 1).

Jensen indicates that businesspeople from all over the world come to the United States to learn and experience the U.S. technology marketplace. They return with that knowledge to their home countries to build their own companies. He believes that venture capitalists follow these entrepreneurs wherever in the world they go (Ibid.).

A recent report from a study jointly undertaken by Deloitte & Touche and the National Venture Capital Association clearly indicates that venture capitalists intend to continue investments both in the United States and in many other parts of the world.

The report is based on the 2005 Global Venture Capital Survey, which was conducted during February, March, and April, 2005. The survey was administered to 545 venture capitalists from the Americas, Europe, the Middle East, and the Asia/Pacific regions. Respondents were asked to indicate which of these categories their operations would be classified in: venture capitalists, buy-out firms, or private equity. The U.S. respondents indicated that they should be considered 91 percent venture capitalists, 8 percent private equity, and 1 percent buy-out firms. Remaining respondents indicated that they were 58 percent venture capitalists, 22 percent private equity, and 20 percent buy-out firms (Deloitte & Touche and the National Venture Capital Association, 2005, 3).

The purpose of the survey was to determine venture capitalists' intentions and attitudes regarding world regions in which they intended to invest. Survey respondents indicated that the United States remains the most desirable target for investment by venture capitalists. Sixty-five percent of respondents indicated that they plan to invest in the United States during the next five years. The venture capitalists, in particular those from the United States, do expect to expand their global investments in the future. China and India were among the top targets for U.S. venture capitalists. Twenty percent of U.S. responders indicated that China was their greatest investment interest over the next five years. India was indicated by 18 percent, and 13 percent indicated continental Europe (Ibid., 1).

The survey found that 20 percent of U.S.-based venture capitalists plan to increase investments abroad, up from 11 percent currently investing abroad. Of these, 42 percent expect to invest abroad only with other investors who have a local presence. Thirty-nine percent will develop projects with experienced foreign-based venture capital firms. And, 30 percent expect to open satellite offices where their investments are made (Ibid., 1, 2).

Foreign investors have an increasing interest in U.S. venture capital firms, according to Mark Jensen. Therefore, he believes that the "industry will be well-fueled to expand globally without diminishing its pace of U.S. investments" (Ibid., 1). Future growth of investments seems to be assured in the years ahead. Past experience indicates that the growth of economies will surely be accompanied by public accounting firm facilitative services and by an expanding global financial system. The following chapter will examine the impact and prospects for improvements in communications and computer systems to assist accountants in meeting increasing future global demands for their services.

8

The Impact of the Internet and Improving Communications Systems

The Internet has been hailed as one of the most important innovations of recent times. The immense impact on society that this communications system is having is becoming ever-more apparent. As it has for many professions, the Internet has become a major tool for accountants. Internet use has become indispensable to practitioners, clients, and information users alike. The growing importance of the Internet as a way of economic life continues to build in complexity and scope. The *Net Impact Study: The Projected Economic Benefits of the Internet in the United States, United Kingdom, France and Germany* does not overstate the case when it avers that: "The internet stands as one of the most important innovations of our time and its impact is just beginning to be measured and understood" (Varian et al., 2002, 9).

H. Varian, R.E. Litan, A. Elder, and J. Shutter, the authors of that study, place the Internet on a par with the innovations of electricity, automobiles, the telegraph, the telephone, and the like. Many new benefits have been created by the Internet. Added efficiency and convenience of communications, social benefits of new ways and forms by which to communicate, new ways of interaction, new communities and forms of expression, and the ability to customize services and products are all examples of Internet improvements in the lives of people around the world.

Many Internet benefits are difficult or impossible to measure, just as benefits from earlier society-changing technologies were. There does seem to be a consensus that Internet applications have increased and will continue to increase global economic productivity growth by at least 0.5 percent annually (Ibid., 2).

Internet Productivity Gains, Cost Reductions

The authors of the *Net Impact Study* found that, despite the fact that the Internet was rapidly gaining ground as essential in social and economic activity, relatively little empirical evidence about the communication system's economic impact had been collected and analyzed (Ibid., 2). They conducted two studies designed to collect data at the firm level. The purposes were to estimate the impact of the Internet to date, to project future impacts on revenue increases and cost savings, and to estimate the Internet's impact on productivity of the U.S., UK, French, and German economies.

Using information from Dun & Bradstreet, 2,065 U.S. entities were selected and stratified into industry segments of health care, wholesale and retail trade, durable and nondurable manufacturing, financial services and service providers, and telecommunications. A sixth group for all other entities made up the study stratifications. The authors believed that this stratification provides effective measurement of the financial impact of Internet business solutions across all U.S. industries. The study defined Internet business solutions as applications that combine Internet technologies, networking, software, and computer hardware to improve existing business processes or create new business (Ibid.). The U.S. study was replicated in the United Kingdom, France, and Germany, where the sample selection was 634 entities (Ibid., 3).

The studies found that organizations of all sizes and across all industries are using the Internet to lower costs and increase revenues. Internet business solutions had been implemented in 61 percent of U.S. entities of all sizes sampled. Larger U.S. entities, which had over 5,000 employees, had a higher adoption rate of 83 percent. In the United Kingdom, France, and Germany, the adoption rate was found to be 47 percent of those sampled. U.S. smaller entities were found to have adopted Internet business solutions at a much higher rate than their counterparts in the United Kingdom, France, and Germany. The studies found that adoption of the Internet was widespread regardless of industry type (Ibid., 4).

Combined cumulative cost savings through 2000 from Internet business solutions of $163.5 billion were estimated to have been attained by entities in the United States, United Kingdom, France, and Germany. A majority of this estimated amount had been saved since 1998. For U.S. entities, the cumulative cost savings had been $155.2 billion. Internet business solutions had also helped U.S. entities increase revenues by an approximate estimate of $444 billion. In the United Kingdom, France, and

Germany, cost savings totaled $8.3 billion, and revenues were enhanced by an estimated $79 billion.

The study reports that U.S. entities that have used Internet business solutions expect that once all Internet business solutions are fully implemented, cumulative cost savings dollars will be more than half a trillion dollars by 2010. The impact of Internet cumulative cost savings is predicted to be 0.43 percentage points of the future annual U.S. productivity growth rate. The study indicates that, if sustained for ten years, these cost savings "will have a very strong positive impact on the standard of living in the United States" (Ibid., 6). Similar expectations were expressed for the United Kingdom, France, and Germany.

In the United States, the Internet impact could account for almost half of the projected U.S. productivity increase during the years 2002 to 2011, the study reported. The U.S. productivity growth rate during the next ten years is estimated by the Congressional Budget Office at 2.1 percent annually, which represents an increase of 0.9 percentage points over the productivity growth rate of 1.2 percent from 1974 to 1995. The study estimated that Internet business solutions could contribute approximately 48 percent of this estimated 0.9-point increase in the rate of growth of U.S. productivity (Ibid., 7). In the United Kingdom, France, and Germany, a 0.11-point effect on the productivity growth rate from Internet business solutions could add more than one-third to the projected increase in the combined growth rate from 2001 to 2011 (Ibid., 8).

Another study concerning the impact of the Internet was carried out by Ron J. McClean, David A. Johnston, and Michael Wade of York University and reported under the Canadian e-Business Initiative titled *New Impact Study Canada, The SMF Experience: A Preliminary Report*, published in November 2002. The study concentrated on small- to medium-sized businesses in Canada. Small- to medium-sized businesses were defined as those having between 50 and 500 full-time employees. The project sought to measure current and anticipated cost savings as well as revenue increases for small- to medium-sized companies resulting from Internet business investments, referred to as "Internet business solutions" in this study, as in the Varian, Litan, Elder, and Shutter study discussed above. Internet business solutions covered by the study were defined as those that combined the Internet with networking, software, and computing hardware for existing or new business processes and opportunities (McClean, Johnston, and Wade, 2002, 1).

In Canada, small- to medium-sized businesses account for approximately 60 percent of economic output, hire 80 percent of Canadian employees, and generate 85 percent of new Canadian jobs. Canadian businesses of small to medium size were thought to lag well behind their U.S. counterparts in adoption of online methods and processes. Owners of small- to medium-sized businesses, according to the study, tend to believe that return on such investments will be insufficient.

A stratified random sample of 1,968 businesses was selected from the following sectors: manufacturing; financial services; public service; communications and Internet service providers; and retail, wholesale, and distribution. These businesses were surveyed by telephone during the summer of 2002 to determine willingness to participate in the study. As a result, 398 businesses were randomly selected to be study participants. Information for the study was obtained from these businesses by the use of interviews. To approximate the universe of Canadian small- to medium-sized businesses, firm responses were weighted by appropriate firm size and industry segment (Ibid., 3).

The study concluded that Internet business solutions were currently being used or implemented by 50.2 percent of Canadian small- to medium-sized businesses. A further 20.3 percent intended to adopt Internet business solutions within the coming three years. Some 28.4 percent of the businesses did not, in fact, intend to adopt Internet business solutions.

Businesses that had adopted Internet business solutions reported that revenues increased 7 percent. Costs of goods sold decreased by 9.5 percent. General and administrative expenses decreased by 7 percent. Only 4 percent of responding businesses indicated that their businesses had no financial impact from adopting Internet business solutions (Ibid., 5). The report used a hypothetical example of a business with total revenue of $10 million, a 20 percent gross margin, and a 10 percent net income margin. If the business attained the average percentage reductions in costs and increases in revenue reported in the study, net profit would have increased by up to 154 percent (Ibid., 2).

Revenue gains were found to be substantially different in the various business sectors studied. The financial services sector, for example, had increased revenue of 12.7 percent, while the retailing, wholesaling, and distribution sectors had increased revenue of 4.4 percent. The highest revenue increases and largest cost reductions were achieved in the areas of acquisition and management of customers, customer development, and e-marketing.

The growth of Internet business solution adoptions peaked between

2000 and 2001, slowing in 2002 (Ibid., 3). The growth of adoptions of Internet business solutions among all responding firms was substantial. The number of total adoptions by year were 56 in 1997, 144 in 1998, 272 in 1999, 456 in 2000, 619 in 2001, and 739 in 2002. The increase was attributed to the fact that the systems and other technologies involved became cheaper and more readily available. The study authors suggest that the rate of adoption had slowed and they predicted that by 2005 the growth rate would stagnate. They concluded that this indicates a saturation point for adoptions of Internet business solutions (Ibid., 12).

The study reported a number of barriers to using Internet business solutions, which included cost, time required to implement, uncertainty over return on investment, and management attitudes. The Internet adoption rate varied among business sectors. In the finance and accounting business sector, 39.9 percent of the businesses had adopted Internet business solutions (Ibid., 4). Manufacturing businesses were slow to adopt such solution areas as sales improvement and reduction in customer-focused operations, but were the largest adopters of e-procurement systems. Businesses that adopted Internet business solutions were reported as having high satisfaction with their investments (Ibid., 2).

In all businesses surveyed, business solutions adopted tended to be Internet applications that were customer-focused as opposed to, for example, back-office operations. This was clearly the case in financial services firms where customer service and support Internet solutions were used in 71 percent of the firms, while a much lower 19.4 percent of these firms had adopted e-procurement solutions (Ibid., 4). Further, as to the financial services industry, 70.2 percent of the businesses reported being satisfied with the results of their Internet business solution investments. Twenty-eight percent of the businesses in this sector, however, reported being ambivalent about the results of their investment, while 1.8 percent were dissatisfied (Ibid., 1).

The percentage of businesses in each sector that had adopted an Internet business solution was as follows: manufacturing 35.8 percent; financial services 58.1 percent; wholesale, retail, and distribution 33.3 percent; communications and Internet service providers 35.7 percent; and public sector 51.2 percent.

A further Canadian report was issued by the same authors in May 2003 titled *Net Impact Study Canada, The International Experience: Interim Report* (McClean, Johnston, and Wade, 2003). This May 2003 study contains comparisons between the Canadian experience reported in the November 2002 study by the same authors with the findings reported in the U.S., UK, France, and Germany studies by Varian, Litan, Elder, and Shutter discussed above. In this second Canadian study report, data from the U.S. and European studies were included only for firms with 50 to 500 employees that were also from five industry sectors: manufacturing; financial services; retail, wholesale, and distribution; communications and Internet service providers; and public service. The final data for the second Canadian study were drawn from 398 Canadian entities from the 2002 Canadian study and 1,011 U.S. entities and 257 European Union (EU) entities from the two studies by Varian, Litan, Elder, and Shutter.

Because of the large differences in relative economic size among the regions studied, data in this second Canadian report are primarily presented in the form of relative differences between regions, making easier analysis of the differences in the items in question among regions. Because of the small number in the sample sizes from the United Kingdom, France, and Germany, these were aggregated into an EU region. Data weights were used to match the sample to the relevant population in terms of organization, size, and industry (McClean, Johnston, and Wade, 2003, 2).

Results from the Canadian international comparative study included the following. Average increases in revenue among small- to medium-sized entities from adopting Internet business solutions were 7.2 percent for Canadian entities, 9 percent for U.S. entities, and 10 percent for EU entities. EU entities were less optimistic about future revenue gains from Internet business solutions than were entities from the United States and Canada. Revenue increases from adoption of Internet business solutions in Canada and the United States came mainly from newly acquired customers. Decreases in cost of goods sold achieved by Canadian entities was 10.7 percent, while U.S. entities achieved decreases in cost of goods sold of 6.9 percent and EU entities achieved decreases of 1.3 percent. Much of the Canadian average decrease came from medium-sized entities, which decreased cost of goods sold by 12.4 percent, compared to 8.8 percent for smaller Canadian entities.

As to Internet business solution types, Canada was dominant in customer development and e-marketing, while the U.S. small- to medium-sized entities adoption rates were higher for sales force automation and supply chain management solutions. Except for the indication that U.S. public small- to medium-sized entities lagged Canadian counterparts in adoption of Internet business solutions, industry differences were not significant (Ibid., 5).

The rapid adoptions of Internet business uses are clear from these three studies. Such adoption rates are indicative of the growing importance and broad sweep of the Internet in global societies as a whole. Accountants appear to have also been adopting Internet business solutions in step with businesses and the environment around them. The discussion below of several surveys of accountants taken in the past ten or so years discloses that, from a slow start, accountants have been progressing in Internet use and in coming to the full realization that the Internet is an important part of their future.

Public Accountant Use of the Internet

Conditions existing in the accounting arena regarding Internet use in 2000 are typified in a Harris Interactive study, "Accountants on the Internet 2000," conducted for CCH Incorporated to determine the value and advantages of the Internet to accountants and their clients. The survey was made during June and July 2000 via live telephone interviews to 600 accountants, 400 from public accounting firms and 200 from corporations with $10 million or more in annual sales (CCH, 2000a, 1).

The survey found that accounting practitioners are benefiting from the "exploding" Internet economy and are adopting "more and more uses for the Internet in their practices" (CCH, 2000b, 1). In this regard, CCH itself can be considered a case in point. CCH, formerly known as Commerce Clearing House, began offering its products and services via the Internet in 1995, yet had been in the business of supplying accountants and others with business information for over four generations. CCH now produces more than 700 electronic and print products for the tax, legal, securities, human resources, health care, and small business markets (Ibid.).

Of the accountants surveyed, 96 percent had access to the Internet in 2000. Eighty-four percent of the accountants used the Internet for business. In 2000, 59 percent of the accountants had used the Internet for business on a daily basis. This was an increase from the CCH 1996 survey in which 51 percent indicated they had used the Internet daily for business and 31 percent conducted business via the Internet (Ibid.).

In the 2000 survey, the accountants accepted the Internet as a reliable source of business information. The Internet was more likely to be used as an information source replacing print or CD versions of information or seminars. In the prior survey, the Internet was listed next to last as a source of information. In the 2000 survey, one in ten of the accountants said the Internet was absolutely essential as a professional information source and 43 percent said it was very important as a professional information source. Over 85 percent of the accountants rated the available information on the Internet as either excellent or good as to timeliness, relevancy, accuracy, reliability, and quality of source (Ibid.).

The 2000 survey report indicated that a majority of accounting firm practitioners use the Internet for e-mail, professional research, business research, downloading software, reading business and professional news, and for purchasing products and services. Just less than half of the firms in each size category indicated that they filed tax returns over the Internet. The Internet was used by a minority of users in all firm size classes to store or manage client data, including payroll data, as well as to access remote applications and for continuing professional education. This proportion of users was a substantial increase over the 1996 survey, in which 1 percent of accountants had used the Internet to seek continuing professional education credit (Ibid.).

Sixty-five percent of Internet users in firms with eleven or more professionals indicated that the Internet was used in marketing their firm. In smaller firms, less than half reported marketing their firm via the Internet. Web home pages have been established by firms of all sizes (Ibid.).

In 2000, 22 percent of corporate accountants indicated that they conducted financial transactions via the Internet. This compared to 10 percent of the public accounting firms. Accountants making purchases over the Internet totaled 52 percent in 2000 compared with 27 percent in the 1996 survey (Ibid.).

In 2000, 70 percent of larger firms had a Web site, while 82 percent planned to have a Web site within one year. For smaller firms, 30 percent currently had Web sites and 50 percent planned to have one within a year. Only 20 percent of firms with one or two professionals had Web sites. Value-added services via the Internet were more likely to have been offered by the smallest firms that have Web sites, than by larger firms. Firms with five or fewer accountants were more likely than larger firms to offer tax or financial news and calculator tools via the Internet. Further, firms with one or two professionals were more likely than larger firms to offer tax-preparation software (Ibid.).

Both responding accountants who anticipated establishing a Web site during the coming year and accountants who already had a Web site had increasing expectations for the Internet. But accountants who anticipated establishing a Web site had much higher expectations about the Internet. Seventy-three percent of those planning new Web sites and 55 percent of those having existing Web sites expected that the Internet would produce new business opportunities for their firms. Seventy-three percent of accountants planning to establish a Web site and 66 percent of those with existing Web sites indicated that they would sell services or products. Sixty-five percent of those planning a Web site and 59 percent of those with existing Web sites wished to provide customer service via the Internet. Seventy percent of the accountants expected the Internet to be of greater use in a business context. Fifty-seven percent of those in public accounting firms anticipated greater use of the Internet for accounting and tax applications (Ibid.). Finally, 22 percent of responding accounting firms indicated that there had been an increase in clients who were largely in e-commerce-based businesses. Forty-two percent of responding accountants with an expanding e-commerce customer list had consulted on technology to "dot-com" clients (Ibid.).

Accountants, it appears, were beginning circa 2000 to see the Internet in a more productive light. Conditions were, however, overtaking the profession. The use of the Internet as the basis for online accounting systems for clients was developing into a runaway business by 2002, according to Don Uhl. Demand was growing so fast that there weren't enough accountants who could efficiently use Internet methods. Fees for online accounting services in 2002 were four to five times traditional fees. Uhl cites Louis Metherne, director of information technology for the American Institute of Certified Public Accountants: "Those who provide traditional types of accounting and tax services are going to be challenged by the new web based competitors providing commodity services cheaper" (Uhl, 2002, 1).

In 2003, Industry Canada prepared an informational Web page on the accounting industry's use of electronic commerce and the Internet: "E-Commerce in the Accounting Industry—Start Yesterday" (Industry Canada, 2003). Projections about Internet use, which had been made by Boston Consulting Group, were reported on that Web page. The Canadian Internet economy, it was projected, would grow from $28 billion to $155 billion by 2003. This is astounding growth with astounding opportunity for accountants. Accountants were exhorted to prepare for this new economy by improving their Internet practices in order to continue to serve their clients (Ibid.).

Robert Gold from the chartered accountant firm of Bennett Gold agreed, advising his colleagues: "The reality is accountants have to get in touch with what is happening" (Ibid., 1). Accountants' practices must be modernized, Robert Gold advised, with technological access if they are to keep abreast of client needs. The Internet must be used by more practitioners to receive data and to carry out a good many tasks that are now done with paper. This is especially so for new business that accountants wish to add to their practices.

The information on the Industry Canada Web page was directed, primarily, to public accountants not using the Internet and not involved in electronic commerce, or those involved in only limited ways. The intended purpose was to illustrate opportunities and benefits that practitioners can derive. The Web page summarizes telephone discussions held with practitioners recommended by the three Canadian national accounting associations, provincial organizations, and knowledgeable practitioners. Those interviewed were recommended by their representative bodies as accounting leaders. They came from firms of all sizes, from sole practitioner to major accounting firm (Ibid.).

As business clients switch their operations to electronic commerce and the Internet, the interviewed practitioners agreed, accountants must adjust or be left behind because they will not be able to meet client expectations and requirements. Electronic commerce was viewed by all the accountants interviewed as enhancing their practices. Any number of examples of enhancements were given. By using electronic filing for tax returns, practitioners indicated that improved productivity in their firms ranged from 25 percent improvement to a doubling of productivity (Ibid.). Electronic filing of personal income tax returns has grown rapidly, with 5.4 million returns filed via the Internet for 1998. The interviews indicated that the great majority of these returns were prepared by professionals (Ibid.).

Transfer of information via e-mail for general information, sales brochures, and other former mail-out items saved substantial costs. Delivery by Internet is instantaneous, saving time and ensuring on-time arrival of time-sensitive documents. The use of secured Internet e-mail or the like for transfer of trial balances, spreadsheets, and other sensitive files enhanced client service significantly, the accountants indicated (Ibid.).

In fact, most public accounting offices are now organized around computers. The Internet is a primary connector of major impact, allowing much greater efficiencies and new avenues of service. Many of today's

Internet systems allow dual access, for client and accountant. This creates a seamless working environment between the client and accountant. The client can log on via the Internet to do data entry. The accountant can log into the system for such work as reviewing the data entry or preparing tax returns or filings. The accountant can work without calling on or receiving materials from the client.

A major trend in accounting systems is moving toward server-based/Internet software in place of installed software on a local hard drive. The advantages include instantaneous software updates and access for users from any location on the Internet. Many of the new software systems are updated in real time, with no need to make updates in multiple files. The cost structure appears to favor Internet accounting packages, as well. Monthly subscription costs have become reasonable. Start-up and training costs for Internet packages are minimal when compared to software packages on local hard drives.

The Internet enables remote site and home office work in place of travel to the practice office. One practitioner in a rural area explained that he has been able to retain his trained staffers by having them work from home, which has been as far as 125 miles from the practice office. Staff, who in the ordinary course of events would have resigned to stay at home with children, or staff who move to a new domicile, can now remain in the employ of the practitioner via Internet and home office use. This is particularly important, he indicates, in rural or other areas where it is difficult to hire competent new staff.

The practitioners also reported that their productivity increased and client support was enhanced as staff experience with and understanding of the technologies being used increased. In a multi-office firm, large cost savings were realized by transfer of files by secured Internet, which allowed spreading of work from overloaded staff to underutilized staff (Ibid.). Further, practice office productivity can be bolstered by client computer systems that are accessible for use by accountants, or by procedures that call for having the client prepare accounting entries using secure Internet connections or e-mail to send the information to the accountant. Clients who are able to perform higher-level functions on their own free up public accountant staff to move to higher skill levels (Ibid.).

Audit software, as well, has advanced to the point where the audit can be virtually paperless. The use of scanners by auditors allows audit evidence to be copied and saved electronically, enhancing both the efficiency and effectiveness of such work paper support. The Internet allows work paper preparation and review from remote locations. The audit software increases reliability of much of the auditor's work, such as analysis of accounts, documentation, charting, and reporting. Major accounting firms have developed proprietary audit software that is made available to firm members via the Internet. There are a number of vendors who now market audit and accounting Internet software (Ibid.).

Internet chat group capabilities allow technical chat groups for audit team use. Practitioners can get answers on technical matters or more quickly be directed by others in the firm to appropriate sources. The Internet allows the practitioner to build knowledge bases that are instantaneously available to the firm's practitioners anywhere in the world. Practitioners can add, at any time, information such as ratings for a Web site as to appropriateness or effectiveness, which is immediately available for others within the firm. There are a plethora of knowledge bases that can be accessed both without charge and through subscription.

Practitioners noted that one big use of their intranets, that is, private leased Internet or similar lines, is for working up proposals for engagements. Firm practitioners, expert in different areas, who may be located around the world, can be included in the practitioner team via intranet at both proposal and engagement work stages. Databases of firm practitioner skill sets can help direct practitioners preparing engagement proposals to firm members with the appropriate skills, wherever they may be located (Ibid.).

Instantaneous access is available, the interviewed practitioners believe, to research and information sites appropriate to the needs of accountants, such as handbook information, articles, analysis of various kinds, government budgets, and regulations. This is important help to practitioners in maintaining and improving their skills, the interviewees believed. Ross Harwood from Deloitte & Touche thinks that "We have to do this to keep up. There is a cost for not being current" (Ibid.).

Most firms do have Web sites today. The practitioners believe that the Web site gives them a competitive edge. Such sites are useful to maintain current clients and to attract new clients. Information can be readily provided in a Web site that demonstrates the firm's professional competence and expertise. It is a good place to differentiate the firm from competitors. Another important Internet advantage for public accounting firms has been the use of search engines on a regular basis to find information that clients are interested in and pass this information along to the clients in question. This has built the firm's presence with clients, the interviewed accountants reported (Ibid.).

Canadian accounting professional associations, much as U.S. accounting bodies, are doing more and more of their business with practitioners and others via the Internet. All three Canadian associations have Web sites for information, products, and member services. CMA Canada has a Virtual Learning Centre that includes Internet-delivered professional courses. All aspects are handled via the Internet, including registration, delivery of courses, billings, and payments. A Virtual University For Small and Medium Enterprise Members is delivering short courses, as well.

The Canadian Institute of Chartered Accountants, together with the American Institute of Certified Public Accountants, has developed an assurance program for clients who engage in electronic commerce called WebTrust. In order to display the Web Trust emblem, businesses must meet all requirements set by the associations and undergo verification by a licensed chartered accountant or U.S. certified public accountant.

The Certified General Accountants Association of Canada, reportedly, was the first accounting body in the world to offer a combination print and Internet program of professional studies. Students use the Internet for delivering and returning assignments, receiving feedback, and for conversing with fellow students in chat rooms. The previous three national conferences of the organization had electronic commerce as a theme. The association maintains an online center where practitioners can assess their professional education needs (Ibid.).

There are any number of opportunities available in the Internet economy for accountants who are prepared with the necessary skills, the interviewed practitioners believe. Advisory services of many kinds will be needed as electronic commerce and the Internet grow to what appears to be great potential. Niche marketing will allow practices to have the expertise to service selected areas of client needs. These will be business-to-business as well as business-to-consumer opportunities. Consulting with clients to assist in designing, developing, implementing, and monitoring systems for electronic commerce is a highly potential market. Technology consulting on assuring secure Internet and computer systems will be needed, including privacy controls (Ibid.).

Demand is growing for audits to be completed in shorter time frames after year-end closings. As an example, Cisco Systems, a large software company with $12.2 billion in revenue for the year ended July 31,

1999, in one day closed its global consolidated accounting books for the month-end and year-end. The auditor's report on those consolidated financial statements was dated August 9, 1999. This was eight days after closing of the books. There seems little doubt that auditors and accountants will increasingly be called upon to complete corporate financial statements, as well as to audit financial statements, in shorter time frames in tomorrow's fully computerized, interconnected business environment (Ibid.).

A look at the future was also provided by the example of a partnership between KPMG and Cisco Systems, which makes equipment for running the Internet. Cisco invested $1 billion dollars in KPMG to assist the public accounting firm to offer business services via the Internet. KPMG reportedly used the resources to hire 4,000 engineers and other professionals to build six technology centers to deliver Internet-based data, voice, and video consulting services to Cisco's clients (Ibid.).

What about the smaller or local public accounting firms? Robert Gold of Bennett Gold advises "more accountants will have to adopt and use the Internet." And, when asked what a smaller practitioner who was not already up to speed on electronic commerce should do, Gold's advice was a succinct "Start yesterday" (Ibid.).

XBRL on the Horizon

Significant help for preparing and auditing financial statements within compressed time frames may be on the global accounting horizon. Many observers believe that a new networking revolution for finance and business reporting, involving XBRL, or Extensible Business Reporting Language, is now unfolding that will provide new capabilities to move information more quickly and with more adaptability. Using the XBRL protocol, each item of information will be embedded with a standardized, computer-readable tag of identification (ID tag). The ID tag will accompany the item of information in question wherever it is used, be it analysis, accounting application, or financial statement presentation.

ID tag protocols must be developed for specific standard uses, for example, the generally accepted accounting principles (GAAP) of a given country, region, or industry. These protocols have been given the name taxonomies by XBRL International. So, for example, U.S. GAAP taxonomies needed to be developed in conjunction with XBRL International. Users knowing the standardized tag ID system will be able to extract via computer individually desired items from XBRL-enabled financial statements, for any and as many companies as desired that use a taxonomy in question.

Currently, the objectives for XBRL efficiency and productivity gains appear to be primarily at the information user end. However, the necessary standardization in the mechanics of financial statement compiling and computer input may allow accountants and auditors to be more efficient in statement compiling and auditing, allowing shorter time frames to be met. This development, of course, remains to be seen, but the prospects are bright.

The emerging XBRL revolutionary paradigm for financial and business reporting consists of sets of computer reporting standards that define and exchange business financial performance information. This innovative business reporting language, it is thought, can be universally applicable and usable on all computer platforms and universally usable in or adaptable to all proprietary business software.

XBRL may cure the reporting problems noted in the newsletter *Chartered Treasury Manager* of June 1, 2003, which was based on the work of Samuel A. DiPiazza Jr. and Robert G. Eccles in their book *Building Public Trust: The Future of Corporate Reporting* (DiPiazza and Eccles, 2002). These authors noted that XBRL may be a solution to the desire of financial statement users to have more information and that it be more user friendly. Financial information and statements have been distributed via the Internet for some time, provided by a number of companies and others, such as the Securities Exchange Commission (SEC), through its EDGAR system. This information, given the technological capabilities available, has been of high quality, easy to obtain, and as trustworthy as information distributed on paper. Yet, as noted in *Chartered Treasury Manager,* it is doubtful that the information as it is currently distributed satisfies a good many users (Association of Chartered Treasury Managers, 2003).

Issuers have used their hard copy financials and other information for Internet-based reporting. They have used PDF files or HTML versions to post the information on the Web. Many issuers have used one large PDF file for their entire financial statements, including footnotes, in some cases. Blunn & Company, in a survey of the top 100 Fortune Global 1,200, found that approximately 30 percent of the companies provided annual reports in a single large PDF file. The number of these companies that provided financials in HTML format had increased. A series of smaller PDF files in place of one large PDF file would be an improvement for usability. The Blunn Company study found that only twenty-five of the surveyed firms used links to related notes from applicable line-item figures. The Blunn survey noted other improvements that are needed. Forty percent of the firms in the Blunn survey presented only their latest company financial statements on the Internet. Statements for the past two or three years were posted by 50 percent of the surveyed firms, while less than 10 percent posted financial reports for the past five years (Ibid.).

In either the PDF or HTML file case, users cannot move the information directly via computer programming into a spreadsheet program, or the like, for analysis. The data must be manually handled, a most time-consuming chore. The replicas of annual reports that have been posted onto the Internet also frequently use large amounts of file space for large graphics and photographs, thus adding to download times and computer space occupied, without a corresponding increase in analysis value (Ibid.).

The XBRL paradigm would solve this problem. Computers need to be provided with instructions, as well as exact information about the information received. Such information about other information is referred to as metadata and can be provided in commuter data tags, the ID tags discussed above. The XBRL language makes the information transmitted more complete as to content and format. The metadata in the identification tags is delivered embedded with the corporation's data. This allows data to be presented in the same format on different computer platforms.

The ID tag can contain considerable metadata information. The data might contain, for example, information that the item is an asset, and also identify its currency basis and the pertinent reporting period or date. XBRL can go beyond financial statements, as well, in its ability to contain any kind of information in ID tags. The information might be industry specific or company specific.

Using XBRL-enabled financials, users can automatically transfer the information desired to data storage in desired form, to analytical software or to decision-making software tools. The data can be directly downloaded into spreadsheets. Microsoft maintains an investor relations site from which Microsoft financial reports can be downloaded directly into Microsoft Excel spreadsheets. Thus, manual operations are not needed. And, at the issuer end, XBRL-enabled information needs to be retrieved only once for many uses thereafter.

Microsoft, an early supporter and adopter, seeks to spread the use of

XBRL by demonstrating its value to other users. The company has the additional goals for XBRL of ensuring credibility and integrity of the financial information, streamlining and reducing the costs of preparing and distributing the company's financial information, and deriving benefits for the company's stakeholders (Ibid.).

XBRL has, in fact, been demonstrated to be both universally applicable and useful in a number of applications. XBRL is one of a family of XML languages. It is a business reporting adaptation using the foundation of XML, or Extensible Markup Language. XML is a computer software standard for electronic exchange of data that uses identifying tags applied to each piece of relevant information in a particular application.

The Internet acts as a nearly instantaneous information transporter. Without XBRL enabling, documents are treated as blocks of text, such as in a standard Internet page. Individual items of information making up transported documents are incapable of being sorted out without prior appropriate programming at both the sending and receiving sites. A user can make or purchase software to do the transporting and sorting jobs. Such software is generally proprietary and is programmed for specific uses.

Without appropriate software, a great deal of hand sorting and accumulating of data are needed to accommodate further uses of information on whole documents, essentially as individual information items sorted and accumulated anew. For standard documents to be sorted by individual document item using any software on any computer platform, there needs to be a standardization of data loading into the document as it is prepared so that it can be retrieved in like fashion. To be of viable use in the global financial system, a standard protocol for major uses is needed that is freely open and not dependent upon proprietary solutions.

XBRL is not the only possible solution but is the top contender to provide these services. It is essentially an electronic communication language for business and financial data. A nonprofit consortium that includes 450 major companies, government agencies, and organizations has been developing the communications language designed to be widely acceptable and universally used throughout the world as an open standard, free of license fees.

To reiterate, instead of treating financial information as a block of text, XBRL provides an identifying tag for each individual item of data. This tag, along with the individual identified item of data, is computer readable. For example, company total assets would have a unique tag. A complete standard tagging scheme, an XBRL taxonomy in the case of business and financial data, must be developed so that all desired information can be loaded along with embedded tags with appropriate metadata, allowing it to be sorted out properly at its destination or point of use. If, for example, each financial statement item is given a unique, standardized tag, then input of the information and sorting can be done so that computer software can both load and sort the standardized data, by ID tag as it were. The introduction of XBRL tags enables automated processing of business information by computer software, cutting out laborious and costly manual or re-entry processes at the information user stage. Software for XBRL applications is flexible and can be embedded in financial applications, as well as provided as separate modules.

Mike Willis, PricewaterhouseCoopers partner and founding chairman of the International Steering Committee of XBRL International, described the problem with the Internet as follows: "What the Internet is missing is universal, software-neutral, non-proprietary standards for presenting, accessing, and moving information safely and securely" (Willis, 2003, 58). The XBRL standards represent to Willis "the next stage in the evolution of human communications" (Ibid., 56) and are already emerging into the corporate reporting world. In a number of implementations in a number of countries, XBRL has already been providing major benefits in preparation, analysis, and communication of business information with great efficiency, improved accuracy and reliability, and cost savings to both those supplying and using business financial data.

More accessible information will improve efficiency and effectiveness of investment decisions. Currently, financial information must be accumulated from each individual financial statement that may or may not be computer readable. There are a number of proprietary software packages to handle this job, but they are not universally available. The job of accumulation of information needed by users is now often inaccurate and very time consuming to obtain. With the XBRL standards in use, desired information can be located and extracted by computer operations almost instantaneously and with greater accuracy in more timely fashion, Willis believes.

Advantages of the XBRL system of standards include greater transparency as greater information in more depth can be retrieved by information users from corporate financial statements. Costs of retrieval, and probably uploading on the provider end as well, will be lowered. Reporting will be more exact and effective since each item of business information will be identified by a predefined tag that any type of business software can recognize. The correct data can therefore be transferred by appropriate programming from and to computers without further human intervention. This allows automatic updating of information, with nearly instantaneous speed, into models, databases, and the like for uses desired by information users.

Data will have to be entered only once, into reporting entity computers. From that point onward computers will be able to recognize and handle the tagged data. This will result in more accurate and direct communications by public companies with their constituents. Willis estimates that annual costs of corporate financial reporting enabled with XBRL could decrease by 40 to 50 percent (Ibid., 57).

The users of financial reporting information now have a very large and growing problem in processing information in a timely and efficient fashion. Corporate stakeholders, regulators, and many other information consumers may receive information via the Internet but cannot process individual data items without re-entry to computers in some form. Before this step can be taken, the appropriate information must be gathered, generally by hand, as well as accumulated in forms appropriate for use. Then, analysis and decision making can go forward, as well as further reporting, which may be necessary. Willis believes that XBRL methods will exponentially improve timeliness and ability to communicate with those who need or desire corporate financial statement information. This will include parties that aggregate corporate information for use by others, such as government agencies, regulators, stock analysts, and the like (Ibid., 58).

XBRL International agrees, indicating on its Web site that data can be "intelligently" treated by computers that use XBRL. The computers can recognize, select, analyze, and store the information as well as exchange it with other computers. The information can be automatically presented in a variety of ways desired by users. The speed of handling financial data is increased dramatically and the chances of error are reduced. XBRL permits automatic information checking. Collecting and reporting of financial information is streamlined at source companies. Users of financial information are able to receive, find, compare, and analyze needed information rapidly and efficiently. A wide variety of users are accommodated, including regulators, investors, analysts, and financial institutions. XBRL operates in any of the different country languages of the world. Different accounting standards are also accommodated. The adaptability and flexibility of XBRL allows many different requirements and uses to be met. Further, transformation of data into XBRL form can be made by suitable mapping software or by direct generation by appropriate software programs (XBRL International, 2006).

In his 2003 article, Willis described the increasing uses of XBRL by regulators such as Germany's Bundesbank, UK Inland Revenue, National Tax Agency of Japan, and the U.S. Federal Deposit Insurance Corporation (Ibid., 57). The need is acute to have XBRL required for reporting to government agencies. Government agencies and departments tend to act as isolated entities. They usually have differing computer systems with different systems requirements. Consequently there is often redundancy in the information collected by different governmental agencies, with resulting inefficiencies, errors, and out-of-date operations (Ibid., 58). Frequently, agencies use incompatible software, often making the use of data from constituents and the sharing of information between agencies untimely, inaccurate, and inefficient.

Willis notes that the situation in the banking industry is worse than the norm because of the past high number of mergers and acquisitions undergone by banks. This has created organizations consisting of consolidated entities that have many separate systems still being used in each formerly separate entity. Many such systems are frequently incompatible between companies that may now have been joined, creating layers of incompatibility as new organizational structures emerge. Similar situations can be expected to have occurred in other industries where merger and acquisition activities have taken place (Ibid.).

Organizations often try to deal with this situation by a form of data warehousing. Data is forwarded by the separate units to centralized locations where it is sorted out for reporting, analysis, and management decision making. In effect, a further layer of inefficiency has been created that is quite costly. Such operations require layers of special-purpose computer software, both at the various units that are the information sources and at the warehousing centers. With XBRL-enabled systems in place, compatibility is assured and information to monitor, manage, and report is readily accumulated (Ibid.).

The XBRL movement has grown substantially since the first meeting of the XBRL Steering Committee in October 1999 in the New York City offices of the American Institute of Certified Public Accountants. Development began at that meeting on the first XBRL taxonomy, which was for financial statements prepared in accordance with U.S. commercial- and industrial-sector generally accepted accounting principles. These sectors included 80 percent of all U.S. public companies (XBRL International, 2006).

XBRL International has grown, in a relatively short time, to be a not-for-profit international consortium with membership totaling over 450 organizations, including regulators, government agencies, software vendors, and others. The international organization is broken out into jurisdictions, which are independent bodies generally organized in a given country that promote and work toward the adoption of XBRL. The jurisdictional bodies develop taxonomies for defining the information exchange needs and requirements in their jurisdictions (Wikipedia, 2006b).

Established jurisdictions in 2006 included fourteen jurisdictions: Australia, Belgium, Canada, Germany, International Accounting Standards Board (IASB), Ireland, Japan, Korea, Netherlands, New Zealand, Spain, United Kingdom, United States, and Developing Jurisdictions Direct Participants. Europe was named as an affiliate organization. Provisional jurisdictions included Denmark, France, Poland, South Africa, Sweden, and United Arab Emirates.

XBRL International has set up the requirements and procedures by which taxonomies designed for XBRL applications can be approved. Taxonomies are the dictionaries used by XBRL that define specific tags for individual items of data. Taxonomies attempt to capture individual reporting element definitions as well as the relationships between elements within a taxonomy and between taxonomies. For different financial reporting purposes, appropriate taxonomies must be developed. Each national jurisdiction, for example, may need to develop a taxonomy to cover their national financial reporting standards. In fact, XBRL taxonomies have already been completed for International Financial Reporting Standards (IFRS) and U.S. Generally Accepted Auditing Standards. Special taxonomies, responsive to their particular needs, may be needed by regulators, companies, industries, or others.

There are two levels of XBRL International recognition for taxonomies: approved and acknowledged. Approved taxonomies must have complied with official XBRL guidelines for the type of taxonomy in question and must have complied with the XBRL specifications. Acknowledged taxonomies need only to have complied with the XBRL specifications. Taxonomies under development may also be listed with the XBRL International organization.

Taxonomies have been recognized for eight countries: Canada, China, Germany, Ireland, Korea, New Zealand, United Kingdom, and United States. Most of these were designed to apply XBRL to financial statements using generally accepted accounting principles of the country in question. Some of the countries have developed more than one taxonomy for differing reports. China, for example, has two taxonomies, one for listed companies and one for fund companies. The United States has different taxonomies for GAAP reporting standards for commercial and industrial, banking and savings, insurance, investment management, brokers and dealers, and pensions. There are also U.S. taxonomies for the management report, the accountant's report, and the Management Discussion and Analysis of Financial Condition report. The International Accounting Standards Board has separate taxonomies for its reporting standards for the years 2003 and 2004. All of the taxonomies are in the acknowledged stage except for eight U.S. taxonomies that have gained the approved stage (XRBL International, 2006).

A very substantial U.S. Federal Deposit Insurance Corporation XBRL project in conjunction with the Federal Reserve Board and the Office of the Comptroller of the Currency was carried out successfully in 2005. The project involved the collection of quarterly bank financial statements, titled Call Reports, from over 8,300 U.S. banks. XBRL was made mandatory for the Call Reports. Resulting data are posted on the Internet publicly for use and analysis. This large U.S. project involving substantial reporting requirements successfully demonstrated that XBRL can provide real business value by reducing reporting burdens and duplication, improving data transparency, and enabling more timely analysis. The Federal Deposit Insurance Corporation Call Report project is the largest use of XBRL in the United States to date (Wikipedia, 2006b).

The U.S. SEC has been quite active in promoting XBRL. The SEC allowed, on a volunteer basis, the use of XBLR-enabled filings that used the approved taxonomies for U.S. GAAP-based financial statements. Such U.S. company SEC filings can be downloaded from EDGAR Online on a subscription basis. Proprietary service companies, such as PR Newswire and Business Wire, provide services to listed companies to allow them to distribute their financial information in XBRL format for a fee (Ibid.).

Further, a pilot XBRL-based program is being sponsored by the U.S. SEC. The program allows volunteer companies to use interactive data in their financial statements filed with the SEC. The program was designed with several purposes in mind. The SEC can assess the new methods for its own purposes. Volunteer companies will be able to gauge the costs of producing the interactive data. Users of information, such as investors and analysts, will have the opportunity to assess company financial statement filings in the XBRL format. Both preparers and users will be able to give feedback to the SEC.

An assessment by SEC chairman Christopher Cox of the project thus far was included in a press release: "As the number of companies voluntarily submitting interactive data continues to grow, it's obviously becoming clear that making information available to investors in a more useful way is also cost effective" (SEC, 2006, 1). The twenty-four companies that have committed to furnish their financial information to the SEC using interactive data now include 3M Company; Altria Group, Inc.; Automatic Data Processing, Inc.; Banco Itaú Holding Financeira SA; Brazilian Petroleum Corporation (aka Petrobras SA); Bristol-Myers Squibb Company; Crystal International Travel Group, Inc.; The Dow Chemical Company; Ford Motor Company; Ford Motor Credit Company; General Electric Company; Gol Intelligent Airlines, Inc.; Infosys Technologies Limited; Microsoft Corporation; Net Servicos De Comunicacao SA; Old Mutual Capital, Inc.; PepsiCo, Inc.; Pfizer, Inc.; RR Donnelley & Sons Company; Radyne Corporation; South Financial Group, Inc.; United Technologies Corporation; Xerox Corporation; and XM Satellite Radio Holdings, Inc. (Ibid.).

Europe has taken a leading role in XBRL implementations. The first XBRL project for the Dutch Waterboards was followed by other successful projects in Spain, Belgium, and other European countries. A major Dutch government project currently in progress to move XBRL reporting into all business and quasi-government organizations such as health institutions and cities will make Holland the first country with a nationwide XBRL implementation (Wikipedia, 2006b).

Swedish small- and medium-sized entities were permitted to file company accounting using XBRL on June 1, 2006, with the Swedish Companies Registration Office. The filings include the primary financial statements, financial statement notes, Directors' Report, and Audit Report. The filings use taxonomies to categorize statement items using Swedish GAAP, which were developed by the Swedish XBRL jurisdiction. One taxonomy is used for annual reports by small- and medium-sized entities and follows a standard format. A second taxonomy is used for Swedish audit reporting. Companies eligible to use XBRL filings number several hundred thousand. Neither Swedish companies listed on stock exchanges that file under International Financial Reporting Standards, nor financial-sector companies, nor companies filing consolidated or interim statements are currently eligible to file XBRL-enabled financial statements with the government regulator. The approval for XBRL-enabled filings will be gradually extended to these companies, beginning with the interim and consolidated reports (Calvert, 2006, 1).

Financial reports enabled with XBRL are already available for a number of companies, including a large range of companies that file on EDGAR Online, as discussed above. Microsoft has issued its financial statements in XBRL since 1996. Reuters has issued XBRL-based financial statements for several years. TSX Group was the first Canadian public company to issue annual financial statements enabled in XBRL format. It appears that XBRL-enabled financial statements will continue to increase as more of the world's regulators permit or require them.

Financial Statements on the Internet

Whether financial statements are posted to the Web site using XBRL or other protocols, problems of auditor oversight arise in conjunction with audited financial statements and related information distributed on the Internet. The posting of financial information by corporations on the Internet has increased rapidly in recent times and this trend is certain to continue. By 1996, in excess of 80 percent of the Fortune 150 companies posted financial information online. Sixty percent of the UK FTSE 100 posted financial information in 1998, up from a reported 54 percent in 1997 (Bagshaw, 2000, 1).

The Internet provides a number of advantages for the distribution of financial information. The substantial costs of printing and mailing annual reports to interested requesters are avoided. A wider audience can be reached using the Internet. Information on Web sites can be updated at any time such that financial information can be kept up-to-date continuously. Advancing technologies, in particular XBRL, allow downloading of financial information from the Web site directly into files appropriate to user needs.

Financial information posted on Web sites varies from company to company. The information may be financial highlights only, interim reports, summary financial statements, full audited financial statements with audit report, or many other variations. On some Web sites, it is difficult to know which information has been audited and which has not. There are few regulations and no definitive rules for Web sites and their content. But, many lawyers believe that publication of financial statements and related information on a Web site carries with it the same stringent requirements that apply to financial reports issued in paper venues (Ibid.).

There does not appear to be sufficient guidance for auditors on information presented in Web sites. Many country professional standards and the International Federation of Accountants standards for auditors do include the prohibition that auditors should not allow their names to be associated with financial statements or related information unless the auditor has complied with applicable professional rules for the information. The auditors must have performed audit or other attestation work appropriate to the situation. In no case may the auditor's name be associated with misleading financial information.

Auditors would be well advised when entering into a client engagement to ensure that the client agrees to seek the public accounting firm's express permission before posting audited information on a Web site. Auditors should take a number of items into consideration when allowing audited financial information to be posted on the company Web site. The Web site information must be secure from tampering. Altered information might become misleading information. Auditors should consider whether the security of the Web site in general should be examined and whether the security of sections containing the audited financial information, in particular, is adequate (Ibid.).

Information with which the auditor's name is associated should be clearly segregated to avoid confusion of what the auditor is and is not responsible for. Particular care is needed when posting complete audited financial statements. The Web site–posted financial statements should be identical to those audited. When the client transfers the financial information to the Web site by scanning the information, the information should be identical, with small chance of error. However, when the transfer is made with HTML protocols, the information has to be keyed in from the original statements, giving rise to possible errors. Controls should be reviewed by the auditor. Any changes made in Web site content should also be reviewed for accuracy by auditors. If hyperlinks are used on the Web site to allow users to automatically move to another page or Web site, the auditor needs to assure that links in the audited information are accurately handled so that the difference between audited and non-audited materials is clear. Local requirements for audited financial statement presentations vary, and the auditor should ensure that Web site presentations are in compliance (Ibid.).

Requirements and standards have been issued in some jurisdictions. Audit guidance in Australia, for example, makes presentation of financial information on corporate Web sites management's responsibility. Presentations on Web sites require the clear distinction between audited and non-audited content. Auditors are expected to ensure the security and control of the Web site in general and to ensure the quality and integrity of financial statements and related content posted on the Web site.

Auditors in the United States have no obligations in regard to Web site financial presentations. Such information is not regarded as "published" information for which the auditor would have responsibilities. In the U.S. litigious environment, however, auditors in all probability need to oversee Web site presentation even though not required by regulators or standards.

A UK discussion paper suggests that Web sites should be separated into restricted and unrestricted parts. Only information upon which an auditor has issued a report should be presented in the restricted section. In the unrestricted Web site area, a notice should state that information in the unrestricted area has not been audited. The restricted areas should not contain hyperlinks. The full annual report should be presented. Highlights or abridged information should not be contained in the restricted Web site area. The Web site should contain the declaration that company directors are responsible for content and security of the Web site. Auditors should review and be satisfied with Web site security (Ibid.).

A number of organizations or groups connected with standard-setting bodies have studied Internet reporting as well as the potential of XBRL. In 1999, the International Accounting Standards Committee (IASC) published a study authored by Andrew Lymer, Robert Debreceny, Glen Gray, and Asheq Rahman titled *Business Reporting on the Internet* as a first step in a project to analyze Internet reporting. The study surveyed Internet reporting practices around the world at that time. Many of the factors about financial information reporting via the Internet discussed above were also observed in this study. Recommendations from the study included, among others, the suggestion that IASC join a consortium effort to develop an electronic reporting language for Internet reporting. It also recommended that the IASC develop a code of conduct for Web-based reporting practices.

The International Accounting Standards Board, successor to the IASC, concluded that the project should be combined with a similar project of the International Federation of Accountants in as much as the subject went beyond accounting standards (Deloitte IAS Plus, 2001). However, the IASB did join the consortium of XBRL International as a member and a jurisdiction. In 2001, the IASB completed the core taxonomy for XBRL-enabled reporting of IFRS-based financial statements. This taxonomy was and continues to be made available to all users of IFRS, including countries throughout the world (Smartpros, 2001, 1). The IASB has, as noted above, continued to update the IFRS taxonomies in subsequent years as changes have been made to IFRS.

The U.S. Financial Accounting Standards Board (Steering Committee, 2000) sponsored a business reporting research project in 2000, titled "Electronic Distribution of Business Reporting Information," designed to gather and analyze information about the kind of information that companies were reporting outside traditional financial statements via the Internet. The study group recognized that the Internet has grown rapidly as a medium for delivering business reporting information and has altered the way information goes from companies to information users. The Internet has expanded the delivery of information to nonspecialist investors at very low or no cost to investors. Today an investor who has a computer and access to the Internet can obtain information that was previously available only to specialists such as professional investment analysts, the financial press, and company officials.

This direct delivery of information should assist companies in making full disclosures and reduce problems caused by information disclosure to user subsets, such as investment banks or analysts. Wider, rapid disclosure of information that is required to be disclosed should assist capital markets in establishing efficient prices. The flow and content of information will continue to change as new technologies are brought to the process (Steering Committee, 2000, vii).

Investor or investor relations sections of company Web sites were found to be the usual location for reporting financial information. These sections were found to have at least the following information: quarterly and annual financial statements, financial histories, SEC filings, stock quotes, press releases, information request forms, and other shareholder information (Ibid., 11). Some companies included information that had historically been prepared for analysts and institutional investors. This information included management presentation transcripts and slides, transcripts or audio archives of conference calls, presentations to analysts or other meeting presentations, online company fact books, earnings commentaries, and investor relations events calendar (Ibid., 12).

Some companies included in their investor section streaming audio or video of analyst conference calls, annual meetings, or similar presentations. An archive of these was provided in some cases (Ibid., 13). At least one company was found, by the study, to have included analytical tools that assisted users in summarizing and analyzing company financial information (Ibid., 12). Many companies provided e-mail alert services for which users could subscribe that provided messages to alert users to some event or change in the investor section, such as press releases, information updates, or company investor events. On some sites, users can sign up to be e-mailed company newsletters (Ibid., 13).

The study group noted that most of the Web sites reviewed use HTML in the presentation of data. They reported that a project, sponsored by the American Institute of Certified Public Accountants, the five largest accounting firms, and other organizations, was under way that was developing new technologies for delivery of financial information now called XBRL. The study group also reported that many third-party Web sites were in existence for the electronic distribution of company and business information. These sites may accumulate and assemble financial and other business information about public companies. They may have been established to service customers who do business via the Internet or they may be traditional entities, such as news services, that have expanded their service menus to meet the new demands arising from the availability of the Internet. Many of these third-party sites give investors access to a plethora of information through accumulation and storage on their own sites or by hyperlinks to others (Ibid., 14).

Data that may be provided include company financial statements, SEC filings, company press releases, and stock quotes. These sites enable the user to search a variety of information sources on an industry, an individual company, or multiple companies. These sites save user time by providing access to desired information at one site. Further, the sites frequently provide all of the features of the company investor sites plus additional analytical tools and Internet compatible formats that facilitate the collection of desired data, such as downloadable data files and hyperlinked tables of content that are annotated (Ibid., 15, 16).

The impact of the Internet on the practice of accounting has been one of new opportunities for improved, more efficient productivity. Communications have been speeded between accountant and client, and between corporation and information user. All of these groups have been enabled to notch up their level of activity and achievement. The dawn of vastly improved financial statement delivery methods with XBRL technologies is rising and should prove to be a major productivity enhancement just as the Internet has proven to be. Accountants have responded with alacrity in taking up these new tools, thereby improving local and global financial reporting systems.

Part III

The Firms in the
New Global Environment

9

Firm Effectiveness in the Face of Emerging Accounting and Auditing Standards

The collapse of Enron took with it the self-regulation of the U.S. public accounting profession. Accountants and public accounting firms were subjected to a deluge of new standards, regulations, and requirements. Many new regulations and requirements were also extended to corporations listing stock on U.S. exchanges and their boards of directors and managements, as the U.S. Congress legislated new approaches to ensure improved financial reporting. By 2006, the plethora of adjustments made by accountants, managements, and boards of directors seemed to be reaping renewed public confidence in the financial reporting process.

Chief executive officers (CEOs) and other corporate officers have been paying considerably more attention, as well as directing substantially more corporate resources, to financial reporting processes, in as much as chief executive officers must now certify financial statements and internal control reports personally. Corporations have directed very large expenditures indeed to the new requirements for internal control over financial reporting, creating, as noted elsewhere in this volume, large amounts of work for corporate and public accountants alike.

The corporate governance structure is showing signs of being strengthened as reports of more independent board of directors actions come into public view. Boards of directors seem to be aware that they too must fulfill their fiduciary duties to corporation shareholders rather than just have allegiance to company management. Independent audit committees appear to be fulfilling their mandated roles in better fashion. The independence of company auditors, both internal and external, has been strengthened. Internal auditors in many corporations have gained new importance and increased responsibility, now reporting to higher corporate levels and frequently reporting to the audit committee of the board.

External auditor independence has been strengthened in several ways. The Sarbanes-Oxley Act prohibitions against non-audit services for audit clients have taken full effect. In many cases, corporations are going further than the requirements of the law by hiring the company's independent auditor only for audit work and for no other services. To aid auditor independence from management, it is now common practice to have the audit committee, instead of corporate management, hire the independent auditor. Further, in most corporations the independent auditor now commonly reports to the audit committee. Oversight of audit matters is maintained by the audit committee. *The Economist* reported in 2004 that the "checks-and-balances" in the financial system have been working better (*The Economist*, 2004b, 1).

Public accounting practitioners report that more exacting, stronger audit procedures have been placed in service by most audit firms in response to Public Company Accounting Oversight Board (PCAOB) oversight and inspections. Internal control has clearly been enhanced with work accomplished to meet Section 404 of the Sarbanes-Oxley Act. All of this speaks to the effectiveness with which accounting firms and their corporate clients have been able to deal with the many changes in their environments.

In 2001 and 2002, many inside and outside of the accounting profession thought that hard times were ahead for accountants and for accounting firms. The vast dimensions of accounting and auditing failures had become apparent to an unsuspecting public. Some were even asking if it were possible that the end was near for the profession. Just eight months after Arthur Andersen client Enron had filed for protection under U.S. bankruptcy laws on December 2, 2001, WorldCom, another Andersen client, filed the largest bankruptcy case in U.S. history on July 21, 2002, after disclosing accounting irregularities that had fraudulently inflated its assets by $11 billion.

The public outcry, first over Enron and then over WorldCom, coming after a long series of other accounting debacles, forced the hand of the U.S. Congress. The Sarbanes-Oxley Act of 2002, also known as the Public Company Accounting Reform and Investor Protection Act of 2002, was passed into law on July 30, 2002. This U.S. reform legislation, as discussed in earlier chapters, was closely followed by accounting reforms by governments around the world. Many questioned whether public accounting firms could ever again be effective in the face of these scandalous debacles, which had lost the long-held public confidence in accountants and had lost U.S. accountants' long-held professional self-regulation.

Accountants Adjust and Are in High Demand

As businesses, regulators, accounting firms, and the general public all adjusted to the new environment, they found that the economic functions performed by accountants were still very much in demand, albeit with new sets of governing rules. The Sarbanes-Oxley Act and related reform legislation around the world had, in fact, set the stage for greater effectiveness of the world's accounting professions and the public accounting firms, as well.

There was greatly increased need for accounting and auditing services from public corporations confronted with new requirements in governance, in internal control, and in financial reporting. Demand for public accounting for both attestation and non-attestation engagements has greatly increased in the years since 2002. Changes set in motion by new legal prohibitions and requirements, as it turns out, have economically benefited accounting firms of all sizes.

Large public corporations had previously been able to work exclusively with a single Big Five accounting firm for all audit and consulting needs around the world. In adjusting to the new legal requirements, large companies had to expand the number of firms hired. They were prohibited from using their auditors for a number of kinds of consulting engagements. Many used other Big Four firms. Many extended engagements into the second tier of firms and beyond, as appropriate to their needs.

The accounting firms, particularly the Big Four, adjusting to the new realities, began, among many other actions, to carefully examine their client lists. The firms, reportedly, used risk models to assess whether such factors as fee revenue generated, gross margins, liability potential, and the like were such that it was advantageous to continue engagements with the clients in question. Further, all audit firms had to divest newly prohibited non-audit engagements with their audit clients. These actions, begun shortly after passage of the Sarbanes-Oxley Act, continued in subsequent years.

Accountancy Age reported that in the first three quarters of 2004, Big Four firms shed 157 U.S. clients. This was three times the number in the prior year. Jim Quigley, CEO of Deloitte & Touche, stated in September 2004 that his firm was "turning down clients at an unprecedented rate" (*New York Times*, 2004).

At the same time, some clients had also been turning away from Big Four firms to use second-tier firms, in many cases because of the high costs associated with implementation of Sarbanes-Oxley Act requirements. Smaller firms claim to offer lower costs and better access to their firm's practitioners. In 2004, client lists decreased for each of the Big Four accounting firms. The client list of Deloitte & Touche, for example, reportedly declined by twenty-five clients in 2004 (Ibid.).

Even though shedding clients, the Big Four firms have more than held their own. In fact, accounting firms of all sizes continued to grow their revenues at a healthy pace throughout the 2001 to 2006 period. They did this by revising their business strategies to fit the new world environment. Recent actions by Sun Microsystems, Inc. may help explain the continuing growth and revised business strategy of the Big Four. In former times, prior to Sarbanes-Oxley requirements, Sun Microsystems used its auditor, Ernst & Young, for all manner of engagements ranging from audit to advice.

After Sarbanes-Oxley, the company found that it needed to increase the number of public accounting firms it engages to complete all of its work. Ernst & Young is still engaged to perform the Sun Microsystems financial statement audit, for which it must maintain independence. Now, however, PricewaterhouseCoopers has been engaged to perform Sun Microsystems internal audit functions. KPMG International has been engaged to test the company's financial controls. Deloitte Touche Tohmatsu prepares the company's tax returns. The Sun Microsystems policy, according to chief financial officer Stephen T. McGowan, is to have the auditor focus specifically on the audit and to engage other public accounting firms for all other work (Borrus and Byrnes, 2004, 1).

Sun Microsystems is but one example of many companies with this policy. Institutional Shareholder Services, which provides proxy advice, has indicated to shareholders that they should vote against retaining their company's audit firm if the auditor's fees for non-audit work are greater than their fees for the audit. Not surprisingly, the percentage of Standard & Poor's 500 stock index companies not meeting this test declined from 60 percent in 2002 to a mere 2 percent in 2004, a tremendous turnaround in the way companies view their auditors. Clearly they believe that the independence of the auditor is important to their cost of capital in today's environment (Ibid.).

Nicholas Moore, retired CEO of PricewaterhouseCoopers, believes that this conservative approach has put upward pressure on audit fees and is an overreaction to the new Sarbanes-Oxley requirements. He thinks that inefficiencies are created when corporations use multiple public accounting firms for services that a single firm could provide. In particular, the tax area is one in which auditors must have a full understanding. To say that the audit firm should not do the tax work for the audit client is wrong, Moore indicates. This does not make the audit firm or the client more productive and instead encumbers both with more costs (Krell, 2003). Such tax work is not on the list of taboo engagements set out by the Sarbanes-Oxley Act.

It is certainly true that the non-audit work must be accomplished even if the auditor cannot do it. For large corporations, much of this work requires large public accounting firms that have the wherewithal to handle large engagements. This means, in many cases, that the work will go to one or more of the remaining three big firms. There is no prohibition in the Sarbanes-Oxley Act against engaging other accounting firms for this work. Thus, revenue growth in the Big Four firms has been greatly aided by non-audit work for non-audit clients. It also seems that competition among the firms for non-audit work has been increasing.

Even though it is in the non-audit category, tax service by the auditor was not prohibited by Sarbanes-Oxley. The law gave boards of directors' audit committees the authority to decide whether auditors could perform non-audit work not explicitly prohibited by the act. Even though tax service is not prohibited, a number of companies, including General Electric, American Express, and Home Depot, are engaging non-auditor firms for tax services, it would seem, to avoid any possible conflicts of interest. The wisdom of this policy was bolstered when the PCAOB acted to restrict certain tax services by auditors in the wake of the admission by KPMG that it had committed fraud in the performance of some of its tax engagements.

This case, the largest criminal tax case of its kind, was filed against the firm of KPMG alleging fraud relating to the design, marketing, and implementation of tax shelters. In 2005, KPMG admitted that the firm had engaged in fraudulent filings of tax returns of at least $11 billion, which cost the U.S. treasury $2.5 billion in evaded taxes. As a result of the firm's pleading, criminal charges of tax fraud and conspiracy were filed against the allegedly responsible KPMG partners, including a KPMG former deputy chairman, two former heads of KPMG tax practice, two other former KPMG partners, as well as a former tax partner of a prominent New York national law firm (Internal Revenue Service, 2005, 1).

KPMG, the individual defendants, and coconspirators allegedly filed, from 1996 through 2003, false tax returns claiming phony tax losses for wealthy individuals who needed $10 million or more in tax losses to offset income upon which taxes would have been due and payable. KPMG was to be paid a percentage of the taxes not paid. KPMG admitted that firm personnel concealed the shelters from the IRS in a number of fraudulent ways. Top leadership of KPMG made decisions to approve and participate in these frauds, notwithstanding significant warnings from KPMG tax experts and others that the shelters were close to frivolous and could not stand up under IRS audit. Further, the warnings included the information that the representations that the wealthy individuals would be making on their tax returns were not credible (Ibid.).

As part of a plea bargain and related agreements with the U.S. Justice Department and the Internal Revenue Service, the prosecution of the firm was deferred until December 31, 2006. KPMG agreed to pay $456 million in fines, restitution, and penalties as well as agreeing to other specifications. If KPMG complies with all of the specifications, the deferred prosecution of the firm will be dismissed. Included, among a number of other requirements, are permanent restrictions on KPMG tax practice. KPMG is banned from involvement in any prepackaged tax products. It must adhere to high tax practice standards in the giving of tax advice and in preparation of tax returns, particularly for wealthy individuals. Acceptance of fees not based on hourly rates is restricted. The firm agreed to be monitored for a period of years (Ibid.).

The PCAOB ruling on tax services identified circumstances in which providing tax services would impair auditor independence. The board's restrictions curb selling tax services to audit clients, ban auditor promotion of aggressive tax shelters to audit clients, prohibit contingent fees based on percentages of client tax savings, and prohibit providing tax services to top company officers of audit clients. The new rules also implement procedures for auditor non-audit tax work to be preapproved by the corporation's audit committee. Auditors must seek approval of tax services by describing proposed tax service work in writing to the audit committee, discussing potential effects of the services on the client firm's independence, and documenting the substance of the discussions with the audit committee. Also included as part of the ethics ruling was a statement that individual accountants can be held responsible when their actions contribute to the firm's violation of applicable laws, rules, or professional standards (PCAOB, 2006b, 1).

Many corporations have been, it seems, well advised to have their tax services performed by other public accounting firms than their audit firm. Paul R. Brown, a member of the audit committee of Dassault Systemes, a French aerospace company, indicated, "When in doubt, I want to turn away from the audit firm for anything except auditing (Borrus and Byrnes, 2004). Much of this movement away from the audit firm for tax services has also been inspired by increased disclosures required for public accounting fees. The result of this change has meant greater competition in the market for corporate tax services, which has in turn resulted in lowering fees for this work.

Sun Microsystems, for example, had paid Ernst & Young $3.5 million a year for expatriate tax services. When it offered the work to the competition, Deloitte did the work for $3 million. According to Glass, Lewis & Co., a proxy research firm, the average fee paid by large U.S. companies for tax services fell 14 percent during 2003. Because of the new PCAOB rulings, Jonathan Hamilton, editor of *Public Accounting Report,* said that fees for tax services by public accountants could drop between 5 and 10 percent in 2005 (Ibid.).

Firms of All Sizes Gain

The competition for tax service engagements, as well as other non-audit work, extends to the second-tier public accounting firms and below. Tax work of various kinds can be effectively split up in parts so that more firms can bid for the engagements. Grant Thornton, for example, was hired to do the state and local tax work for RR Donnelley & Sons and Marriott International (Ibid.).

Second-tier firms have grown quite rapidly in the new environment. BDO Seidman, LLP, a U.S. national firm that provides the full range of assurance, tax, financial advisory, and consulting services, reported that revenues increased 27 percent in its fiscal year ended June 30, 2006. This increase came on top of a cumulative increase of 53 percent over the prior two years. The firm's revenues in 2006 totaled $558 million, with all business lines showing increases. Assurance services revenue, which was 62 percent of the firm's total business, increased by 28 percent in 2006. Tax revenue, which was 23 percent of the firm's business, increased by 10 percent. And, specialized services, which were 15 percent of the total revenues, increased 55 percent.

These are by any measure large gains. BDO Seidman reported that it continues to have unprecedented increases in its core assurance business. In the past three years, the firm's gain in Securities Exchange Commission (SEC) clients was larger than for any other accounting firm. There has been a marked increase in the firm's engagement revenue for initial public offerings caused by clients turning to the firm as an alternative to Big Four firms. Jack Weisbaum, CEO of BDO Seidman, explained that during the past year the firm achieved strong growth in both the tax business and specialized services business lines by adding client work from Big Four audit clients. The specialized services growth has come, in the past year, from increased demand for the firm's services in litigation support, fraud investigations, and business restructurings (Accountinweb, 2006d, 1).

Smaller firms, as well, grew substantially. Richard J. Caturano, chair of the PCPS Executive Committee, reported, "local and regional CPA [certified public accountant] firms are thriving in the current business environment (Smartpros, 2004b, 1). Ken Stephens, with the regional accounting firm Rothstein Kass in Roseland, New Jersey, indicated that his firm has had new opportunities to provide services in different capacities for mid-sized and smaller client firms (Wolosky, 2004, 1).

A national survey of regional and local CPA firms, the National Management of Accounting Practice (MAP) Survey, is jointly sponsored by the American Institute of Certified Public Accountant's (AICPA's) Private Companies Practice Section and the Texas Society of Certified Public Accountants. In the 2004 survey, U.S. local and regional firms reported expanding core services, revenue growth, and increasing salaries. Of the 2,373 regional and local firms surveyed, 32 percent had increased 2004 revenue by at least 10 percent, with 14 percent of surveyed firms experiencing revenue increases greater than 20 percent over prior year revenue (Smartpros, 2004b, 1).

Responding firms indicated that, as in the prior year, tax services, compilations, and write-up/data processing were the top three revenue-generating practice areas. Tax services were 48.5 percent of total firm revenues, 12.5 percent came from compilations, and 12 percent from write-up work and data processing. Average profits for the responding firms had increased slightly to 36.8 from 36 percent in the prior year. Average annual base salaries for firm employees increased 5.2 percent, with bonus remuneration averaging 5.3 percent of total salary (Ibid.).

About 16 percent of responding firms indicated that they would consider outsourcing individual tax returns while 75 percent would not. This would seem to indicate that, while such work could be done more cheaply by outsourcing perhaps to overseas preparers, the practitioners valued quality control more. By continuing to prepare tax returns in house, the firms could ensure that the quality of the work was up to firm standards.

Partners in public accounting firms were reported to be 75 percent male. In past years, female partners were rare indeed. So, this percentage is actually a major improvement on the part of the firms. In addition, the majority of nonpartner CPA staff among the reporting firms was female. These facts indicate the adjustments that the formerly all-male firms have made. Since the majority of staff is female, the accounting firms' progress in hiring and using female talent seems quite improved and improvements in this area seem most likely to continue.

While 13 percent of the reporting firms indicated that they would not go paperless in their operations, 20 percent of the firms reported that their operations were already paperless. An additional 41 percent would consider going to paperless operations. One-quarter of the firms had actual plans to go to paperless operations. This would seem to be indicative of the response the firms are making and have made to become more efficient in their operations. While paperless records bring potential problems of possible demands to produce significantly more quantities and more detailed records in court cases or other proceedings, the efficiencies and the effectiveness of using computers for recording and storage of firm documents, work papers, and the like seems to be winning out.

Working partnerships and alliances have been created by 55 percent of the responding firms (Ibid.). The trend to band together for mutual support seems to have grown substantially. This growing trend to form relationships with large groups of other public accounting firms indicates that the firms are responding to the new environment where they need greater support services, enlarged knowledge bases, improved worldwide connections to service clients in enlarged geographic spheres, and the like. Most of these affiliations are made by looser arrangements than selling or swapping equity, allowing firm ownership and control to remain intact. These alliances and working partner arrangements allow flexibility in future operations while retaining autonomy and separate ownership. Such factors are important to, and preferred by, a great many small- and medium-sized firms.

Smaller firms believed that their price advantage helps them in obtaining engagements previously held by larger firms, particularly as adjustment to new restrictions on non-audit work worked through the accounting services markets. Some predicted that audit fees would also increase. Ken McCrory, partner in the firm McCrory & McDowell, believed that corporations that are clients of the big name accounting firms needed to be prepared to pay higher audit fees. He thought that with profitable consulting services for audit clients off-limits, Big Four fees for audit services would have to rise.

His reasoning was that the audit had been used for some time as a loss leader to gain access to sell more profitable consulting services. McCrory anticipated that audits would be priced more fairly. McCrory's view reflected the feeling, expressed by others as well, that pricing audits as a loss leader is unfair competition. This certainly seemed to be quite plausible at the time and in fact did turn out to be the case (Winnick, 2002, 1).

Accounting Fees and Salaries Rising

Fees did rise rather substantially after 2002. The higher prices for audits are justified, many believe, because audits have become more thorough and therefore time consuming under the jurisdiction of the PCAOB. It seems that public expectations for better auditing are driving hours worked on a given audit to increase, thereby causing higher costs. According to Pennsylvania State University accounting professor Ed Ketz, higher audit fees may be worth the cost because "the public is going to demand that audited statements be more truthful" (Ibid.).

Neil Lebovits, president and chief operating officer (COO) of a financial services staffing unit of Adecco SA, a large employment company, indicates that there has been a dramatic increase in demand that resulted from Sarbanes-Oxley Act requirements. Grant Thornton, for example, increased its hiring 25 percent in 2005 over the prior year. Plans for 2006 call for another substantial increase. Lebovits thinks that a mild panic exists in the market for accountants (Chasan and Nag, 2005). Lebovits reported that one in five U.S. accountants have resigned their positions, further exacerbating the shortage. "There are a lot of disgruntled accountants out there who have been asked to do way too much with way too little resources," Lebovits said (Ibid.). In the past year, he believes that long hours on grueling assignments have caused many accountants to burn out and that this has been a major contributing factor to the shortage of accountants. Lebovits indicated that many of those who left accounting firms went into other types of consulting firms or into part-time work.

In the face of the shortage, some U.S. corporations have begun to rely on consulting firms that also do accounting work. Two such consulting firms were reported to have increased their profits by approximately 45 percent in the second quarter of 2005 (Ibid.).

Both public accounting and corporate accounting positions, it is certain, now require more experienced, talented people. Frank Fusaro, CPA and an accountant recruiter for Forum Personnel, Inc. in New York City, stated, "Audits conducted today require 50 percent more talent compared to three to four years ago" (Ibid.). The increasing demands for accounting services and accountants have caused salaries to rise. Over the past three years, the salary for a Big Four firm accountant with five years' experience increased by 30 percent. PricewaterhouseCoopers was reported to have paid $85,000 to $90,000 annually for accountants with five years' experience, when three years before the salary paid was $65,000. Salary.com, a Web site for tracking employment trends, indicated that recruiters offered 35 percent increases in annual salaries for both accounting graduates and experienced practitioners. New hires with three years' experience at other than the Big Four firms were being offered around $75,000 annual salaries compared to two years ago, when $55,000 was the level.

Accountants in Short Supply

The dearth of accounting graduates from U.S. colleges during this period in the face of the rapidly escalating demand has been an additional problem for employers. An AICPA survey of graduates showed the total number of accounting graduates to be 53,760 in 2004. This was down from 61,220 a decade before, in 1994, a 12 percent decline. College accounting enrollments have recently increased, apparently in response to the unmet demand and rising salaries, but an accounting degree may take up to five years, and certainly four years of college work. Recruiters are anticipating a long delay before there are sufficient accountants to meet market demand. Grant Thornton recruiter Tom Rogowski confirmed these trends, observing "Today we have to work much harder to recruit from schools" (Chasan and Nag, 2005). And, of course, the shortage is not just in public accounting. Auditors and accountants of all types have been in short supply and greater demand.

The rapid growth in the ranks of internal auditors since the passage of the Sarbanes-Oxley Act has continued unabated. Reflecting this, the Institute of Internal Auditors experienced unprecedented growth, with members now standing at over 115,000 worldwide. Membership grew by 15.4 percent in 2005. In 1995, membership totaled 53,000. By 2000, membership in the institute had grown at a healthy pace to 71,000 (Institute of Internal Auditors, 2006, 1). Candidates sitting for the institute-certified internal auditor examination increased to 38,000 in 2006, up from 30,634 in the prior year. Internal auditors have been elevated in the corporate business environment since the Sarbanes-Oxley Act passed. Internal auditors now frequently report directly or with direct access to the board of directors or the CEO. The internal audit position has always been one from which people could move to important jobs in corporations. The Sarbanes-Oxley effect has made it even more of a respected position and a launching pad for enhanced careers in other parts of corporations (Accountingweb, 2006b, 1).

Sarbanes-Oxley Section 404 Is Controversial

Much of the increasing demand for accountants and auditors has certainly come from implementation of Section 404 of the Sarbanes-Oxley Act. In 2005, approximately 3,700 large-capitalization companies, those with $75 million or more, implemented Section 404 procedures and underwent internal control audits. Companies with market capitalization under $75 million are scheduled to begin internal control examinations by public accountants for fiscal years ending after July 15, 2007. In a report from AMR Research, total accumulated compliance costs for Sarbanes-Oxley up to the end of 2006 were estimated to be $20 billion. A *Wall Street Journal* article indicated that the feelings of many businesses toward the act were: "Expensive, onerous and unnecessary—those are a few of the complaints U.S. publicly traded companies have leveled at the Sarbanes-Oxley Act, designed to keep companies honest" (Badal and Dvorak, 2006, B3).

One recent survey of corporate chief financial officers (CEOs) indicated that 56 percent believed that, as a result of Section 404, investors do have more confidence in the reliability and accuracy of corporate financial reports. Nevertheless, eight of ten respondents did not think that the increased confidence was worth the cost, in particular because their companies had not seen reductions in cost of capital. Another more recent survey found that seven of ten public company financial executives do believe that their organizations have had some benefit from the Section 404 implementation. Ninety-three percent of these executives cited business-process improvements for their companies (O'Sullivan, 2006, 1).

Yet, many of these financial executives, as well, did not believe that improvements in business processes were worth the cost. Decreases in cost of capital, which a few executives indicated had occurred for their firms, would be needed to justify the expenditures. This was a view generally held by responding company officials. For example, in the view of Sharon Tetlow, from biotechnology company Cell Genesys, the costs of compliance with Section 404 were misspent and "are large enough that they affect our ability to conduct business" (Ibid.). This is money that, she believes, should have been spent on clinical trials. Proposals for changes to the Sarbanes-Oxley Act were put forward, in particular for exemption of smaller companies and foreign registrants from the Section 404 requirements because of the comparatively higher costs for those entities (Ibid.). The official response thus far has been the SEC delay of Section 404 implementation for smaller companies and for foreign companies listed on U.S. stock exchanges.

Many corporate finance managers projected that the high costs of Section 404 compliance would decrease after the first year. A study by the Financial Executives International organization indicated that costs in 2005 were expected to decline over 2004 costs by 39 percent for non-audit fees and 26 percent for audit fees. Actual decline was found to be 34.5 percent for non-audit fees and 13 percent for audit fees (Ibid.).

In 2005, out of 3,900 reporting companies, fully 1,500 indicated that their companies had internal control material weaknesses. A further 16 percent of the respondents indicated that their operations had internal control weaknesses but the problems did not rise to the level of a material weakness (Ibid.). Improvements in corporate internal control were clearly overdue, judging from this large number of firms reporting problems with their internal control systems. Improvements in internal control should certainly lead to lower problems with financial reporting in the future and can be expected to help restore public confidence in financial reporting.

KPMG reported that a survey of corporate board of directors members disclosed that 74 percent were not surprised by the number of internal-control weaknesses identified by the Section 404 work. Sixteen percent of the companies had disclosed internal control weaknesses during the second year of Section 404 implementations (Ibid.), indicating that they had not been able to clear up their internal control problems even though they were in the second year of the required evaluations.

Proponents of the Section 404 internal control strengthening point out that the purpose of the requirements is to restore faith in financial reporting. California Public Employees' Retirement System (CALPERS) investment officer Christy Wood pointed out that the Section 404 costs were necessary for ensuring the integrity of financial reports. When considering the need to have true and fair financial reports, she asked, "How much is too much?" (Ibid.).

A major problem with measuring the benefits of internal control is that the causes of changes in cost of capital are difficult to measure. Ryan LaFond, from MIT's Sloan School of Management, studied the effects of company announcement of internal control deficiencies on the cost of capital. His study disclosed that the median cost of capital increased by 1 percent for corporations that made internal control problem announcements versus those that did not make such announcements. When the companies addressed the internal control deficiencies and received a clear auditor's report, the costs of capital decreased by a median of 1.3 percent, the study report disclosed. For companies that receive unqualified opinions on their internal controls, the decrease in cost of capital was reported as 0.58 percent. Professor LaFond points out that if a company is a good firm and the market already values the good internal controls of the company, benefits of Section 404 as measured by lowered cost of capital would be limited. LeFond indicated that he was comfortable with saying that economically meaningful benefits accrue from the Section 404 implementations. But, he cannot say whether these benefits are greater than the costs or not (Ibid.).

Mark Haskins, a professor of business administration at the University of Virginia's Darden Graduate School of Business Administration, indicated that markets appear to be valuing the discovery and correction of material internal control weaknesses. He pointed out, "There may be a positive response to the fact that the company found the weakness" (Ibid.).

The securities markets of the United States, as discussed elsewhere in this volume, are the most regulated in the world for the protection of investors. The Sarbanes-Oxley requirements have added additional regulations. Some foreign companies avoid the U.S. market because of these regulations. Nasdaq CFO David Warren points out that the benefits of raising capital in the United States outweigh the costs of additional regulation compliance. Ohio State University professor Andrew Karolyi, after studying the problem area, said that valuation of foreign company securities listed in the U.S. markets is 30 percent higher than securities listed only in the home country securities markets. And, the valuation premium increased for companies from countries with fewer legal protections for minority shareholders and less-developed financial markets (Ibid.).

Professor Karolyi adds that the premium is for the entire monitoring system in U.S. capital markets in total and not just regulation. He sees the valuation premium as arising from the securities laws and the integrity they bring to the U.S. markets. If these laws are diluted, the premium may decline and disappear. Movements to soften the provisions of the SEC laws and the Sarbanes-Oxley Act for foreign companies or small businesses may lead to such dilution of U.S. market benefits (Ibid.).

Christy Wood, CALPERS investment officer, views U.S. regulation costs as the toll for using U.S. markets. The requirements are guarantees for the public to invest their life savings and retirement funds in securities markets, she believes. Further, it is the toll to receive the valuation premium present in the U.S. markets. If companies want to list their securities on foreign securities markets because of the less-stringent regulation, in Wood's view, the investor in the foreign market will be taking a greater risk, which the U.S. investor does not want to take. She believes that U.S. regulators should not seek to retain U.S. stock market listings for such companies. Woods also suggested that the private markets for funds are better suited for those firms that say that the Sarbanes-Oxley costs threaten their ability to carry on their core businesses (Ibid.).

Private Companies Adopt Sarbanes-Oxley Procedures

The private company market does continue to be an important service area for public accounting firms, even as they deal with the many changes in the public company sector. PricewaterhouseCoopers, for example, instituted in July 2006 an industry sector for private company services. This is a dedicated group of the firm's practitioners who offer the full range of audit, tax compliance, and planning and business advisory services to private companies and their owners. The group indicates that it offers services throughout the business life cycle, which are aimed at aiding clients in improving cash flow and increasing wealth accumulation (PricewaterhouseCoopers, 2006b, 1).

James Mattie, PricewaterhouseCoopers partner in the new industry group, indicates that, even though they are not required by law to do so, about one-fourth of his private company clients are in the process of adopting parts of the Sarbanes-Oxley requirements. And, other private companies are seeking advice on appropriate parts of Sarbanes-Oxley that should be adopted.

Mattie believes that many measures within the Sarbanes-Oxley Act have potential benefits for private companies as well as for public companies. The private company must determine which parts of Sarbanes-Oxley will provide benefits that exceed the costs and whether the practices fit company strategies, objectives, and goals. Mattie points out that many private companies can improve critical areas of their company's operations by following Sarbanes-Oxley selectively (SmartPros, 2005, 1).

A number of the companies that are privately owned now do seem to be selectively adopting at least parts of the Sarbanes-Oxley requirements. An article in the *Wall Street Journal* authored by Jaclyne Badal and Phred Dvorak agrees with Mattie's observations, reporting that the voluntary adoption of some Sarbanes-Oxley requirements is increasing among private-sector companies. There appear to be a variety of reasons for private company use of the public company requirements. A number of private-sector firms see the requirements as beneficial, thinking that their businesses will be more efficient and effective by adoption of selected requirements. Some of these firms expect to go public in the near future. Others expect to buy out and merge with public companies, and they seek system compatibility. Pressure from lenders, customers, and government agencies, who view the requirements as beneficial, convince some of the voluntary adopters (Badal and Dvorak, 2006, B3).

CFO Joe Gaynor of Goss International, a printing-press manufacturer, indicated that his company had adopted Sarbanes-Oxley internal control requirements to standardize procedures and policies across its eight business units. The units had operated independently of one another and followed varying procedures. Internal control over human resources was of concern among the units, for example, ensuring that employees received proper pay only for hours actually worked.

The primary shareholder of Goss International, MatlinPatterson Global Advisers LLC, had just taken another company under their control public. During that process, complying with Sarbanes-Oxley requirements had to be rushed to completion. Although there were no immediate plans for Goss to go public, MatlinPatterson encouraged the company to comply with Sarbanes-Oxley internal control provisions designed to reduce errors and prevent fraud. Goss reviewed internal controls, improved the computer and software technology, and strengthened its audit committee, making meetings more regular. By the end of 2007, Gaynor plans to have a Big Four firm review the actions taken. He believes that internal control aids companies in following approved company policies. Such internal control items may be simple as, when buying a big-ticket item, requiring a purchase order, or as complex as a detailed inventory processing system (Ibid.).

PricewaterhouseCoopers' James Mattie indicated that some private companies that adopt Sarbanes-Oxley requirements need to demonstrate strong internal controls when they do business with government agencies. He cites the example of a client that provided government consulting services. The government agency, in an effort to ensure that it was not being overcharged, sought to review the client's billing control procedures. Other private companies face pressure from customers or suppliers that are public companies. The public companies must now demonstrate compliance, and this sometimes extends to the network of companies with which they do business (Ibid.).

Another incentive to adopt Sarbanes-Oxley internal control requirements is that raising money can be done at lower costs. Ryan LaFond of MIT's Sloan School of Management believes that good internal controls in private companies should work in the same way as good internal controls in public companies. In his study, he tracked 221 public companies that had reported internal control weaknesses and subsequently corrected the controls and received an auditor's clean opinion. He found that the company's costs to borrow were lower after correction of the internal control problems. While these were public companies, LaFond believes that it would hold true for private companies as well. Mike Loughlin, chief credit officer at Wells Fargo & Co., said that his company routinely factors in internal control when making loan approval decisions. Potential customers are asked about their internal controls and corporate-governance practices, even though Sarbanes-Oxley compliance is not required (Ibid.).

The CFO of Financial Engines, Inc, an investment adviser and portfolio manager with $5 billion under management, Ray Sims, said that his firm, while not hiring an audit firm to independently report on internal controls, needs to maintain controls similar to Sarbanes-Oxley, which are used as a guide. Financial Engines' board has both an audit committee and a compensation committee independent of management. Sims indicates that lenders and institutional investors want to be able to audit controls and ensure that information systems are up-to-date (Ibid.).

PricewaterhouseCoopers' Trendsetter Barometer, which is a quarterly survey taken since 1991 to gauge opinion and innovation in the fastest-growing American companies, interviewed the CEOs of 341 private service and product companies identified as among the fastest-growing U.S. businesses in 2005. The companies had revenue or sales of between $5 million and $150 million. Three out of ten of these companies are looking to benefit from provisions of the Sarbanes-Oxley Act. The CEOs of the private companies that are voluntarily adopting Sarbanes-Oxley requirements see such adoptions as best business practices with the purpose of heading off future problems, not necessarily to solve current problems (SmartPros, 2005, 1).

Seventeen percent of the interviewed companies have been impacted by the Sarbanes-Oxley Act over the past one to two years, and a further 13 percent believe their businesses will be impacted within the near future. Of companies with a current Sarbanes-Oxley–related project, 26 percent expect that benefits will exceed costs. Twenty-two percent expect to break even, and 43 percent believe that costs will be greater than benefits received. Sixty-four percent of companies with an existing Sarbanes-Oxley project indicate that they are improving company control documentation and testing. Fifty-three percent are updating governance procedures, while 50 percent are strengthening their code of conduct or code of ethics.

The companies that were currently adopting Sarbanes-Oxley initiatives tended to be larger, with average revenues of $46.2 million versus $28.8 million for non-adopters. The adopters were faster growing, increasing revenues by 387 percent over the past five years, as opposed to 303 percent for the non-adopters. Among industries surveyed, technology companies were more likely to have a Sarbanes-Oxley project. Twenty-two percent of interviewed technology companies were adopters versus 12 percent for nontechnology company adopters (Ibid.).

In viewing their growth and competitive adjustments in the markets for non-audit services, one must agree that public accounting firms have proven quite successful and effective in adjusting their business models and menus of services to the new demands of the Sarbanes-Oxley Act. In fact, the firms have facilitated the spread of the advantages offered by newly required practices and procedures for public companies to private clients that are not required to adopt them.

Accountants Favor Sarbanes-Oxley and PCAOB

A survey by Nancy T. Hill, John E. McEnroe, and Kevin T. Stevens, accounting professors at DePaul University, was taken among CPAs from small, medium, and large accounting firms in 2005 to study accountants' opinions of some key provisions of the Sarbanes-Oxley Act (Hill, McEnroe, and Stevens, 2005). Responses totaled 336 of 1,200 questionnaires mailed. The CPAs indicated by 73 percent to 18 percent that an independent third party, such as the PCAOB, should conduct investigations and disciplinary proceedings of auditors. A majority of responding CPAs were in agreement with having PCAOB set standards for independence by 69 percent indicating yes to 23 percent indicating no; having PCAOB set standards for ethics by 66 percent yes to 25 percent no; and having PCAOB set standards for quality control by 54 percent yes to 32 percent no. CPAs from large firms were stronger in support of PCAOB setting standards, with 85 percent in support of PCAOB setting independence standards, 83 percent in support of PCAOB setting ethics standards, and 74 percent in support of PCAOB setting quality control standards (Ibid.).

Responses became negative, however, when the questions were the following: Should the PCAOB set auditing standards?, with 56 percent no and 36 percent yes, and Should the PCAOB set accounting standards?, with 61 percent no and 31 percent yes. Comments from respondents indicated a general opinion that the accounting and auditing scandals were not caused by a lack in the accounting and auditing standards but because there was failure to properly monitor accounting and auditing performance in accordance with the standards. Respondents also believed that vigorous punishments of unethical behavior were lacking (Ibid.).

Responses were even more negative for questions about membership composition of the PCAOB. When asked whether the respondent agreed that a maximum of two of five PCAOB members should be CPAs, 72 percent responded no and 16 percent yes. To the question of whether the PCAOB chair, if a CPA, should not have practiced for at least five years prior to appointment as chair, 72 percent responded no and 15 percent yes.

Respondents' objections to PCAOB membership being made up primarily of non-CPAs were reported by the authors as the primary reason for the negative responses. Of those respondents who disagreed with the limit of two CPAs serving on the PCAOB, 23 percent recommended the board be entirely comprised of CPAs, 17 percent recommended that it include four CPAs, and 60 percent recommended three CPAs. And, over 80 percent of respondents said that a break of no more than one or two years from practice as a CPA was sufficient for the PCAOB chair (Ibid.).

A number of comments from the CPA respondents indicated preference for CPAs rather than lawyers on the PCAOB. One CPA's opinion, which is likely to be shared by many other CPAs, was: "Can you imagine an oversight board created for the legal profession comprised of a majority of nonlawyers?" (Ibid.). The CPAs thought that nonpracticing CPAs were unlikely to fully understand the problems and scope of the work accountants and auditors perform. With too few CPAs on the PCAOB, respondents felt that there was no assurance that members of the board understand the issues involved. Further, they did not like the implication "that CPAs in practice cannot be trusted" (Ibid.).

The CPA respondents were in agreement that improved audit record-keeping was beneficial. The Sarbanes-Oxley requirement to maintain audit work papers for seven years was agreed with by 86 percent of the CPAs. Only 50 percent of them, however, thought that internal control testing results and findings should be disclosed publicly (Ibid.).

As to the Sarbanes-Oxley prohibitions of specified non-audit services to audit clients, the survey report showed that more than a majority of respondents agreed with the prohibition of four of the eight non-audit services to audit clients. Eighty percent agreed that, for audit clients, broker-dealer, investment adviser, and investment banking services should not be allowed. The prohibition of internal auditing services for audit clients was thought proper by 69 percent of respondents. The banning of appraisal or valuation services for audit clients was seen as prudent by 59 percent. Sixty-three percent indicated agreement with the prohibition of bookkeeping or related services for audit clients. Of the remaining four prohibited services, approximately half of respondents agreed with the prohibitions for human resource services, legal or expert witness services, actuarial services, or financial information system design and implementation services (Ibid.).

Opinions about the prohibition of some non-audit services varied between CPAs from large versus those from smaller accounting firms. The large-firm CPAs indicated by 96 percent that bookkeeping and related services should be banned for audit clients, while only 53 percent of CPAs from smaller firms agreed with the ban. The prohibition of financial information system design and implementation was agreed with by 64 percent of the CPAs from large firms, while only 44 percent of CPAs from smaller firms agreed with banning this area of engagements with audit clients (Ibid.).

This survey indicates that the overwhelming majority of CPAs think that the Sarbanes-Oxley provision for an independent board, such as the PCAOB, is needed. They are of the opinion that the scandals and frauds were caused by lack of monitoring of standards and a lack of appropriate punishment for those who violated ethical and independence standards. They agree with the PCAOB setting and monitoring standards for ethics, independence, and quality control. But, the CPAs do not agree that the PCAOB should set the standards for accounting or for auditing. This opposition, the survey report indicates, is because of the lack of CPA representation on the PCAOB (Ibid.).

The SEC Assesses Public Accounting and Looks to the Future

The PCAOB has been moving ahead in its U.S. regulatory role for auditors of public companies with what appears to be full cooperation from public accounting firms and the AICPA. The AICPA has continued its role in self-regulation of private company service areas. The SEC, PCAOB, and AICPA have been working hand in hand with the accounting firms. Indicative of this close cooperation, an annual conference is sponsored by the AICPA concerning SEC developments. The AICPA asserts that this is its biggest conference of the year and always sells out (AICPA, 2006b).

At the December 2004 conference, over 2,000 attended from accounting firms, private industry, and government. Speakers were from the SEC, PCAOB, AICPA, Financial Accounting Standards Board (FASB), and International Accounting Standards Board (IASB) (Victor and Levitin, 2005, 1). Harvey Goldschmid, SEC commissioner, said that he was satisfied with the progress made since Congress passed the Sarbanes-Oxley Act. He believes that, over time, the benefits of the act's implementation and compliance will outweigh its costs. He noted that disclosures made in financial statements have improved significantly since CEOs and CFOs are required to certify the statements (Ibid.).

Charles D. Niemeier, PCAOB member, praised the accountants for responding to the calls for change. The accounting profession, in his view, looked at past accounting scandal involvements and agreed that there was a need for change. The profession has faced up to past shortcomings and has learned from them. Accountants have, in Niemeier's view, begun a new period in which the minimum compliance approach to reporting is replaced with best practices. He believes that accountants will promote best practices and no longer permit incorrect financial reporting just because a substantial client is involved or because the method is not prohibited in the rules or the area in question is not a high priority of the SEC. Donald Nicolaisen, SEC chief accountant, said that the accounting profession appeared to have turned the corner but had much remaining work to do, noting continued problems of business ethics and disclosures to shareholders (Ibid.).

PCAOB director of registration and inspections George Diacont disclosed that PCAOB inspectors in 2003 and 2004 were particularly concerned to examine the following areas of registered public accounting firm operations: tone at the top of the firm; partner evaluations, compensation, and promotion; independence of the firm from clients; client acceptance and retention policies; internal firm inspection programs; internal quality control review deficiency responses and corrections; communication within the firm of firm procedures and policies; and assessment of the work of foreign affiliates. Diacont indicated that the deficiencies found that were most pervasive among firms were a failure to document significant audit and accounting issues and to document audit evidence properly, in particular evidence for contingencies, accruals, and deferred tax assets (Ibid.).

At the 2005 AICPA National Conference on Current SEC and PCAOB Developments in Washington, DC, on December 5–7, 2005, the earlier reports on PCAOB inspections issued to the Big Four accounting firms in 2004 were said to contain "significant accounting and audit issues" that needed to be addressed by the firms in question within twelve months of report issuance (Accountingweb, 2006e, 1). In March 2006, the PCAOB was reported by Market Watch to believe that the firms had made progress addressing issues raised. Bill Gradison, acting chairman of PCAOB at the time, indicated that the board's initial experiences with the inspection process had generally validated the premise of the approach included in the Sarbanes-Oxley Act. The board believed that the large firms had been responsive by undertaking processes and steps, which, if carried out, will benefit audit quality (Ibid.).

In his address to the 2005 AICPA conference, Christopher Cox, chairman of the SEC, noted that the membership growth of the accountancy profession from a few hundred members to over a third of a million in 2005 reflects the rise of America as a great industrial power. He commended the profession for having a solid reputation among the public and business decision makers, which, he asserted, is a testament to accountants' professional competence and integrity. He noted that accountants received a favorable rating of 95 percent from business executives, while investors gave them a favorable rating of 97 percent. Cox cautioned that these very high favorable ratings do not mean that complacency is in order. He said that accountants must be vigilant in protecting their reputation and their future (Cox, 2005, 1).

According to Cox, the SEC, together with the PCAOB and FASB, has embarked on a major national effort to make the financial reporting system more clear, straightforward, and transparent. He feels that accounting needs to be less complex. Rules and their applications for the entire process from audits to financial reports need to be understandable by the using publics. Cox stressed that the SEC needs the help of the accounting profession and the AICPA in this effort. The importance of this effort has been made extremely clear by "the accounting scandals that our nation and the world have now mostly weathered" (Ibid.). These scandals were in part made possible by the overwhelming complexity of the standards, rules, and procedures that needed to be applied by accounting practitioners and auditors. Fraud and other criminal conduct were hidden in these complexities with attendant details. The rules were so complex that they became a sword to use against investors instead of a protective shield.

The complexities of accounting rules were built up over time. Cox believes that the U.S. financial system is shaped by the accumulation of pressures from different constituency preferences. This is one of the strengths of the system, being able to respond to changing economic and market conditions. Modern financial transactions have often called for complex detailed standards and regulatory requirements. The accretion of details responding to user needs has led to today's extreme complexity. The usefulness of financial reports and the systems that produce them have been damaged by the complexity and convolutions (Ibid.).

According to Cox, a number of efforts are under way to improve the situation. For example, the FASB has begun a reassessment of major areas where specific accounting standards have not provided transparent information for users. Another project has begun to codify all existing authoritative generally accepted accounting literature into a single source for users. The FASB has been taking measures to reduce the proliferation of new pronouncements from multiple sources (Ibid.). Accountants will be needed in all of these simplification efforts.

Progress is needed, Cox believes, on other problem areas as well, where accountants are in the forefront. More choice in the auditing of large corporations is needed, along with more competition in that market. Further development and implementation are needed for computerized systems to make financial information interactive for the benefit of investors and other users. In sum, Cox told the accountants, "The truth is, in the 21st century as much as the 19th; our nation desperately needs you" (Ibid.).

10

The Firms and the Practical
Issues of Adjustment
in the Global Economy

Accounting firms and the accounting profession have been responding to change in a positive fashion. They have adjusted their operations into conformity with new requirements of the post–Enron-Andersen environment, and at the same time pursued the many opportunities that presented themselves to advance their businesses. Growth described in the previous chapter has propelled the firms to new revenue heights. Accountants have regained much of the public confidence lost, albeit with wary acceptance by the investing public. As is generally the case at any time in history, very significant challenges remain ahead. For the accounting profession, these challenges are in both national and international settings. Many of the challenges have been discussed as this volume has progressed.

For some challenges, there are promising solutions; others remain more intractable. The conflict-of-interest problems that public accountants had with audit clients seem to be abating as responsibility for external audit is shifted away from corporate managements. The Sarbanes-Oxley–endorsed approach of having corporate independent audit committees hire and supervise independent auditors, in place of corporate management, seems to be taking hold. Audit committees seem to be making progress in accepting their responsibilities in other ways, as well.

Auditors have adjusted to the prohibition against non-audit engagements for audit clients. This has opened up competition for many types of service engagements. Internal control weaknesses within corporation operations have been addressed in large corporations and seem to be on the way to improvement in most large public corporations. Corporate managements have been brought front and center into the public financial reporting process by their need to sign off on financial statements and internal control reports. However, there remain some intractable problems facing the accounting profession around the world that are likely to continue for some time to come.

Our analysis and discussions of public accounting firms and the public accounting profession will conclude with four of these problems, which we see as being of primary importance: concentration of the market for large corporation audits in a few large auditing firms, increasing numbers of restatements of prior year financial statements, continuing growth in accounting and auditor litigation liability, and an ineffective peer-review system in the private-engagement sector of public accounting.

Concentration of the Market for Large Company Audits

In the area of market concentration, little headway seems to have been made. If anything, the situation may have darkened. Solutions are not apparent. Nearly all of the world's largest corporations rely upon the Big Four public accounting firms for their audits. As noted elsewhere, about 97 percent of U.S. public companies with revenue over $250 million annually are audited by Big Four firms. In Japan, for example, the concentration is 80 percent of public companies. In Canada, fully two-thirds of public companies employ Big Four firms for required annual auditing. In the European market, the firms collect in excess of 70 percent of large corporate audit fee income. All of the largest 100 British companies are Big Four audit clients (*The Economist,* 2004a, 1).

Before 1970, there was little thought of problems of market concentration. Audits were voluntary in the United States before 1933. Upon passage of the Securities Act of 1933 and the Securities Exchange Act of 1934, as discussed elsewhere in this volume, audited financial statements were required by public corporations for the first time. The Federal Trade Commission in the 1970s required the accounting profession to change its rules for competition and related matters. Strong competition ensued among public accounting firms, frequently based on price competition. The audit fees set in the audit services markets seemed to cause the public accounting firms to move more into consulting engagements, which were more lucrative. As their corporate clients grew larger and more complex with operations on a global scale, the accounting firms consolidated into eight firms that dominated the market for large company audits. The number of firms in the market decreased to five by 1998 and, with the fall of Andersen, to four in 2002.

This tight oligopoly in public accounting services for the largest companies has caused concerns that competition has been stifled. Because client corporations have few alternatives, costs for accounting services may be higher and quality of auditing and other services lower. A continuing concern is that one of the Big Four will fail and the oligopoly would go to only three public accounting firms capable of worldwide large company audits. In some industries, the market situation is even tighter. For example, the *Public Accounting Report* indicated that 97.3 percent of companies in the oil and gas industry are audited by three of the Big Four. Two of the Big Four accounting firms service 88.2 percent of the casino industry. *The Economist* reported that other industries, such as air transportation and coal, have similar concentrations (*The Economist,* 2004a).

Paul Danos, dean of Dartmouth College's Tuck Business School, believes, "These are shaky foundations for financial markets" (Ibid.). In fact, some observers believe that financial markets could suffer great damage to their operations from failure of one of these firms. Cono Fusco, Grant Thornton partner, holds the view that a Big Four firm collapse "could cause paralysis in financial markets" (Ibid.). This is particularly a threat if such a failure occurred close to the deadlines for annual financial statements to be filed. The fact that 1,300 or so corporations had to find new auditors when Andersen collapsed adds credibility to Fusco's opinion.

The General Accounting Office report to Congress in 2003, fortunately, did not find that Big Four firms were colluding or that audit quality had declined. Nevertheless, the general view remains that an accounting services market for large corporations that had only three big firms would not be favorable for economic growth. Regulators, as discussed elsewhere, appear to have been constrained by these facts in assessing penalties for certified public accountant (CPA) firm infractions. KPMG paid a heavy fine plus penalties and agreed to constraints on the firm's business practices for its fraudulent tax service acts (Mumma and Donmoyer, 2005, 1). In the Ernst & Young conflict-of-interest case with PeopleSoft, a six-month ban on new business was levied. Jim Cox of Duke University believes, "The reality is that the Big Four is very likely too big to fail. Regulators know this—and that is a huge moral hazard" (*The Economist,* 2004a).

The reduction of concentration in the market for large company audits clearly remains a practical issue in the global economy, but successful adjustment seems problematic. *The Economist* asked, "Can anything be done to shore up the audit profession's latent instability?" (Ibid.). It would seem that the market should correct itself in due course. The American Enterprise Institute's Peter Wallison indicates that new entrants can be expected to emerge "where profits are to be made" (Ibid.).

Barriers to entry into the market for audits of large corporations, however, are very high. A huge international network of public accounting firms must be built. Capital is difficult to obtain for public accounting firms, particularly since in many countries audit firms may only be formed as partnerships. With the existing regulatory environment, the costs of performing public company audits have risen considerably. Moreover, audit clients believe that their cost of capital is lower when a Big Four auditor is engaged to add credibility to financial statements.

The second-tier firms, by their own assessment, do not have the capacity for worldwide corporate auditing engagements. The General Accounting Office (GAO) report agreed with that assessment, indicating that even if the five largest firms after the Big Four were to merge, such a firm would not be able to compete on the same scale (Ibid.). Nor do the second-tier firms desire to take on the task, given that their profitability is already high by providing services to medium-sized corporate clients. BDO Seidman, for example, has 100 audit clients that are in the Fortune 500 companies list, although all are ranked below the Fortune 100 companies. Grant Thornton indicates that it has audit clients that rank as high as the bottom of the Fortune 250 companies list.

Some have suggested that government action may be needed to force the Big Four to become the Big Six or Eight. Others suggest that rotation of audit firms be made mandatory, that non-audit service limitations be made steeper, or that caps be placed on Big Four firm audits of middle-market-sized corporations. These actions, it is claimed, would assist the second-tier firms to develop areas of expertise in which they could compete with Big Four firms (Ibid.). Such government actions would restrict corporate choice further and are not looked upon with favor by many second-tier firms. Some observers think that, in the event of failure of an existing Big Four firm, a system of government auditing for corporations might be installed, with attendant decline in financial market performance over the long term. In fact, some observers believe that the current state of regulation already appears to be moving into a more heavily regulated or nationalized audit industry (Ibid.).

Worldwide alliances of mid-sized public accounting firms have been growing, as discussed elsewhere in this volume. The alliances consist of large networks of accounting firms that act to benefit members and clients by giving their consortium world-spanning reach as well as increasing resource pools. Some see these alliances as a step in the direction of entry to the market for audit of large corporations. Baker Tilly International, for example, has 125 allied firms worldwide. Together with three other networks—Moores Rowland North America, Leading Edge Alliance, and Moore Stephens North America—these alliance members include approximately two-thirds of the top 100 U.S. accounting firms.

A group of twenty-two mid-sized accounting firms that will market itself as one firm, named Baker Tilly USA, opened for business in mid-October 2006 with the intention of drawing business from the Big Four. On the occasion of Baker Tilly USA opening for business, Geoff Barnes, Baker Tilly International chief executive, declared, "We're coming at a time when the business market is crying out for alternatives to the Big Four, and we believe our structure can fill that void" (Hart, 2006, 1). The new alliance firm indicates that it will offer tax, audit, and consulting work to "capture more of the accounting market" (Ibid.). Moreover, the other three large alliances were reported to be planning similar moves into the market as alternatives to the Big Four in the near future.

Baker Tilly, with a total of approximately 8,000 practitioners in 93 offices, could have some amount of difficulty competing with the larger firms in their main arena, it would seem. Ernst & Young, for example, has about 26,000 practitioners in 140 offices, while PricewaterhouseCoopers consists of 30,000 practitioners in 140 offices (Ibid.). The new organization may find it easier to compete with second-tier public accounting firms. It remains to be seen whether the alliance movement will become a path for creation of competitors for the audit of large, world-spanning corporations.

Restatements on the Rise

The reputation of public accounting firms has improved considerably, but increased volume of prior-year financial statement restatements carries significant negative effects on companies, investors, and auditors. Improvement in financial statement preparation and auditing is an important problem that both corporations and their auditors must address. In 2002, the U.S. General Accounting Office reported that, from 1997 to June 2002, restatements caused by accounting irregularities grew approximately 145 percent, and that number was expected to rise to 170 percent by the end of

2002. The number of restatements rose from 92 in 1997 to 225 in 2001. The percentage of firms listed on U.S. stock exchanges that restated their financial reports in 1997 was 0.89 percent, which grew to 2.5 percent in 2002, and was expected to grow to 3 percent in 2002. During the period from January 1997 to June 2002, approximately 10 percent of listed U.S. companies had announced at least one restatement (U.S. GAO, 2002, 4). This is a rather remarkable number, given the costs that were expended to prepare and audit the statements in the first place.

The effects of these restatements were not trivial. Of the 689 companies that restated between January 1997 and March 2002, market capitalization of an estimated $100 billion was lost in trading days close to the restatement announcement. Of the companies analyzed by the GAO, stock prices fell almost 10 percent on average from the trading day before to the trading day after the restatement announcement. Further, the average market capitalization of corporations restating increased from $500 million in 1997 to $2 billion in 2002, indicating that larger companies were restating their financial results in 2002.

The GAO study reported that restatements were instigated by company auditors, the Securities Exchange Commission (SEC), or the company itself. Reasons for restatement were many. Examples cited were to address securities-related issues or to adjust revenue, costs, or expenses. Thirty-eight percent of announced restatements between January 1997 and June 2002 involved revenue recognition, either misreported or not reported. Revenue recognition problems were the leading cause of restatements in each year studied and were responsible for over 50 percent of immediate stock market losses. Further, the GAO reported that, although measurement was more difficult for longer-term losses, there was evidence that longer-term losses, that is, for sixty trading days before and after the restatement announcements, had an even greater negative stock price impact (Ibid.).

Restatements since 2002 have become even more of a problem, according to a study conducted by Glass, Lewis & Co., a corporate governance research firm. In 2005, public company restatements hit a record high of 1,295—almost double the 2004 total of 650. Companies filing restatements totaled 1,195, or 8.5 percent of all U.S. public companies. Among the audit firms, Grant Thornton had the highest percentage of audit clients that restated their financial statements, 12 percent. KPMG had the highest percentage of client restatements among the Big Four firms at 7.1 percent (Ibid., 1).

These were restatements of financial statements upon which an auditor had reported, presumably issuing a clean opinion. The 2005 total was triple the number of restatements for 2002. In the period from 1997 through 2005, restatements to correct accounting errors totaled 3,642. On average this means that about 30 percent of all U.S. public companies filed restatements in the nine-year period (Taub, 2006, 1).

In 2005 alone, one out of every twelve companies issued incorrect financial statements that needed to be restated. This was up from an average of one out of twenty-three companies in 2004. Surely, if one of twenty-three financial reports is inaccurate, investors cannot be sure of the reliability of reporting or of corporate results. When the inaccuracy gets to one of twelve companies, the quality of information investors are receiving can only be called unreliable. So long as financial statements need to be recalled and restated on the scale now being seen, corporations and public accounting firms cannot be said to be finished with the job of reformation of their ways.

Some companies have placed blame on the "overreaching requirements" of the Sarbanes-Oxley Act (Ibid.). The Glass, Lewis & Co. research team believes the opposite is true. The heightened Sarbanes-Oxley requirements, in particular the Section 404 strengthening of internal controls over financial reporting, have resulted in discovery of misstatements in prior-year reports. To support this view, the study disclosed that in 2005, over half of the companies that restated their financial statements had also disclosed at least one material weakness in their internal controls over financial reporting (Ibid.).

The researchers believe that if the SEC had not delayed the implementation of Section 404 for public companies with a stock market value of less than $75 million until 2007, restatements would have been even higher. Smaller companies have historically been where most problems occurred, and their study indicated that small companies are twice as likely to restate financial results. The study found that corporations that were audited by the smallest audit firms were six times more likely to have to restate their financial statements than corporations that had been audited by Big Four firms (Ibid.).

The study also found, remarkably, that 14 percent of total corporate restatements are made without the corporations in question filing amended reports, Form 8-Ks, or other public announcements. Such so-called stealth restatements are reportedly on the rise. Stealth restatements seem to fly in the face of proper reporting by the corporations in question and their auditors (Ibid.).

The *New York Times* reported that Audit Analytics indicated that in the first half of 2006, 928 companies announced prior-period financial statement restatements. Of these, 424 companies were clients of the eight largest accounting firms. This represented a drop of 31 percent from the prior-year period in restatements for clients of the largest eight public accounting firms. Unfortunately, the remaining 504 restatements for clients of smaller firms were more than double that for the corresponding prior-year period. The *Times* conjectured that this substantial percentage increase among the smaller firms may have resulted from the fact that the smaller audit firms are now being audited themselves by the Public Company Accounting Oversight Board (PCAOB) every three years. Smaller audit firms may have tightened up on detailed auditing in anticipation of, or as a result of, PCAOB inspections (Accountingweb, 2006f, 1).

If, in fact, the large increase in prior-period financial statement restatements is the flushing out of problems long neglected, the numbers should begin to decline. Whatever the cause may be, corporations and their auditors must do a better job of issuing accurate, correct financial statements. The large market value losses resulting from unsuspected false information contained on financial statements are inexcusable. They indicate that the auditors and the corporations have not been doing an honest job of reporting. Audit practitioners can themselves correct this problem.

Auditor Liability a Major Hurdle

Litigation involving the accounting profession continues to be a major problem facing public accounting practitioners in the current world environment. Auditors can reduce litigation and the attendant costs by performing adequate audits, but cannot, of course, completely control such costs. Neil Lerner of KPMG estimated that there are $50 billion in claims outstanding against Big Four firms alone. Settlements can be enormous. KPMG's payment of over $458 million in settlement of its fraud conviction is a case in point. There seems no reason why such a settlement needed to be paid in the first place, if the firm had avoided its fraudulent actions. The best defense against these legal actions is, of course, to perform in a duly diligent manner.

The top ten settlements with shareholders of client corporations through 2004 were reported by *The Economist* using the *Public Accounting Report* as the source. The highest settlement of $335 million was paid by Ernst & Young to shareholders of Cendant, followed by $217 million by Arthur Andersen to Baptist Foundation of Arizona shareholders; $125 million by KPMG to Rite Aid shareholders; $115 million by KPMG to Lernout & Hauspie shareholders; $110 million by Arthur Andersen to Sunbeam shareholders; $90 million by Arthur Andersen to Colonial Realty shareholders; $75 million by KPMG to Oxford Health Plans shareholders; $75 million by Arthur Andersen to Waste Management shareholders; $55 million by PricewaterhouseCoopers to MicroStrategy shareholders; and $34 million by Ernst & Young to Informix shareholders (*The Economist,* 2004a).

Litigation costs and settlement payouts have increased over the years. In the post–Enron-Andersen era, these costs have jumped substantially. Bill Parrett of Deloitte declared that litigation and settlement costs have "spiked like a hockey stick" (Ibid.). Litigation costs, for insurance, settlements, and the like now routinely run from 10 to 20 percent of Big Four firm audit revenues. These costs, of course, are passed on to clients in the form of higher fees. The Big Four firms reportedly have substantial difficulties arranging for professional liability insurance, particularly for catastrophic, unpredictable risks. Tom McGrath, Ernst & Young partner, said that there are now ten commercial insurance companies that will provide major auditor insurance where there were 150 such carriers ten years ago (Ibid.).

Auditors believe that they should pay their share of any settlements made where they are to blame, *The Economist* reports. They believe that financial statement fraud and misstatement are caused by managers of client companies, not by auditors. Yet because the Big Four audit firms have deep pockets and are frequently the only defendants with resources, these firms have been picking up much more than their share of settlement and litigation costs. Sam DiPiazza of PricewaterhouseCoopers said that the auditors are often "the last man standing." Cono Fusco, Grant Thornton partner, believes that the process can be likened to writing an unhedged option. He declared, "You get unlimited exposure for a limited reward." The effect, the accountants say, is that auditors are the insurers for financial statements. Others don't see the situation in that manner. They point out that the purpose of the audit is to add credibility and a form of guarantee for financial statements (Ibid.).

The accountants believe that the mountain of litigation that they must contend with has caused audit quality to decrease. As was discussed in an earlier chapter, accounting standards have become increasingly rule based and prescriptive because, it is asserted, principles-based standards open up more litigation risks. A check-the-box approach to auditing is taken, it is said, which adheres strictly to rule-based standards in an attempt to improve the auditors' ability to prove that audits were done in a duly diligent manner. Auditors seek not to exercise judgment for fear of being second-guessed in courtrooms and, of course, now by the PCAOB. Accountants' outsized litigation risks aggravate other problems, including causing difficulty in recruitment and retention of "the best and brightest" graduates into accounting. The outsized liability risks have also been cited as a cause of the industry concentration problem since potentially large losses can only be sustained by very large accounting firms (Ibid.).

Remedies for outsized litigation settlements have been instituted in some jurisdictions. Some European countries have placed limits on auditor liability. Germany capped auditor liability exposure to 4 million deutschemarks or US$5.2 million. Non–Big Four public accountant firms audit 67 of the 300 largest German corporations, representing much less concentration than in the U.S. market. The same decrease in market concentration was seen in Greece, where auditor liability was capped at five times the salary of the Supreme Court president. Non–Big Four firms audit twenty-seven of the sixty Athens stock exchange–listed corporations, a considerable improvement in the concentration problem (Ibid.).

Caps for auditor liability were examined and rejected by the United Kingdom's Office of Fair Trading. That office, according to *The Economist,* had not found evidence sufficient to show that such liability caps would encourage competition or reduce the risk of demise of a Big Four public accounting firm. Reasoning cited was that since larger firms have much larger exposure to liability litigation than smaller firms, a cap on liability settlements would benefit larger entities and not help smaller ones advance.

In similar fashion to most of the rest of the world, U.S. accountant liability arises from either legislation or common law. As discussed earlier in this volume, the Securities Act of 1933 and the Securities Exchange Act of 1934 are the primary pieces of legislation under which auditor liability arises nationally. Prior to the Private Securities Litigation Reform Act of 1995, which amended securities acts, accountants and other defendants were held jointly and severally liable for all plaintiff losses for which the defendants were held responsible. This legal concept holds a class of defendants jointly responsible for judgment losses attributable to the class as a whole. That is, should some defendants be unable to pay their share of the judgment, remaining financially able defendants in the class must pay the total owed to plaintiffs. Frequently, this results in public accountants paying entire judgment amounts because they are the only defendants remaining able to pay.

The Private Securities Litigation Reform Act of 1995 replaced joint and several liability with a form of proportionate liability under which defendants, including auditors, have joint and several liability only to certain small investors. As to all other investors, the total judgment owed is prorated by the court to individual defendants based on the percentage for which the court holds each defendant responsible. Should any defendant be unable to pay its pro rata share, each of remaining defendants must pay an additional pro rata amount, but the additional amount is capped at 50 percent of the defendant's original pro rata share of losses in question. For example, if a plaintiff judgment totaling $100,000 allocated 90 percent to client management and 10 percent to the auditor, the auditor would owe $10,000. If client management was bankrupt and could not pay, and assuming no small investors' claims, the auditor would have to pay a total of $15,000, instead of the entire judgment of $100,000, which would have been due under the joint and several rule.

This statutory reform of auditor liability was a major step toward equitable treatment, as it places costs on those responsible with a limit of 50 percent over their pro rata share of the losses caused. For suits brought under federal securities acts, the proportionate liability concept should result in much more manageable costs for public accountants. But, the reform does not apply to suits brought in state courts under common law.

Under common law, professionals ordinarily owe contractual duties only to someone who is party to a professional service contract. Therefore, most professionals do not have to be concerned about financial liability except to their clients. The client is in a contractual relationship with the professional and is owed the duty of performing the contracted services with due care. To have rights, third parties must ordinarily be in privity of the contract in question, that is, named in the contract as being a beneficiary of the contract.

A public accountant's work products, audit reports on financial statements, make the relationships with third parties more complex than for other professionals because the audit report and the financial statements are generally meant to be used by third-party beneficiaries as well as third parties not in privity of the contract in question. Auditors, unlike other professionals, face the situation in which they are potentially liable to third parties who rely on audit reports and financial statements for business decisions but who are perhaps unknown and unspecified to auditors.

In the 1931 case of *Ultramares v. Touche & Co.,* the New York Court of Appeals found that auditors are not liable for ordinary negligence to third parties not in privity of contract. But, the court did hold that auditors are liable to third parties not in privity of the contract for acts of fraud or gross negligence in the performance of the contract in question. This means that auditors in states upholding *Ultramares v. Touche & Co.* have liability for ordinary negligence to clients and to third parties in privity of contract as well as liability for gross negligence and fraud to all other third parties. This is assuming that the auditor's unsatisfactory performance was the proximate cause of plaintiff's loss.

Seven states were reported by Michael R. Lane in 1989 to still be following the *Ultramares* concept. In the other states that do not now follow the *Ultramares* precedent, the number of third parties to which the auditor owes due diligence has expanded as courts have needed to determine what the extent of auditor duties should be beyond client duty. The Restatement of Torts approach expands auditor liability for ordinary negligence to a specific limited class of third parties known by the auditor, although not identified individually, to be using the audited financial statements for a specific business purpose. For example, if the auditor knew that the audited financial statements were to be used by clients to add support for obtaining bank loans, the limited class would consist of all banks using the financial statements for the stated purpose, even though names of individual banks were unknown to the auditor. Most states follow the Restatement of Torts approach or a variant (Lane, 1989).

Four states have gone further in granting rights to third parties. New Jersey, Wisconsin, California, and Mississippi follow the Foreseeable Third Party Approach, in which the duty of due care is owed to any third party using audited financial statements in the ordinary course of business. The client does not have to identify the third party to the auditor nor does the fact that the financial statements have been distributed to the third party need to be known by the auditor. The purpose of the court in approving the Foreseeable Third Party Approach was thought to be to place responsibility on the party most capable of preventing the negligence proximately causing plaintiff loss. The results from this approach are seen as dramatically increasing the number of third parties to whom auditors can be held liable for ordinary negligence (Ibid.).

The concept of joint and several liability, discussed above, is still followed under common law. Audit firms, having "deep pockets," frequently are sued by third-party plaintiffs along with any other defendants, such as client companies, company managers, company lawyers, and others. When codefendants are unable to pay, auditors are held responsible for entire plaintiff court judgments, even when the major cause of plaintiff loss was not auditor failure.

Settlements have been made by audit firms in a great many cases to contain the costs of litigation. Even when the auditors are not liable, it is frequently cheaper to settle before court costs and judgments rise. Once the court judgment is rendered, there appear to be no remedies on the horizon for the joint and several kinds of third-party liability costs. Some firms have developed changes in their contract with clients that may help to contain rising litigation costs when the client company is the plaintiff.

Engagement Letter Contract Provisions
May Reduce Litigation Costs

Some Big Four firms have developed an innovative approach to limitations on costs of possible punitive damages and legal expenses that might arise when clients assert claims against their auditors. The approach consists of an alternative form of dispute resolution and a prohibition of punitive damages clause that the firms began including in private executory contracts with clients as long as ten years ago. This contract, in the parlance of auditing called the engagement letter, is usually drawn up in some detail before an audit is begun. Engagement letters are legally binding when signed by both auditors and client company representatives, increasingly the board of directors' audit committee. Engagement letters, being private contracts, have not been publicly disclosed in the past. Therefore, the new provisions had not come to investors' attention.

In November 2005, a *Wall Street Journal* article by Michael Rapoport noted that the issue was first briefly brought to public notice in spring 2005 by a warning from the Federal Financial Institutions Examination Council that financial institutions should not allow the provisions. The article reported that Sun Microsystems in September 2005 and, shortly thereafter, Silicon Graphics Inc. had "parted the curtain" on this previously nondisclosed but growing practice. The two companies described in their proxy statements that company engagement letter agreements with their auditor, Ernst & Young in both cases, contained provisions that subject the contracting parties to alternative dispute resolution procedures and punitive damage exclusion. The companies stated that they provided this information in their proxy statements to enable shareholders to include it in their consideration of whether to vote to retain the auditor (Rapoport, 2005, 1).

Rapoport interpreted the agreements as barring the corporation from taking the public accounting firm to court in the case of a "botched audit." Instead mediation and arbitration must be used. The punitive damage exclusion was seen as limiting damages to actual compensatory damages that might be related to the auditor's conduct of the contract. The provisions, Rapoport reports, were put in the contract by Ernst & Young to limit auditor liability to the client. He indicates that auditors have used these provisions in the past. And, "a dispute over them between regulators and accounting firms has been bubbling for months" (Ibid.).

Investors in general had been, it seems, largely or completely unaware of the new provisions to which corporations had been agreeing, until the issuance of the Sun Microsystems and Silicon Graphics proxy statements. Some corporations, reportedly, felt that they were pressured by the audit firm and had little or no choice but to agree or risk being "dumped" by the audit firm. Sun Microsystems audit committee chair and former SEC chief accountant Lynn Turner indicated that "all four accounting firms are demanding the companies include these liability caps clauses in their contracts" (Ibid.). He believes that company audit committees have little or no choice but to sign the agreements. Arkansas Best Corporation's chief financial officer (CFO) indicated that Arkansas Best did not believe that it had leverage to remove the provisions, although the company does not necessarily oppose the provisions (Reilly, 2006, 1).

The disclosure by Sun Microsystems was, apparently, the first by an individual company. Cynthia Richson of Ohio Public Employees Retirement System does not see the provisions to be in companies' or investors' best interests. Ted White of the Council of Institutional Investors believes that more disclosure is needed. Because of the lack of public disclosure, it is difficult to estimate how widespread the provisions have become. However, they could be widely used indeed (Rapoport, 2005, 1).

Ken Kerrigan, a spokesman for Ernst & Young, said that the provisions are a part of the firm's standard client agreements and have been that way for some time. In Kerrigan's view, the provisions do not limit investor rights to seek redress (Ibid.). In a 2006 article by David Reilly of *The Wall Street Journal,* Ernst & Young asserted that the punitive damage waiver is consistent with securities legislation that does not allow punitive damages. Arbitration requirements have been in Ernst & Young engagement letters for over ten years, the firm confirmed. These agreements, in the firm's view, are not liability limits upon either party. The provisions apply only to the client and do not apply in any way to shareholder claims made under security legislation or to class action suits (Reilly, 2006, 1).

Nevertheless, the Ohio Public Employees Retirement System as well as other shareholders voted against retaining Ernst & Young as auditors of Sun Microsystems, even though the majority voted to retain. Dow Jones Newswires reportedly had seen sample engagement letters from two other Big Four firms, KPMG and Deloitte & Touche, which did have the provisions. Ted White believes that the audit firms have asked most, if not all, of their clients to agree to the provisions (Rapoport, 2005, 1).

Those questioning the practice see the provisions as lowering auditor responsibility. Further, they point out that there is a conflict of interest independence issue. The agreements threaten the arm's-length dealings that auditor and client must have. If a company agrees to let the accounting firm lower its potential liability, might not the auditor in some future time be in a position where he or she is pressured to return the client favor when needed by management? Is this a conflict of interest that would impair auditor independence?

KPMG does not see the requirement for arbitration that way. Rather, the provision is a way to control costs normally associated with litigation for both parties to the contract. The KPMG spokesman stated, "We believe alternative dispute resolution is consistent with maintaining auditor independence" (Reilly, 2006, 1). A spokesman for PricewaterhouseCoopers declared that no limitations had been placed in engagement letters with public clients of the firm. This, of course, leaves private companies, which may have agreed to limitations. Deloitte & Touche's Robert Kueppers believes that the provisions provide a mechanism for settling disputes between client companies and auditors. They do not in any way limit investors from suing auditors (Reilly, 2006, 1).

By 2006, an increasing number of companies were disclosing similar agreements with their auditors that prevent the companies from taking the auditor to court or seeking punitive damages for failure to perform audit work with due diligence. The SEC or the PCAOB have not officially taken a position on such agreements. The Web publication *Inside*

Sarbanes-Oxley reported that SEC staff have been considering the issue. A PCAOB advisory group was reported to be split on the harmfulness of such agreements for arbitration of disputes and waiver of punitive damages (*Inside Sarbanes-Oxley,* 2006, 1). A member of the group, Nick Cyprus of Interpublic Group, stated that it was not yet clear whether agreements to limit punitive damage awards will actually limit liability. In other words, the agreements may not stand up in court. The outcome of this avenue for containing auditor liability and litigation costs remains to be seen. But, the large amount of auditor liability litigation is certainly an overriding concern that practitioners must view as a major problem area, now and in the future.

Peer Reviews

Peer reviews represent another area of unresolved controversy for accountants. The U.S. peer review system prior to the Sarbanes-Oxley Act was exclusively carried out by the profession under the aegis of the American Institute of Certified Public Accountants (AICPA). The process of having one CPA firm conduct peer review of another was a major part of accountant self-governance. The AICPA created the Public Oversight Board (POB) in 1977 in the wake of audit failures in the 1970s to forestall stronger government actions (Levitt, 2002, 126). The board was intended ostensibly to carry out self-regulatory oversight of the profession. The peer review system was among its responsibilities. As noted earlier in this volume, Arthur Levitt wrote that he believed that "self-regulation by the accounting profession is a bad joke" (Ibid., 127). In Levitt's words, "They wanted the POB to remain a gentlemen's debating society and planned to keep it on a tight leash" (Ibid.). The character of the peer reviews carried out, as typified by the Deloitte & Touche 2001 peer review of Arthur Andersen, bears out Levitt's assertion that "The firms would never subject themselves to scrutiny unless forced to do so" (Ibid.).

Few details of peer review findings were made public. This was in accordance with AICPA bylaw changes establishing peer review. Noam Scheiber (2002) noted in his *New Republic* article "How Arthur Andersen Got Away With It. Peer Revue" that the 2001 Andersen peer review report prepared by Deloitte & Touche did indicate that there were three issues raised. But these issues were deemed not significant enough to change the peer review report from its "without qualifications" designation. In fact, not a single major accounting firm had ever received a failing grade on an AICPA peer review report. The three issues raised in the Andersen report were not disclosed.

Not deterred, Scheiber continued his analysis of the AICPA peer review process and requirements (Scheiber, 2002, 1). He described a number of problems that indicated that the peer review process was inadequate at best, and probably closer to Arthur Levitt's description of accounting profession self-regulation.

The peer review process excluded audits for which there was pending litigation. This is akin, Scheiber indicates, to computing the grade-point average of a college student without including any courses in which he had received low grades. Any review done of Andersen that did not include Enron would have been useless, in Scheiber's view. However, whether or not the Enron audit had been included in the Deloitte & Touche review was irrelevant because of other flaws in the peer review process. Review guidelines lacked requirements needed to ensure that adequate audits had been performed. Although 3 to 6 percent of previous-year total audit hours were required to be covered by the review, audit work papers, reportedly, were rarely examined. And, when work papers were looked at, the purpose was to ensure that the numbers that the original auditors recorded "looked plausible." There was, in Scheiber's words, no "re-audit" or looking at judgments by which audit decisions were made. Reviews of work papers were primarily reviews of what had been recorded by the auditor (Ibid.).

Judgment calls were at the heart of the problem with Andersen's flawed approach at Enron. Scheiber cited the example of Andersen's 1997 agreement to go along with Enron management's statement of earnings at $105 million, even though Andersen audit work indicated earnings were $54 million. This flawed judgment call was justified on the basis that the difference was not material to a corporation of Enron's size. The peer review processes being used had little probability of unearthing the flawed practices. The Enron audit would have had to have been picked as part of the review process. The working papers would have had to be looked at, which was rarely done. And the reasoning behind the judgment would have had to be recorded by the auditor in the first place.

As accounting for large corporations became more lax in the years after 1997, Scheiber thinks that even if the peer review system had been capable of disclosing the many instances of sham accounting, the Big Five firms would not have exposed one another's faults because they "often behaved less like competitors than corporate partners" (Ibid.).

They worked together for mutual protection. They were, after all, in the same insurance pool. Scheiber believes that peer review should have been the final fail-safe, but was not.

Scheiber's observations are logical and pertinent. Unfortunately, the AICPA peer review system was not designed to provide the kind of auditing of the auditor that he very correctly observed is needed. Peer reviews under AICPA protocols at the time were designed to determine the adequacy of established quality control policies of the firm in question. Tests made were to determine the extent to which the firm complied with established policies. The peer review was not intended to determine whether the firm's audits had been adequate or defective. The established quality control policies were gauged against professional standards in areas of client acceptance, employment of professional personnel, staffing of engagements, continuing education of firm personnel, and promotions of employees.

The reviewer's objective was a report with an opinion about firm quality control system adequacy. A letter of comment, where necessary, was issued to the firm with any recommendations for improvement in systems of quality control. If a reviewed firm did not take appropriate corrective actions based on the reviewer letter of comment, sanctions could be imposed, such as admonishments, requiring additional continuing education, or suspension from AICPA membership (Whittington and Pany, 2006, 46–47). Of course, the PCAOB inspections for auditors of public companies are another matter altogether.

Scheiber was one of many critics of the peer review system. In another example, on February 6, 2002, problems with peer review from their viewpoint were enumerated by the New York State Board for Public Accountancy in testimony before the New York Senate Higher Education Committee. First, the board indicated, the audit of publicly traded corporations was carried out primarily by eight firms. These eight firms audited 80 percent of all publicly traded corporations. Peer review was carried out by having these eight firms review other firms within the group. This limited pool of peer review firms may have compromised the process. "Firms may hesitate to report quality control violations on the very firm that may be conducting their firm's peer review, believing that criticism invites criticism"(New York State Public Accountancy Board, 2002). Secondly, such peer reviews were only required on a triennial basis. Reviews are needed at least annually "to ensure that quality control standards are continually met" (Ibid.). The New York State Board's

2002 specific objections that applied to public company auditors were in effect cleared up by the Sarbanes-Oxley Act.

Robert Bunting, in his 2004 article in the *CPA Journal Online,* described the history of peer review in the United States. At each step, it appears, the accounting profession was, in fact, reluctant to have others judge them, although they themselves were responsible for judging corporate financial reports. As seems common in the history of the U.S. accounting profession, congressional hearings and regulators pressured the AICPA to reorganize in 1977, adding the Division for CPA Firms. The new organizational arm was to ensure, for the first time, that all firms providing audit services followed the same set of generally accepted auditing standards. The voluntary peer review program was set up to monitor adherence through triennial reviews. Both joining the new Division for CPA Firms and joining the new peer review program were voluntary. Bunting reports that the peer review process was highly successful, being recognized as a rigorous process producing "tangible results." Yet, the voluntary nature of the program did little to support the argument that accounting profession self-regulation was adequate (Bunting, 2004).

By the mid-1980s, in response again to heavy pressure from the U.S. Congress and regulatory agencies after high-profile corporation bankruptcies and bank failures in the late 1970s, the profession's leaders concluded that to avoid congressional action, peer review "would have to become mandatory" (Ibid.). This required changes to the AICPA organizational bylaws passed by vote of the entire membership.

The bylaw changes were passed in 1988, establishing a new code of conduct, new college-level education requirements, continuing professional education, and mandatory peer review. The peer review process was set up to be confidential throughout and only to be directed at educational and corrective actions (Ibid.). Herbert Vessel describes these measures as two promises made to convince AICPA members to vote for the referendum: "Peer reviews were to be remedial rather than punitive. Peer review findings were to be kept confidential, except to those administering the program" (Vessel, 2006).

There were two distinctly different peer review programs established. For firms with audit clients, on-site reviews were mandated to evaluate the quality control system followed by each subject firm. For firms that performed compilation and review services but not audit services, peer reviews were conducted off-site to determine compliance with applicable professional standards. A firm review file was prepared that included the peer review report. Some files included reviewer letters of comments with responses from the reviewed firm (Bunting, 2004).

In 1995, the AICPA Peer Review Program was adopted to encompass previously separate programs run for the various groups within the AICPA structure. Substantial revisions were proposed in 2003 that became effective in 2005. All AICPA members in public practice now must undergo peer review by working for a firm that is enrolled in an AICPA-approved practice monitoring program or by enrolling in such a program individually (Russell and Armitage, 2006). Programs are administered through state boards of accountancy.

Peer review is required every three years and consists of three different review types. The first two types, called engagement reviews and report reviews, are required for firms with limited-scope engagements such as financial statement reviews and compilations. The third type, which is more generally applicable, called a system review, is comprehensive and is for CPA firms with engagements that fall under the Statements on Auditing Standards, Government Auditing Standards, or prospective statement examination under the Statements on Standards for Attestation Engagements. A system review must consist of evaluation of firm quality control policies as well as examination of a cross section of firm accounting and auditing engagements. The examination must include work paper review and be for a cross section of all firm accounting and auditing engagements, with emphasis on engagements with high peer-review risk assessments (Jentho and Beddow, 2005).

The reviewer's report, which may be unmodified, modified for notable deficiencies, or adverse, states whether the system of quality control is in accordance with AICPA Statements of Quality Control Standards and whether the firm is complying with quality control measures in a way as to have reasonable assurance of complying with all relevant standards.

The new 2005 standards require that the reviewed firm provide representations to the reviewing firm that all state regulatory requirements were complied with and that a complete list of all engagements subject to peer review had been provided to the reviewer. Any communications received by the reviewed firm within the prior three years as a result of investigations must be disclosed to the reviewer. No engagements can be excluded from the peer process without causing a scope limitation on the review engagement report (Ibid.).

Reviewer reports for system reviews now must state whether the reviewed firm, in the opinion of the reviewer, demonstrated competencies necessary to perform the engagements that were subject to peer review. Two weeks before the review begins, the reviewer is required to notify the reviewed firm of all but one of the engagements that will be reviewed. The remaining engagement must be selected after the engagement has begun (Russell and Armitage, 2006).

Other procedures for the peer review have been changed as well. The peer reviewer must now determine whether the reviewed firm appropriately identified high-risk engagement areas and performed and documented required procedures related to the high-risk areas. Areas of high risk are considered to be fraud occurrences, estimates, emerging issues, and the like.

The peer review is designed to cover a one-year period, with all engagements in that year becoming the pool from which the reviewer selects. State CPA societies administer the AICPA Peer Review Program in most jurisdictions. The state society establishes a peer review committee with responsibility for the program. Firms needing to be reviewed self-select their reviewers and communicate arrangements to state peer-review committees. When the peer review process is completed, the reviewed firm must file with the state committee a copy of the report with any letters of comment together with a response to any letters of comment in which corrective actions are outlined. This letter of response must be approved by the reviewer prior to filing with the peer review committee. Where deficiencies have been noted, the peer review committee may require corrective measures, including requiring the reviewed firm to agree to other actions, for example, submitting a monitoring report or having a revisit by the reviewer (Ibid.).

The revisions put into effect in 2005 do strengthen the peer review process. Changes made should correct some of the pre-Enron shortcomings, including some of those cited by Noam Scheiber above. All engagements are now subject to review except when special procedures are followed in which the reviewed firm formally requests exclusion of an engagement and the reviewer agrees that a particular engagement need not be included in the review pool. Work papers for all selected engagements are now required to be examined during the review. One direct purpose of the review is to determine whether the firm is complying with quality control measures such that there is reasonable assurance that the firm is complying with all relevant standards. The reviewer must state in the review report whether the firm demonstrated competencies necessary to perform its engagements. These are improvements, but other problems remain. The new provisions still permit a CPA firm to perform reviews for comparable firms. The review still does not address whether a sample of engagements were performed adequately. And, the fact that the reviewed firm can select its reviewer leaves the process open to question.

It is clear that the procedures are nowhere near as strong as those for public company examinations by the PCAOB. At least one state board of accountancy has, in its own words, been "unable to embrace" (Sos, 2005) the AICPA Peer Review Program. The California Board indicates that after considerable efforts to work with the AICPA to make improvements, there are unresolved scope problems in the AICPA Peer Review Program. The California Board also believes that there is insufficient transparency in the AICPA program. An ancillary problem is that the board believes that California consumers would be done a disservice to continue to exempt small firms and sole proprietors from mandatory peer review, as current California state law provides.

These problems keep the board from recommending implementation of mandatory peer review in California. The board intends to continue to work on the problem and make a recommendation to the California Legislature as part of the board's 2009 Sunset Review. In a study report on the issue, the board indicated that it supported the 2005 changes made to the peer review procedures but did not think that the changes went far enough to address the board's concerns stated to the AICPA. The board was unclear whether the new standards had significantly expanded the scope of engagements that will be subject to review. It was clear to the board, however, that the new procedures do not provide for transparency of peer review documents. The board clearly states that "transparency is of critical importance" (California Board of Accountancy, 2005, 8).

Peer review results and details have not been made available to the public, which the California Board had requested as long ago as 2002. The board expressed its concern that the AICPA had not yet "provided for public reporting of peer review reports and findings; nor has the AICPA responded meaningfully to most of the other concerns expressed by this Board in its comment letters" (Ibid.). The board's study task force was unable to determine whether California consumers would be sufficiently protected by the AICPA Peer Review Program (Ibid., 9). At the same time, the study indicated that consumer education is needed to communicate that public accounting peer review is not a punitive process nor can it be expected to "prevent audit failures" (Ibid., 11) as it is primarily an educational tool to use in improving the quality of professional practices.

The National Association of State Boards of Accountancy (NASBA) has made it clear, as well, that transparency is needed by boards of accountancy in general (Sadler, 2005, 1). NASBA believes that U.S. peer review has evolved from a voluntary educational effort into a mandatory, regulatory, and firm-licensing matter. NASBA recently established its Compliance Assurance Review Board to give independent oversight and monitoring for the administration of standards for peer reviews on behalf of all state boards that do not conduct their own oversight and monitoring. State boards need complete access to the results of peer review, in NASBA's view. While NASBA states that thirty-nine jurisdictions now accept the AICPA peer review system, none has "direct and unfettered access to the peer review reports that they require" (WebCPA, 2006, 1).

The Case for Peer Review Results Transparency

CPA members of the AICPA organization have not yet agreed to make their peer review results public across the board. A major controversy has arisen over whether the peer review system should have transparency, that is, whether to make peer review findings available to the public. In order to take this step, the AICPA indicates that it must hold a referendum among its membership. When peer reviews, as noted above, were instituted by agreement of the membership in 1988, two promises were made: peer review findings were to be kept confidential except to those administering the peer review program; and peer reviews were to be remedial rather than punitive in nature (Vessel, 2006).

A variety of authorities outside the AICPA in addition to the state boards of accountancy now want peer review results disclosed to them, including bank regulators, pension plan administrators, and the U.S. Department of Labor. Firms with engagements that come under the jurisdiction of Government Auditing Standards, commonly referred to as the "Yellow Book," are now required to provide audit clients with copies of their peer review reports if they want to do those engagements. The Government Auditing Standards are applicable for audits of federal entities and the wide range of entities that receive federal funds.

An AICPA 2005 poll found that, of 2,350 CPA respondents, only 41 percent supported making peer reviews public, with 43 percent opposed. Robert L. Bunting, then vice chairman of the AICPA, indicated that in 2004 nearly 35,000 public accounting firms in the United States "now rely on the peer review program to demonstrate that their accounting and auditing practices meet the highest of standards" (Bunting, 2004, 1). Yet, peer reviews are still by AICPA bylaw kept confidential within the review process except with the consent of the reviewed firm.

For firms that do not follow the recommendations in peer reviews, further actions by the AICPA could be taken to terminate firm enrollment in the Peer Review Program, with resultant loss of AICPA membership and membership in some state CPA societies (Vessel, 2006). Changes for both the existing policies on confidentiality and on the nonpunitive nature of peer review would have to be agreed to by the AICPA membership.

To be sure, the peer review programs were at first meant and designed to be educational and corrective, helping to provide improved services and to prevent problems from coming to fruition. They were not meant to be enforcement tools. Problems noted within a firm were to stay confidential with the firm and the reviewers. Yet, in each of the cases where change was agreed to, the profession was essentially forced to accept the changing of professional rules or accept even more undesirable government regulation (Bunting, 2004).

Robert Bunting believes that the times have once again changed and that transparency is inevitable. The range of users of public accounting services is much wider today. Users now expect to have as much transparency as possible to evaluate audit and accounting service providers. Credit grantors are ever more important users of accounting and auditing services, as are regulators and governmental authorities of various types. Many firms have begun to use peer reviews as badges of honor "to trumpet their positive reviews to clients and others" (Ibid.). In place of a system to aid improvement, peer review is now viewed almost as a grading system in which pass or fail are the alternatives.

State boards are increasingly requiring peer reviews and the submission of peer review information as part of the licensure process. In 2006, as a condition of licensing, forty-six of fifty-four U.S. states and territories had already instituted mandatory peer review, or were moving in that direction. Twenty of these require submission of peer review–related information in order to be licensed. NASBA has recommended changes to the Uniform Accountancy Act that will give state accountancy boards unfettered access to peer review reports. It seems clear that the peer review process is no longer viewed as an improvement and remediation tool by the state boards. Bunting indicates that all of this is indicative of an "inexorable march toward greater transparency" (Ibid.).

The AICPA has embarked upon an educational program to inform members about transparency-related issues similar to the educational campaign undertaken before the referendum in which peer review was made mandatory (Ibid.). It would seem that the profession is once again approaching the juncture where a choice must be made between approving the lesser evil of improved peer review with greater transparency and a more punitive nature, or accepting government intervention.

A viable peer review system is vital to adequate self-regulation of the profession. The public company sector has been lost to self-regulation and likely will remain under the current or a similar government regime. Existing AICPA peer review is important if the profession does not want government regulation extended. There are substantial organizations that do not fall under PCAOB oversight that the self-governing profession continues to serve. Private companies of all sizes, not-for-profit organizations, and governmental entities at all levels—federal, state, and local—all rely upon public accountants. The peer review system in its pre–Enron-Andersen state was a clear failure. It is not clear yet whether the profession is willing to strengthen self-governance sufficiently to prevent failures to clients and to future publics.

The time may be fast approaching when peer reviews will be placed in the hands of state boards of accountancy. The need for serious, tough, enforceable peer review for auditors not under the PCAOB has been highlighted by recent, serious, and high-profile audit failures in New York, including failed audits of New York public school districts. This speaks to the fact that meaningful peer review is needed for all accounting and auditing firms, not just public company auditors. This environment may be right to change peer review and attach it to the state CPA licensing processes.

A New York State Society of CPAs (NYSSCPA) report recommended just such action. The report concluded that the state should establish disciplinary procedures for firms and CPAs that do not receive adequate peer review reports. Further, the peer review process needs to be strengthened, with increased scope and depth. This is a completely different peer review process, meant to determine whether adequate audits have been rendered, not simply for the education and improvement of CPAs.

Lou Grumet, executive director of the 33,000-member NYSSCPA, stated that "the AICPA's discipline is more training, while we say that in some cases there should be serious disciplinary sanctions, including the loss of license" (Accountingweb, 2006g, 1). In Grumet's view, the AICPA peer review system fits with what New York State does but does not go far enough. The state society issued a report earlier in 2006 that found the AICPA processes to have "gaping shortcomings" (Ibid.). Only thirty-nine states now tie peer review to licensing procedures. The New York society report calls on all state boards of accountancy to make peer review a mandatory part of CPA licensing processes.

Problems Difficult but Not Insurmountable

This chapter has presented several problem areas in addition to peer review that also need continuing attention by the profession. The market concentration for audits of large public companies has not yet hobbled the world economy. But, it may be just a matter of time. Market concentration may be the most intractable challenge that now faces the profession.

The volume of restatements of prior financial statements surely must be brought under control. This should be possible with improved auditing and accounting within public accounting firms and corporations. Should restatements continue at the current rate for very long, public confidence will again erode, with resulting governmental actions of one sort or another.

The continuing problem of excessive professional liabilities from litigation has been growing for many years. With legislated relief coming from the Private Securities Litigation Reform Act of 1995, which replaced joint and several liability with less-onerous and less-expensive proportionate liability, the buildup of excessive liability may now be reversible. The new engagement letter client and auditor agreement for arbitration of legal claims and the punitive damage waivers may prove to be acceptable to the government and the public. Improvements in performance of audit duties should also help reduce the profession's litigation liability problem.

None of these problems seem insurmountable, particularly when the accomplishments of the recent past are taken into consideration. The profession adapted to dramatic change in losing Arthur Andersen & Co., which had been a main pillar of the worldwide profession. The need for a change in direction back to putting public responsibility first was accepted as reforms swept the globe. Both practitioners and firms have adapted to this new environment of increased government direction and regulation. In fact, the adjustments have been such that firms of all size are benefiting handsomely from the increased competition and opportunities in the accounting and consulting markets.

References

Accountancy Age. 2005. "Big Four Non-Audit Fees Soar" (February 18). Available at: http://www.accountancyage.com/articles/print/2036898.

Accounting Standards Board. 2007. "Financial Reporting Standard for Smaller Entities." Available at: http://www.frc.org.uk/documents/pagemanager/asb /FRSSE-Jan2007%20web%20Optimized.pdf.

Accountingweb. 2003. "Andersen's Duncan Sentencing Likely to Be Delayed— Again." Available at: http://www.accountingweb.com/egibin/item.cgi?id =98344&d=815&h=817&f=816&dat.

———. 2004a. "Professional Fees in Enron Bankruptcy to $780M." Available at: http://www.accountingweb.com/cgi-bin/item.cgi?id=100263&d=659.

———. 2004b. "WorldCom Whistleblower to Be Inducted into Hall of Fame for CPAs" (October 17–26). Available at: http://www.accountingweb.com/cgi-bin /item.cgi?id=99954.

———. 2004c. "Ernst & Young Disciplined by California Accountancy Board." Available at: http://www.accountingweb.com/cgi-bin/item.cgi?id=99798.

———. 2004d. "Business Groups Begin Quiet Campaign to Oust SEC's Donaldson." Available at: http://www.accountingweb.com/cgi-bin/item.cgi?id=100230&d =659&h=660&f=661.

———. 2004e. "Big Four Accounting Firms Express Their Support of the FASB to Congress." Available at: http://www.accountingweb.com/cgibin/item.cgi?id =98903&d=659&h=660&f=661.

———. 2005. "Ebbers Found Guilty in Massive WorldCom Fraud Case." Available at: http://accountingweb.com/cgi-bin/item.cgi?id=100670&d=659.

———. 2006a. "PCAOB & Sarbanes-Oxley Under Fire." Available at: http://www .accountingweb.com/cgi-bin/item.cgi?id=101792&d=659&h=660&f=661.

———. 2006b. "Internal Auditing Gaining in Popularity." Available at: http:// www.accountingweb.com/cgi-bin/item.cgi?id=102032&d=659&h=660&f =661.

———. 2006c. "Consolidation Ahead for Accounting Firms." Available at: http://www .accountingweb.com/cgi-bin/item.cgi?id=102514&d=659&h=660&f=661.

———. 2006d. "BDO Seidman LLP Reports Revenue Growth Exceeding 25 Percent in 2006." Available at: http://www.accountingweb.com/cgi-bin/item .cgi?id=102372&d=659&h=660&f=661.

———. 2006e. "PCAOB Find Their Audit Concerns Addressed." Available at: http://www.accountingweb.com/cgi-bin/item.cgi?id=101941&d=815&h=817 &f=816&dateformat=%250%20%25B%20%25Y.

————. 2006f. "More Restatements in 2006 for Smaller Accounting Firms—Update 1." Available at: http://www.accountingweb.com/.

————. 2006g. "AICPA and NYSSCPA Differ Slightly on Peer Review." Available at: http://www.accountingweb.com/cgi-bin/item.cgi?id=101889&d=815&h=817&f=816&dateformat=%250%20%25B%20%25Y.

AICPA News Update. 2003. "AICPA Provides Guidance on AICPA and PCAOB Standards in One Resource." Available at: http://www.aicpa.org/download/info/aicpa_news_update_73.pdf#search=%22AICPA%20and%20PCAOB%22.

American Institute of Certified Public Accountants. 2002. *A Brief History of Self-Regulation.* New York: American Institute of Certified Public Accountants. Available at: http://thecaq.aicpa.org/Resources/Sarbanes+Oxley/Archive++A+Brief+History+of+Self+Regulation.htm.

————. 2004. A Bird's Eye View of the Enron Debacle. Available at: http://pcps.aicpa.org/Resources/Closely-Held+Companies/A+Birds+Eye+View+of+the+Enron+Debacle.htm.

————. 2005. AICPA and SEC Independence Rule Comparison. Available at: http://www.aicpa.org/download/ethics/11_2003_AICPA_SEC_Independence RulesComparison.pdf.

————. 2006a. AICPA Code of Professional Conduct. New York: American Institute of Certified Public Accountants. Available at: htttp://www.aicpa.org/about/code/index.html.

————. 2006b. "National Conference on Current SEC and PCAOB Developments." Available at: http://www.cpa2biz.com/CS2000/Products/CPA2BIZ/Conferences/National+Conference+on+Current+SEC+and+PCAOB+Developments.htm?wtlink=hpbestseller3.

————. 2007. "Auditing Standards Board, ASBs Operating Procedures, Including Its Authority and Mission." Available at: http://www.aicpa.org/Professional+Resources/Accounting+and+Auditing/Audit+and+Attest+Standards/Auditing+Standards+Board/.

AMR Research. 2004. "Study: SOX Spending Will Reach $5.8 Billion in 2005." Available at: http://www.smartpros.com/x45870.xml.

Arens, Alvin A., Randal J. Elder, and Mark S. Beasley. 2004. *Overview of the Sarbanes-Oxley Act of 2002 with Other Changes in Auditing and the Public Accounting Profession.* Upper Saddle River, NJ: Pearson Prentice Hall.

Association of Chartered Treasury Managers. 2003. "Emerging Trends in Financial Reporting on the Internet." *Chartered Treasury Manager* 4, no. 10 (June 1–14). Available at: http://www.actm.org/actmnl/jun14/web/coverstory.htm.

Badal, Jaclyne, and Phred Dvorak. 2006. "Sarbanes-Oxley Gains Adherents: Closely Held Companies Embrace Internal Controls as Incentives, Pressures Rise." *Wall Street Journal,* August 14, B3. Available at: http://online.wsj.com/article/SB115551450520734692.html?mod=DAT.

Bagshaw, Katherine. 2000. "Financial Reporting on the Internet." Association of *Certified Chartered Accountants (Student Accountant)* (August 1). Available at: www.accaglobal.com/archive/sa_oldarticles/31113.

Baker, Richard H. 2001. "Hearings on International Accounting Standards." *U.S. House of Representatives, Subcommittee on Capital Markets, Insurance, and Government Sponsored Organizations,* (June 7). Available at: http://financialservices.house.gov/media/pdf/060701ba.pdf.

Beck, Rachel. 2005. "Accounting Rules Show Their Worth." *Modesto Bee,* April 5, D-3.

Beltran, Luisa. 2002. "Andersen Merger Hopes Dim." *CNN/Money* (March 13). Available at: http://money.cnn.com/2002/03/13/news/companies/andersen/index. htm.

Beltran, Luisa, Brett Gering, and Alice Martin. 2002. "Andersen Guilty: Once Grand Accounting Firm Now Faces Five Years Probation, $500,000 Fine and Possibly Its Own End." *CNN/Money* (June 16). Available at: http://money.cnn. com/2002/06/13/news/andersen_verdict/.

Benston, George J., and Al L. Hartgraves. 2002. "ENRON: What Happened and What We Can Learn From It." *Journal of Accounting and Public Policy* 21, no. 2 (Summer): 105–127.

Berenson, Alex. 2003. *The Number: How the Drive for Quarterly Earnings Corrupted Wall Street and Corporate America.* New York: Random House.

Bishop, William G., III. 1998. "Letter to Arthur Siegel, Executive Director, Independence Standards Board." Available at: http://www.theiia.org/iia/index. cfm?doc_id=661.

———. 2000. "Letter to Jonathan G. Katz, Secretary, Securities and Exchange Commission on Revision of the Commission's Auditor Independence Requirements" (September 5). Available at: http://www.sec.gov/rules/proposed/s71300 /testimony/bishop1.htm.

Borrus, Amy, and Nanette Byrnes. 2004. "Auditors: The Leash Gets Shorter." *BusinessWeek Online,* December 27. Available at: http://www.businessweek. com/magazine/content/04_52/b3914040_mz011.htm.

Braiotta, Louis, Jr. 2005. "An Overview of the EU 8th Directive: The European Union Prepares to Issue Its Response to Corporate Malfeasance." *Internal Auditor* (April). Available at: http://www.findarticles.com/p/articles/mi_m4153/is_2_62 /ai_n13821969/print.

Brewer, Lynn, with Matthew Scott Hansen. 2002. *House of Cards: Confessions of an Enron Executive.* College Station, TX: Virtualbookworm.com Publishing Inc.

Brewster, Mike. 2003. *Unaccountable: How the Accounting Profession Forfeited a Public Trust.* Hoboken, NJ: John Wiley & Sons, Inc.

Bryce, Robert. 2002. *Pipe Dreams: Greed, Ego, and the Death of Enron.* New York: Public Affairs.

Buffet, Warren. 2002. "Who Really Cooked the Books?" *New York Times,* July 24: Op-Ed.

Bunting, Robert L. 2004. "Transparency: The New Peer Review Watchword." *The CPA Journal Online* (October). Available at: http://www.nysscpa.org /cpajournal/2004/1004/perspectives/p6.htm.

BusinessWeek. 2002a. "Accounting: Bloodied but Rich." *BusinessWeek* (June 3). Available at: http://www.businessweek.com/magazine/content/02_22/b3785095. htm.

———. 2002b. "A Major Boon for Accounting's Minor League." *BusinessWeek* (April 1). Available at: http://www.businessweek.com/magazine/content/02_13 /b3776056.htm.

California Board of Accountancy. 2005. *2005 Peer Review Report.* Sacramento, CA: California Board of Accountancy. Available at: http://www.dca.ca.gov/cba /forms/pr.pdf.

Calvert, Peter. 2006. "Swedish Regulator Launches Service for Filing of Company Accounts in XBRL." *XBRL International* (July 11). Available at: http://www .xbrl.org/Announcements/Sweden-filing-11July06.htm.

CBS News. 2002. "Deloitte Snags Andersen Tax Partners." *CBS News* (April 4). Available at: http://www.cbsnews.com/stories/2002/04/04/national/main505438. shtml.

CCH Incorporated. 2000a. "Accountants on the Internet 2000." Available at: http:// www.cch.com/press/news/2000/20000823t.asp.

———. 2000b. "Accounting Professionals Have Embraced the Internet, Are Moving Quickly to Reap the Benefits, Says CCH Survey." Available at: http://www.cch .com/press/news/2000/2000082301t.asp.

Chasan, Emily, and Arindam Nag. 2005. "U.S. Accountant Shortage Drives Salaries up Sharply." *The Epoch Times* (July 18). Available at: http://www.theepochtimes .com/news/5-7–18/30411.html.

Clark, Kim, and Marianne Lavelle. 2006. "Guilty as Charged!" *U.S. News & World Report,* June 5: 44–45.

CNN/Money. 2002. "Andersen in DOJ Settlement." *CNN/Money* (March 11). Available at: http://money.cnn.com/2002/03/11/news/companies/andersen/index. htm.

———. 2005. "Andersen Conviction Overturned." *CNN/Money* (May 31). Available at: http://money.cnn.com/2005/05/31/news/midcaps/scandal_andersen_scotus /index.htm.

Commission of the European Communities. 2000. *EU Financial Reporting Strategy: The Way Forward, Communication from the Commission to the Council and the European Parliament.* Available at: http://www.iasplus.com/resource/cec. pdf#search=%22EU%20Financial%20Reporting%20Strategy%3A%20the% 20Way%20Forward%22.

Committee for Economic Development. 2006. *Private Enterprise, Public Trust: The State of Corporate America After Sarbanes-Oxley.* Washington, DC: Committee for Economic Development. Available at: http://www.ced.org/publications /subject.shtml.

Cox, Christopher. 2005. "Remarks Before the 2005 AICPA National Conference on Current SEC and PCAOB Developments." Available at: http://www.sec. gov/news/speech/spch120505cc.htm.

CPA Letter. 2004. "Auditing Standards Available on AICPA and PCAOB Web Sites." (November). Available at: http://www.findarticles.com/p/articles/mi_m0HYW /is_11_84/ai_n7635774.

CRA International. 2006. "Sarbanes-Oxley Section 404 Costs and Implementation Issues: Spring 2006 Survey Update." Available at: http://www.deloitte.com/dtt /cda/doc/content/us_investorcenter_CRAIIIFINAL.pdf.

Deloitte & Touche. 2005a. *The New Azeri Manat.* New York: Deloitte & Touche. Available at: http://www.deloitte.com/dtt/cda/doc/content/AzeriManat_eng .pdf.

———. 2005b. "U.S. VCs to Expand Global Investments; China and India Top Global Targets." Press Release, June 22. Available at: http://www.nvca.org/pdf /VC%20Survey%20PR%20FINAL%206–22–05.pdf.

———. 2006. "China: Firm History." Available at: http://www.deloitte.com/dtt /leadership/0,1045,sid%253D89662,00.html.

Deloitte & Touche, and the National Venture Capital Association. 2005. *Global*

Trends in Venture Capital: A Close-Up View. New York: Deloitte Development LLP. Available at: http://www.altassets.com/knowledgebank/surveys/2005 /nz7198.php.

Deloitte IAS Plus. 2001. "Business Reporting on the Internet." Available at: http:// www.iasplus.com/agenda/internet.htm.

———. 2002. "Europe Adopts Regulation Requiring IAS by 2005." Available at: http://www.iasplus.com/restruct/eur02002.htm#jun2002.

———. 2006a. "Use of IFRSs for Reporting by Domestic Listed and Unlisted Companies." Available at: http://www.iasplus.com/country/useias.htm.

———. 2006b. "Chronology of IASC and IASB." Available at: http://www.iasplus. com/index.htm.

———. 2006c. "A Roadmap for Convergence between IFRSs and US GAAP— 2006–2008: Memorandum of Understanding between the FASB and the IASB" (February 27). Available at: http://www.iasplus.com/pressrel/0602roadmapmou. pdf.

———. 2006d. "IFRS for Small and Medium-sized Entities" (April 1). Available at: http://www.iasplus.com/agenda/sme.htm.

DiPiazza, Samuel A., Jr., and Robert G. Eccles. 2002. *Building Public Trust: The Future of Corporate Reporting.* New York: John Wiley & Sons.

The Economist. 2004a. "The Future of Auditing: Called to Account" (November 20). Available at: http://www.economist.com/business/displayStory.cfm?story _id=3398724.

———. 2004b. "All Together Now." *Global Agenda* (December 28). Available at: http://www.accessmylibrary.com/comsite5/bin/comsite5.pl.

Ernst & Young. 2005. "The EU 8th Directive New Rules for Statutory Audits in Europe" (November). Available at: http://www.tecbrand.com/eyrisk/151105 /eynewsletter151105/feateu8thdirective.html.

———. 2006a. "About Ernst & Young." Available at: http://www.ey.com/global /content.nsf/International/About_EY.

———. 2006b. *Cross-Border Transactions: Spotlight on China.* Available at: http://www.ey.com/global/download.nsf/International/EY_TAS_Spotlight-China_June2006/$file/EY_TAS_SpotlightChina_Jun06.pdf.

Financial Accounting Standards Board. 2006a. "FASB Response to SEC Study on Arrangements with Off-Balance Sheet Implications, Special Purpose Entities, and Transparency of Filings by Issuers." Available at: http://www.fasb. org/fasb_response_sec_study_obs.pdf.

———. 2006b. "Overview of FASB's International Activities." Available at: http:// www.fasb.org/intl/index.shtml.

Financial Reporting Council. 2006. "The FRC." Available at: http://www.frc.org. uk/about/.

Fonda, Daren. 2004. "Revenge of the Bean Counters." *Time* (March 29). Available at: http://www.time.com/time/magazine/article/0,9171,993690,00.html.

Fusaro, Peter C., and Ross M. Miller. 2002. *What Went Wrong at Enron.* Hoboken, NJ: John Wiley & Sons, Inc.

Giles, Jill P., Elizabeth K. Venuti, and Richard C. Jones. 2004. "The PCAOB and Convergence of the Global Auditing and Accounting Profession." *CPA Journal* (September). Available at: http://www.nysscpa.org/cpajournal/2004/904 /essentials/p36.htm.

Glater, Jonathan D. 2002. "Big Merger Could Hinder Push for Change in Industry."

New York Times, March 11. Available at: http://www.globalpolicy.org/socecon/tncs/mergers/accountingreform.htm.

Goff, John. 2004. "They Might be Giants." *CFO Asia* (February). Available at: http://www.cfoasia.com/_others/archives.htm.

Goldschmid, Harvey J. 2003. "Speech by SEC Commissioner: A Lawyer's Role in Corporate Governance: The Myth of Absolute Confidentiality and the Complexity of the Counseling Task" (November 17). U.S. Securities and Exchange Commission. Available at: http://www.sec.gov/news/speech/spch111703hjg.htm.

Granof, Michael H., and Stephen A. Zeff. 2002. "Follow the Money, See How Congress Paved Way for Enron." *New York Times,* January 23. Available at: http://www.mccombs.utexas.edu/news/pressreleases/granof.asp.

Gullapalli, Diya. 2004. "Heard on the Street: Andersen Survivors at Huron Aim to Benefit From Scandals." *Wall Street Journal,* September 14, C1. Available at: http://accounting.cba.uic.edu/Articles/Accounting-Profession/Andersen%20Survivors%20at%20Huron%20Aim%20to%20Benefit%20From%20Scandals.htm.

Hartgraves, Al L., and George J. Benston. 2002. "The Evolving Accounting Standards for Special Purpose Entities and Consolidations." *Accounting Horizons,* September: 245–258.

Harris Interactive. 2000. "Accounting Professionals Have Embraced the Internet, Are Moving Quickly to Reap the Benefit" (August 23). Available at: http://www.cch.com/press/news/2000/20000823011t.asp.

Hart, Kim. 2006. "Accounting Firms Ally to Take on the Big 4." *Washington Post,* October 16, D01. Available at: http://www.washingtonpost.com/wp-dyn/content/article/2006/10/15/AR2006101500599_pf.html.

Hayes, Rick, Roger Dassen, Arnold Schilder, and Philip Wallage. 2005. *Principles of Auditing.* New York: Pearson Education United.

Hill, Nancy T., John E. McEnroe, and Kevin T. Stevens. 2005. "Auditors' Reactions to Sarbanes-Oxley and the PCAOB." *CPA Journal* (November). Available at: http://www.nysscpa.org/cpajournal/2005/1105/special_issue/essentials/p32.htm.

Horstmann, Charles A. 2005. "Playing a Leadership Role in International Convergence: A Chance to Set an Example on the World Stage." *Journal of Accountancy* (October). Available at: http://findarticles.com/p/articles/mi_m6280/is_4_200.

Industry Canada. 2003. "E-Commerce in the Accounting Industry—Start Yesterday." Available at: http://strategis.ic.gc.ca/epic/internet/inecom-come.nsf/en/qy00027e.html#skipnav.

Inside Sarbanes-Oxley. 2006. "Audit-Engagement Provisions Raise Queries" (March 6). Available at: http://www.insidesarbanesoxley.com/2006/03/audit-engagement-provisions-raise.asp.

Institute of Internal Auditors. 2006. "Internal Audit Profession Remains in Global Business Spotlight in Post-Enron Era." News release (February 22). Available at: http://www.theiia.org/index.cfm?doc_id=5469.

Internal Revenue Service. 2005. "KPMG to Pay $456 Million for Criminal Violations." News release (August 29). Available at: http://www.irs.gov/newsroom/article/0,,id=146999,00.html.

International Auditing and Assurance Standards Board. 2006. *Modifications to International Standards of the International Auditing and Assurance Standards Board (IAASB): A Guide for National Standard Setters that Adopt IAASB's International Standards but Find It Necessary to Make Limited Modifications.*

New York: International Federation of Accountants. Available at: http://www
.ifac.org/IAASB/downloads/Modification_Policy_Position.pdf.

———. 2007. *International Standard on Auditing 700: The Independent Auditor's Report on a Complete Set of General Purpose Financial Statements.* Available at: http://www.ifac.org/Members/Source_Files/Auditing_Related_Services/2007 _Handbook/2007_A195_ISA_700.pdf.

International Accounting Standards Board. 2001. "Preface to International Financial Reporting Standards." London: IASB. Available at: http://www.iasplus. com/standard/preface.htm.

———. 2006. "Release Ceremony for Chinese Accounting Standards" (February 22). IASB. Available at: http://www.iasb.org/News/Announcements+and+Speeches /Release+Ceremony+for+Chinese+Accounting+Standards.htm.

International Federation of Accountants. 2004. *Statements of Membership Obligations.* New York: International Federation of Accountants. Available at: http:// www.ifac.org/Members/DownLoads/SMO_Final.pdf.

_____. 2006a. *Handbook of International Auditing, Assurance, and Ethics Pronouncements.* New York: International Federation of Accountants. Available at: http://www.ifac.org/Store/Category.mpl?Category=Auditing%2C%20Assurance %20%26%20Related%20Services.

———. 2006b. *Compliance Advisory Program.* New York: International Federation of Accountants. Available at: http://www.ifac.org/Compliance/.

———. 2006c. *Forum of Firms.* New York: International Federation of Accountants. Available at: http://www.ifac.org/Forum_of_Firms/index.php.

International Federation of Accountants Ethics Committee. 2005. *Code of Ethics for Professional Accountants.* New York: International Federation of Accountants.

International Standards Committee Foundation. 2006. "IFRS—General Purpose Taxonomy: 2006 Final." Available at: http://xbrl.iasb.org/int/fr/ifrs/gp/2006 –08–15/summary_page.html.

Jentho, David, and Dean Beddow. 2005. "Peer Review Is Stronger and Better Now." *Journal of Accountancy Online* (April). Available at: http://www.aicpa. org/PUBS/JOFA/apr2005/jentho.htm.

Johnson, Carrie. 2005. "Public Companies Complain to SEC About Audit Costs." *Washington Post,* April 9, E01. Available at: http://www.washingtonpost.com /ac2/wp-dyn/A38809–2005Apr9?language=printer.

Karmin, Craig, and Aaron Lucchetti. 2006. "New York Loses Edge in Snagging Foreign Listings." *Wall Street Journal Online,* January 26. Available at: http:// online.wsj.com/article/SB113824819390656771.html.

Ketz, J. Edward. 2003. *Hidden Financial Risk: Understanding Off-Balance Sheet Accounting.* Hoboken, NJ: John Wiley & Sons, Inc.

KPMG. 2006a. "Where We Are Located." Available at: http://www.kpmg.com /About/Where/.

———. 2006b. "About KPMG in China and Hong Kong SAR." Available at: http:// www.kpmg.com.cn/.

Krell, Eric. 2003. "Auditor Consolidations: Few Choices, Big Implications." *Business Finance,* November: 33–38. Available at: http://www.businessfinancemag. com/magazine/archives/listArticles.html?action=issue&issueID=382.

Kudlow, Larry. 2002. "Riding on Volcker's Wagon." *National Review Online.* Available at: http://www.nationalreview.com/kudlow/kudlow032702.asp.

Labaton, Stephen. 2006. "Four Years Later, Enron's Shadow Lingers as Change

Comes Slowly." *New York Times,* January 1. Available at: http://www.nytimes.com/2006/01/05/business/05govern.html?ex=1294113600&en=47ad7c7877a9eac6&ei=5088&partner=rssnyt&emc=rss.

Lander, Guy P. 2004. *What Is Sarbanes-Oxley?* New York: McGraw-Hill.

Lane, Michael R. 1989. "Legislating Accountants' Third-Party Liability." *CPA Journal Online* (June). Available at: http://www.nysscpa.org/cpajournal/old/07551220.htm.

Levitt, Arthur. 2002. *Take on the Street.* New York: Pantheon Books.

Levy, Leon, with Eugene Linden. 2002. *The Mind of Wall Street.* New York: PublicAffairs, Perseus Books Group.

Lymer, Andrew, Robert Debreceny, Glen Gray, and Asheq Rahman. 1999. *Business Reporting on the Internet.* New York: International Accounting Standards Committee.

Maiello, Michael. 2002. "Tower of Babel." *Forbes.* Available at: http://www.keepmedia.com/pubs/Forbes/2002/07/22/198705.

McClean, Ron J., David A. Johnston, and Michael Wade. 2002. *New Impact Study Canada, The SMF Experience: A Preliminary Report.* Canadian e-Business Initiative (November). Available at: http://cebi.ca/Public/Team1/Docs/net_impact.pdf#search=%22net%20impact%20study%20Canada%22.

———. 2003. *Net Impact Study Canada, The International Experience: Interim Report.* Canadian e-Business Initiative (May). Available at: http://www.cebi.ca/Public/Team1/Docs/netimpact_report.pdf.

McCrone, Linda, and Marcia Hein. 2004. "The Future of Peer Review: It Is a Misconception That the CBA Requires Peer Review." *California CPA* (January–February). Available at: http://www.findarticles.com/p/articles/mi_m0ICC/is_7_72/ai_n6145334.

McGrath, Susan, Arthur Siegel, Thomas W. Dunfee, Alan S. Glazer, and Henry R. Jaenicke. 2001. "A Framework for Auditor Independence." *Journal of Accountancy* (January). Available at: http://www.findarticles.com/p/articles/mi_m6280/is_1_191/ai_69372738.

McKee, David L., and Don E. Garner. 1992. *Accounting Services, the International Economy, and Third World Development.* Westport, CT: Praeger Publishers.

———. 1996. *Accounting Services, Growth, and Change in the Pacific Basin.* Westport, CT: Quorum Books.

McKee, David L., Don E. Garner, and Yosra AbuAmara McKee. 2002. *Crisis, Recovery, and the Role of Accounting Firms in the Pacific Basin.* Westport, CT: Quorum Books.

McNamee, Mike, with Kerry Capell. 2002. "FASB: Rewriting the Book on Bookkeeping." *BusinessWeek,* May 20. Available at: http://www.keepmedia.com/pubs/BusinessWeek/2002/05/20/21145.

Mumma, Christopher, and Ryan J. Donmoyer. 2005. "KPMG Will Pay $456 Million to Defer Tax-Fraud Charges (Update 4)." Bloomberg.com (August 29). Available at: http://www.bloomberg.com/apps/news?pid=10000103&sid=a2De2PdPIjMU&refer=us.

New York State Public Accountancy Board. 2002. "Testimony before the New York State Senate Higher Education Committee." *Current Issues in Public Accountancy* (February 6). Available at: http://www.op.nysed.gov/cpasenatetestimony0202.htm.

New York Times. 1999. "Company News: H & R Block Is in Deal for Most of McGladrey & Pullen," June 30. Available at: http://query.nytimes.com/gst /fullpage.html?res=9F06EFD61F3AF933A05755C0A96F958260.

———. 2004. "Deloitte & Touche USA LLP." Job Market. Available at: http://jobs .nytimes.com/texis/company?compid=42cc448a57cc50.

O'Sullivan, Kate. 2006. "The Case for Clarity." *CFO Magazine,* September 1. Available at: http://www.cfo.com/article.cfm/7851741?f=search.

Oversight Systems Inc. 2004. *The 2004 Oversight Systems Financial Executive Report on Sarbanes-Oxley.* Available at: http://www.oversightsystems.com.

Panal on Audit Effectiveness. 2000. The Panel on Audit Effectiveness Report and Recommendations (August 31). Available at: www.iasplus.com/resource /pobaudit.pdf

Powers, William, Jr. 2002. *Report of the Special Investigation Committee of the Board of Directors of Enron Corp* (February 1). Available at: http://f11.findlaw .com/news.findlaw.com/wp/docs/enron/specinv020102rpt1.pdf.

Prada, Michel. 2006. "Recent Developments and Challenges Regarding Convergence, Harmonization and Reconciliations of Accounting Standards." Keynote address, Financial Stability Forum Roundtable on Financial Reporting and Auditing, Paris, February 16. Available at: http://www.iasplus.com/europe/0602prada.pdf.

PricewaterhouseCoopers. 2005. *Doing Business in Azerbaijan.* New York: PricewaterhouseCoopers. Available at: http://www.pwc.com/cs/eng/ins-sol/publ /pwc_az_businessguide.pdf.

———. 2006a. China Home Page. New York: PricewaterhouseCoopers. Available at: http://www.pwccn.com/home/eng/contactus.html.

———. 2006b. "Private Company Services." Available at: http://www.pwc.com /extweb/service.nsf/docid/0382f83f7a20a08d85256fa100675cd0.

Public Company Accounting Oversight Board. 2003. "SEC Sets PCAOB Determination." Washington, DC: Public Company Accounting Oversight Board. Available at: http://www.pcaob.org/News_and_Events/News/2003/04-25a.aspx.

———. 2006a. "Auditing Standard No. 4—Reporting on Whether a Previously Reported Material Weakness Continues to Exist." Washington, DC: Public Company Accounting Oversight Board. Available at: http://www.pcaob.org/Standards/Standards_and_Related_Rules/Auditing_Standard_No.4.aspx.

———. 2006b. "SEC Approves PCAOB Rules on Auditor Ethics, Independence and Tax Services." Available at: http://www.pcaob.org/News_and_Events /News/2006/04-21.aspx.

Public Oversight Board, Panel on Audit Effectiveness. 2000. "Final Report and Recommendations." Available at: http://www.pobauditpanel.org.

Rankin, Ken. 2004. "PCAOB Unveils Plan for Non-U.S. Auditors." WebCPA. Available at: http://www.webcpa.com/article.cfm?articleid=1305.

Rapoport, Michael. 2005. "Auditing 'Liability Caps' Face Fire." *Wall Street Journal Online* (November 28). Available at: http://online.wsj.com/article_print /SB113313103433907589.html.

Reilly, David. 2006. "Audit-Engagement Provisions Raise Queries." *Pittsburgh Post Dispatch,* March 6. Available at: http://www.post-gazette.com/pg/06065/666054.stm.

RHR International. 2004. "SOX Costs Average $16 Million Per Company." Available at: http://www.smartpros.com/x45907.xml.

Russell, Joshua, and Jack Armitage. 2006. "Peer Review Effectiveness: An Analysis of Potential Loopholes Within the USA Peer Review Program." *Managerial Auditing Journal* 21, no. 1: 46–62. Available at: http://www.emeraldinsight.com/Insight/ViewContentServlet?Filename=Published/EmeraldFullTextArticle/Articles/0510210104.html.

Sadler, Thomas J. 2005. "NASBA Stepping Up on Peer Review." WebCPA. Available at: http://www.webcpa.com/article.cfm?articleid=16561&pg=acctoday.

Scheiber, Noam. 2002. "How Arthur Andersen Got Away With It. Peer Revue." *The New Republic Online,* January 28. Available at: http://www.tnr.com/doc.mhtml?i=20020128&s=scheiber012802.

Schilit, Howard. 2002. *Financial Shenanigans.* New York: McGraw-Hill.

Scott, A. 2003. "Update: Audit Fees Expected to Rise." *Internal Auditor* (August): 13–14.

Securities Exchange Commission. 1997. "Policy Statement: The Establishment and Improvement of Standards Related to Auditor Independence." Available at: http://www.sec.gov/rules/policy/33-7507.htm.

———. 2001. "Final Rule: Revision of the Commission's Auditor Independence Requirements." Available at: http://www.sec.gov/rules/final/33-7919.htm.

———. 2002. "Report of the Securities and Exchange Commission: Section 703 of the Sarbanes-Oxley Act of 2002: Study and Report on Violations by Securities Professionals." Available at: http://www.sec.gov/news/studies/sox703report.pdf.

———. 2003. "Study Pursuant to Section 108(d) of the Sarbanes-Oxley Act of 2002 on the Adoption by the United States Financial Reporting System of a Principles-Based Accounting System." Available at: http://www.sec.gov/news/studies/principlesbasedstand.htm.

———. 2004. Public Company Accounting Oversight Board. "Order Approving Proposed Rules Relating to Oversight of Non-U.S. Registered Public Accounting Firms." Available at: http://www.sec.gov/rules/pcaob/34-50291.htm.

———. 2006. "More Companies Join SEC's Program to Use Interactive Data for Financial Statements." Press Release (June 20). Available at: http://www.sec.gov/news/press/2006/2006-99.htm.

Shea, Joe. 2002. "Andersen & Co. Worked on Pooh Case During Shredding at Disney." *Albion Monitor,* February 2. Available at: http://www.monitor.net/monitor.net/monitor/0202a/pooh3.html.

Sheard, Paul. 2006. "Japanese Corporate Governance in Comparative Perspective." Available at: http://wb-cu.car.chula.ac.th/papers/corpgov/cg075.htm.

Smartpros. 2001. "IASB Provides XBRL Global Spec for Financial Statements." Available at: http://accounting.smartpros.com/x31502.xml.

———. 2004a. "SEC Could Slow Rulemaking Pace in Coming Months." Available at: http://www.smartpros.com/x46096.xml.

———. 2004b. "MAP Survey Shows Revenue Growth for CPA Firms." Available at: http://www.smartpros.com/x46125.xml.

———. 2005. "Private Companies Applying SOX Principles as Best Practice." Available at: http://accounting.smartpros.com/x48713.xml.

Sos, Rent M. 2005. "CPA Exam, Mandatory Peer Review." *California CPA* (September). Available at: http://www.findarticles.com/p/articles/mi_m0ICC/is_3_74/ai_n15693658.

Steering Committee. 2000. "Electronic Distribution of Business Reporting Information." Financial Accounting Standards Board, January 31. Available at: http://www.fasb.org/brrp/brrp1.shtml.

Sylph, James. 2005. "Global Convergence—Near or Far?" Presented at American Accounting Association Auditing Section Mid-Year Conference, New Orleans, January 14. Available at: http://www.ifac.org/MediaCenter/?q=node /view/72.

Task Force on Rebuilding Public Confidence in Financial Reporting. 2003. *Rebuilding Public Confidence in Financial Reporting.* New York: International Federation of Accountants.

Taub, Stephen. 2004. "Europe's Tough New Auditing Standards." CFO.com (March 18). Available at: http://www.cfo.com/article.cfm/3012665.

———. 2006. "Restatements Surged in 2005, Says Study." CFO.com (March 3). Available at: http://www.cfo.com/printable/article.cfm/5591688?f=options.

The Trusted Professional. 1999. "H & R Block Acquires McGladrey & Pullen." *The Trusted Professional* (July). Available at: http://www.luca.com/trustedprof/0799 /tpa8.htm.

Tweedie, David. 2006a. "Statement of Sir David Tweedie, Chairman, International Accounting Standards Board." International Accounting Standards Board. Available at: http://www.iasb.org/News/Announcements+and+Speeches/Prepared +Testimony+of+Sir+David+Tweedie+before+the+US+Senate+Committee+on +Banking+Housing+and+Urban.htm.

———. 2006b. "Prepared Statement of Sir David Tweedie, Chairman of the International Accounting Standards Board before the Economic and Monetary Affairs Committee of the European Parliament, 31 January 2006." International Accounting Standards Board. Available at: http://www.iasb.org/News/Announce ments+and+Speeches/The+IASB+Chairman+Addresses+European+Parliament +-+read+the+full+address.htm.

Uhl, Don. 2002. "Online Accounting—The Runaway Business in the Accounting Industry." Available at: http://www.afdcenter.com/IndustryOpportunities /ArticleViews/index.asp?ArtID=26.

United States Congress. 2002. *Sarbanes-Oxley Act* (Public Law 107–204), July.

United States General Accounting Office. 2002. *Financial Statement Restatements: Trends, Market Impacts, Regulatory Responses, and Remaining Challenges* (October). Washington, DC: U.S. General Accounting Office. Available at: http://www.gao.gov/new.items/d03138.pdf.

———. 2003. *Public Accounting Firms: Mandated Study on Consolidations and Competition.* Washington, DC: U.S. General Accounting Office. Available at: http://www.gao.gov/new.items/d03864.pdf.

Varian, H., R.E. Litan, A. Elder, and J. Shutter. 2002. *The Net Impact Study: The Projected Economic Benefits of the Internet in the United States, United Kingdom, France and Germany,* V2.0, January. Available at: http://www.netimpactstudy.com.

Vessel, Herbert. 2006. "Is the Public Ready for Transparent Peer Reviews?" *CPA Journal* (July). Available at: http://www.nysscpa.org/cpajournal/2006/706 /perspectives/p9.htm.

Victor, George L., and Moshe S. Levitin. 2005. "Current SEC and PCAOB Developments: CPAs Urged to 'Get Back to the Basics.'" *CPA Journal* (November). Available at: http://www.nysscpa.org/cpajournal/2005/1105/essentials/p28.htm.

Volcker, Paul A. 2002. "Finally, a Time for Auditing Reform." Remarks, Conference on Credible Financial Disclosures, Northwestern University Kellogg School of Management, June 25.

Washington Post. 2005. "Accounting Firms Report Slower Revenue Growth." Accountancy.com. Available at: http://www.accountancy.com.pk/pr_pg_newsprac. asp?newsid=71.

WebCPA. 2006. "NASBA Weighing in on Peer Review," October 1. Available at: http://www.webcpa.com/article.cfm?articleid=21952&pg=pracacc&page=1.

Wei, Lingling. 2006. "CPA Alliances Become Fashionable As Firms Seek To Grow." *Dow Jones Newswires.* Available at: http://www.bakertillyinternational.com /default.aspx?page=1428.

Whittington, O. Ray, and Kurt Pany. 2006. *Principles of Auditing and Other Assurance Services,* 14th ed. New York: McGraw-Hill Irwin.

Wikipedia. 2002. "Public Company Accounting Oversight Board." Available at: http://en.wikipedia.org/wiki/Public_Company_Accounting_Oversight_Board.

———. 2006a. "Public Company Oversight Board." Available at: http://en.wikipedia .org/wiki/Public_Company_Accounting_Oversight_Board.

———. 2006b. "XBRL." Available at: http://en.wikipedia.org/wiki/XBRL.

———. 2006c. "KPMG Tax Shelter Fraud." Available at: http://en.wikipedia.org /wiki/KPMG_tax_shelter_fraud.

———. 2006d. "Arthur Andersen." Available at: http://en.wikipedia.org/wiki /Arthur_Andersen.

Willis, Mike. 2003. "Corporate Reporting Enters the Information Age." *Regulation* (Fall): 56–60. Available at: http://www.cato.org/pubs/regulation/regv26n3/v26n3 -13.pdf#search=%22Corporate%20Reporting%20and%20the%20Internet%22.

Winnick, Pamela. 2002. "Big Accounting Firms Shedding Dual Roles." *Post-Gazette. com* (August 11). Available at: http://www.post-gazette.com/businessnews /20020811accounting0811bnp3.asp.

Wolosky, Howard W. 2004. "Cash in on Sarbanes-Oxley." *The Practical Accountant* (January 1): 24. Available at: http://www.webcpa.com/article. cfm?articleId=6149.

Wong, Peter. 2004. *Challenges and Successes in Implementing International Standards: Achieving Convergence to IFRSS and ISAS.* New York: International Federation of Accountants. Available at: http://www.ifac.org/Store/Details. tmpl?SID=10957196043618091.

Woolfe, Jeremy. 2004a. "IAS Convergence Threatens European Capital Market." *Accounting Today* (May 3). Available at: http://www.keepmedia.com/pubs /AccountingToday/2004/05/03/531459/.

———. 2004b. "Europe's Accounting Standards Are Coming Together Piecemeal." *Accounting Today* (November 8). Available at: http://www.keepmedia.com/pubs /AccountingToday/2004/11/08/643474/.

———. 2006. "Bumpy Ride Expected Over Convergence of GAAP, IFRS." *Accounting Today* (January 9). Available at: http://www.keepmedia.com/pubs /AccountingToday/2006/01/09/1147128/.

Wyatt, Arthur R. 2003. "Accounting Professionalism—They Just Don't Get It." Address at the American Accounting Association Annual Meeting, Honolulu, Hawaii, August 4. Available at: http://aaahq.org/AM2003/WyattSpeech.pdf.

XBRL International. 2006. "Welcome to XBRL International." Available at: http:// www.xbrl.org/Home/.

Index

About the Authors

Don E. Garner is professor and former chair of the Department of Accounting in the College of Business at California State University, Stanislaus, where he specializes in the area of auditing and accounting. He is a certified public accountant and a certified internal auditor. His most recent books coauthored with David L. McKee and Yosra AbuAmara McKee are *Crisis, Recovery, and the Role of Accounting Firms in the Pacific Basin* (2002), *Offshore Financial Centers, Accounting Services and the Global Economy* (2000), *Accounting Services, the Islamic Middle East, and the Global Economy* (1999), and *Accounting Services and Growth in Small Economies* (1998), all published by Quorum Books.

David L. McKee is professor of economics in the Graduate School of Management at Kent State University, where he specializes in development economics and economic change. He has published widely in those and other areas of economics and business.

Yosra AbuAmara McKee is an adjunct faculty member in economics at Kent State University. Her work on international trade and services, economic integration, and regional development has been aired in various professional publications and presentations.